Aims and Scope

The purpose of the *Technical and Vocational Education and Training: Issues, Concerns and Prospects* Book Series is to meet the needs of those interested in an in-depth analysis of current developments concerning various aspects of education for the world of work with particular reference to technical and vocational education and training. The Series examines areas that are at the 'cutting edge' of the field and are innovative in nature. It presents best and innovative practice, explores controversial topics and uses case studies as examples.

The audience includes policymakers, practitioners, administrators, planners, researchers, teachers, teacher educators, students and colleagues in other fields interested in learning about TVET, in both developed and developing countries, countries in transition and countries in a post-conflict situation. The Series complements the *International Handbook of Technical and Vocational Education and Training*, with the elaboration of specific topics, themes and case studies in greater breadth and depth than is possible in the Handbook. Topics covered include training for the informal economy in developing countries; education of adolescents and youth for academic and vocational work; financing education for work; lifelong learning in the workplace; women and girls in technical and vocational education and training; effectively harnessing ICTs in support of TVET; planning of education systems to promote education for the world of work; recognition, evaluation and assessment; education and training of demobilized soldiers in post-conflict situations; TVET research; and school to work transition.

More information about this series at http://www.springer.com/series/6969

Madhu Singh

Global Perspectives on Recognising Non-formal and Informal Learning

Why Recognition Matters

 Springer Open

Madhu Singh
UNESCO Institute for Lifelong Learning
Hamburg, Germany

ISSN 1871-3041   ISSN 2213-221X   (electronic)
Technical and Vocational Education and Training: Issues, Concerns and Prospects
ISBN 978-3-319-15277-6   ISBN 978-3-319-15278-3   (eBook)
DOI 10.1007/978-3-319-15278-3

Library of Congress Control Number: 2015937732

Springer Cham Heidelberg New York Dordrecht London

Printed on acid-free paper

Springer International Publishing AG Switzerland is part of Springer Science+Business Media (www.springer.com)

Foreword

The United Nations Educational, Scientific and Cultural Organization (UNESCO) continues to play a central role in the international vision of developing and extending lifelong learning across the globe. Since 1972 and the release of the path-breaking *Learning to Be* report by UNESCO, the Organization has provided detailed and timely research into lifelong learning with a strong focus on promoting equality and meaningful development around the world.

In UNESCO, the importance of recognition, validation and accreditation of non-formal and informal learning (RVA) has been discussed since the UNESCO General Conference in 2005.[1] In this context, the UNESCO Institute for Lifelong Learning located in Hamburg, Germany, conducted analyses of national policies and practice of RVA drawing on data from Member States. More recently, the Belém Framework for Action highlighted UNESCO's role by developing guidelines on all learning outcomes including those acquired through non-formal and informal learning so that these may be recognised and validated. At the same time, it called on member states to develop or improve structures and mechanisms for the recognition of all forms of learning by establishing equivalency frameworks.

Launching from this broad research base, the publication presented here on Global perspectives on recognising non-formal and informal Learning: Why recognition matters provides a thorough, wide-ranging and accessible analysis of Member States' experiences with RVA. It approaches the recognition of lifelong learning pathways by investigating critical factors conducive for RVA's implementation, its strategic policy objectives, best practice features and the challenges and the ways forward as reported by Member States and perhaps most importantly RVA's role in promoting equality and inclusiveness both in education and across society more generally.

The overall aim of the study is to advance a body of knowledge that allows us to share experience, expertise and lessons that concern in-country RVA practices across Member States. It is presented in such a way that enables its effective and immediate

---

[1] 33C/Resolution 10 of the 33rd session of the General Conference (2005).

use across the full spectrum of country contexts whether in the developing or developed world. It is our hope that Global perspectives on non-formal and informal Learning will promote a proper understanding of the opportunities and challenges offered by RVA in different contexts to policy-makers, educators, researchers and anyone with an interest in lifelong learning and the recognition of non-formal and informal learning. For every country that seeks to enable its citizens, build capacity and cultivate human capital, the understanding promoted in this study will be of genuine significance for the sharing of mutual benefit across international borders.

Director   Arne Carlsen
UNESCO Institute for Lifelong Learning, Hamburg, Germany
April 2015

Acknowledgements

This book represents a part of UNESCO Institute for Lifelong Learning's work on "Recognition, Validation and Accreditation of the Outcomes of Non-formal and Informal Learning". I would like to take this opportunity to acknowledge all the colleagues at the Institute for their continued support throughout and for making this publication possible.

An international study like this one is always a major challenge and relies on the collaboration with several individuals and organisations. I have had the privilege to be able to draw on the long-standing working relationships with several of these people and organisations that I cite in the text. They have greatly contributed to the policy debate on recognising, validating and accrediting non-formal and informal learning. Their data and their continual commitment and involvement in necessary and responsible education reforms have greatly contributed to my understanding of the challenges and opportunities that we face in relation to recognising existing talent and in respect to access to education for disadvantaged people.

Most of all, I would like to thank all the peer reviewers for their constructive feedback on the various drafts and for their invaluable expertise and guidance.

My grateful thanks go out to Marcus Brainard for copy-editing the introduction and to Damian Harrison for copy-editing the rest of the publication. I am grateful to Stephen Roche, head of the publications unit at UIL, for overseeing the entire publication. Finally, I am thankful to Marianne Wenger for helping with the bibliographic references.

Hamburg, Germany   Madhu Singh
April 2015

Springer Book Series Technical and Vocational Education and Training: Issues, Concerns and Prospects

Series Editors Introduction

Worldwide, countries are examining what role education and schooling can play in contributing to a more just, equitable and peaceful world, where there is sustainable economic and social development for all, and the end of poverty. In doing this countries recognize a need to re-engineer education for change: that is, rather than just 'tinkering with the existing system', to examine the fundamental, often taken for granted and unexamined values and practices upon which current education and schooling systems are built, and to modify (or even rebuild) these from their foundation upwards. Countries already know the range of education challenges and stumbling blocks that need to be confronted to achieve the improvement of education and schooling for change. These are well researched and documented. But do countries have the courage and commitment, and political will, to take the necessary action?

These are amongst the matters addressed by Madhu Singh, a researcher at the UNESCO Institute for Lifelong Learning in Hamburg, in this important book which examines the importance of re-engineering education for change by moving away from the limited notion of 'education' for all, to that of 'learning' for all, and to placing an increasing emphasis on non-formal and informal learning, rather than largely focusing on learning that occurs in the formal education system in institutions such as schools and colleges.

Singh surveys global perspectives on the importance of non-formal and informal learning, and of giving greater recognition to such forms of learning, rather than just that which occurs in formal education institutions, which traditionally tends to be the emphasis of researchers, policy makers and practitioners. The reason is that much of the most important learning that occurs for individuals and groups in societies worldwide is not that which occurs in formal settings in schools or colleges, but that which occurs through informal and non-formal means, from family, friends, the mass media and 'on the job' in the workplace. This is particularly true when it comes to the knowledge, skills and understandings individuals learn and develop with regard to citizenship and in the area of employment.

In essence, the overall aim of the study presented in this book is to share experience, expertise and lessons concerning the importance of recognition, validation and accreditation of non-formal and informal learning by establishing mechanisms and frameworks to enable this to happen. Singh identifies global best and innovative practices in the belief that what works in one country can, with suitable adjustments to take account of different national contexts, also work elsewhere. The book examines the changing nature of lifelong and shared learning across countries, both developed and developing; the importance of adopting a holistic approach to lifelong learning; the role of the recognition, validation and accreditation of non-formal and informal learning (RVA) in education, working life and society; importance of the coordination and stakeholder interests and motivations; and, features of best practices drawn from country examples.

We believe that the study reported on in this important and timely book will be of considerable interest to a wide audience of education policy makers, researchers and practitioners, as they seek out most effective directions to reengineer education for change to improve the relevance, effectiveness and quality of learning.

Hong Kong	Rupert Maclean
Tokyo	Ryo Watanabe
Malaysia	Lorraine Symaco
31 December, 2014	

Contents

Acronyms

ABE	Adult Basic Education
ABET	Adult Basic Education and Training
ACBS	Academic Credit Bank System
ACE	American Council on Education
ADF	French Development Agency (Agence Française de Développement)
AET	Adult Education and Training
ALS	Alternative Learning System
AMU	Adult Continuing (Post-secondary) Vocational Training Programme (Denmark)
ANKOM	Anrechnung beruflicher Kompetenzen auf Hochschulstudiengänge (Germany)
APCL	Accreditation of Prior Certificated Learning
ANTA	Australian National Training Authority
APL	Accreditation of Prior Learning
APEL	Accreditation of Prior Experiential Learning
AQF	Australian Qualifications Framework
AQFC	Australian Qualifications Framework Council
AVU	Subjects within general adult education (at primary or lower secondary levels) (Denmark)
VUC	Adult Education Centres (Denmark)
BALS	Bureau of Alternative System, (Department of Education (Philippines)
BMBF	Federal Ministry of Education and Science (Germany)
CACE	Certification in Adult and Continuing Education (Canada)
CAEL	Council for Adult and Experiential Learning (United States of America)
CAPLA	Canadian Association for Prior Learning Assessment
CAF	Common Assessment Framework (Portugal)
CAS	Career Advice Service (South Africa)
CAT	Credit Accumulation and Transfer

CCL	Canadian Council of Learning
CEDEFOP	European Centre for the Development of Vocational Training
CHED	Commission on Higher Education (Philippines)
CIC	Citizenship and Immigration Canada Government of Canada
CIDEC	Interdisciplinary Centre of Economic Studies (Portugal)
CLEP	College Level Examinations Programme (United States of America)
CMEC	Council of Ministers of Education, Canada
CNAA	Council for National Academic Awards (United Kingdom)
CNCP	Catalogue of Qualifications (France)
CoC	Certificate of Competency (Philippines)
CONFINTEA	UNESCO's International Conference on Adult Education
CONOCER	National Council for Standardisation and Certification of Labour Competences (Mexico)
CQFW	Credit and Qualifications Framework for Wales
CQP	Vocational Skills Certificate (Certificats de Qualification Professionnelle) (Benin)
CQM	Occupational Skills Certificate (Certificats de Qualification de Métier) (Benin)
CREDIT	College Credit Recommendation Service (United States of America)
CT	Career Technical Credit Transfer, Ohio (United States of America)
CV	Curriculum Vitae
CVET	Continuing Vocational Education and Training
DACUM	Developing a Curriculum
DAEA	Danish Adult Education Association
DBE	Department of Basic Education (South Africa)
DEST	Department of Education, Science and Training (Australia).
DEEWR	Department of Education Employment and Workplace Relations (Australia)
DHET	Department of Higher Education and Training (South Africa)
DIE	German Institute for Adult Education
ELL	English Language Learners
ECTs	European Credit Transfer System
ESD	Education for Sustainable Development
ETF	European Training Foundation
EQF	European Qualifications Framework
ETEEAP	Expanded Tertiary Education Equivalency and Accreditation Program (Philippines)
EU	European Union
EVA	Danish Institute for Evaluation
EVC	Erkenning van Competenties (Netherlands)
FET	Further Education and Training
FHEQ	Higher Education Qualifications (Wales)

FNTI	First Nations Technical Institute
FPSPP	Funds Paritaire de Sécurisation des Parcours Professionnels (Joint Fund for Career Security) (France)
GED	General Education Department (United States of America)
GET	General Education and Training
GVU	Adult Basic Vocational Education Programme (Denmark)
HEFCE	Higher Education Funding Council for England
HRSDC	Human Resources and Skills Development Canada
ICTs	Information and Communication Technologies
IGNOU	Indira Gandhi National Open University (India)
ILO	International Labour Organization
INEA	National Institute for Adult Education (Mexico)
InfEd	Informal Education Program (Philippines)
KMK	The Standing Conference of the Ministers of Education and Cultural Affairs of the Länder in the Federal Republic of Germany (Kultusministerkonferenz)
KOMPAZ	The competence profile of the Adult Education Centre Linz, Austria
KQF	Korean Qualifications Framework
KSS	Korean Skills Standards
LEA	Lifelong Education Act (Republic of Korea)
LLAS	Lifelong Learning Account System (Republic of Korea)
LO	Norwegian Confederation of Trade Unions
MDGs	Millennium Development Goals
MEVyT	Modelo Educación para la Vida y el trabajo (Educational Model for Life and Work) (Mexico)
MEXT	Ministry of Education, Culture, Sports, Science and Technology (Japan)
MOOCs	Massive Open Online Courses
MQA	Mauritius Qualifications Authority
NAAL	Norwegian Association for Adult Learning
NAMCOL	Namibian College of Open Learning
NC	National Certificate (Philippines)
NCVER	National Centre for Vocational Education Research (Australia)
NFE	Non-Formal Education
NFE	A&E Non-Formal Education Accreditation and Equivalency (Philippines)
NHO	Confederation of Norwegian Enterprise
NILE	National Institute of Lifelong Education (Republic of Korea)
NOI	New Opportunités Initiative (Portugal)
NPOs	Non-Profit Organisations
NPVC	National Pre-Vocational Certificate (Bangladesh)
NQA	Namibia Qualifications Authority
NQF	National Qualifications Framework
NSCS	National System of Competency Standards (Mexico)

NTA	National Training Agency (Namibia)
NTVQF	National Technical and Vocational Qualifications Framework (Bangladesh)
NVL	Nordic Validation Network
NVQ	National Vocational Qualifications (United Kingdom)
NVR	National Knowledge Centre for Validation for Prior Learning (Denmark)
NZQA	New Zealand Qualifications Authority
OCNs	Open College Networks (England and Wales)
OCTO	Quality Council for Trades and Occupations (South Africa)
ODL	Open and Distance Learning
OECD	Organisation for Economic Co-operation and Development
OFFT	Office fédéral de la formation professionnelle et de la technologie (Switzerland)
ONIE	Office of Non-Formal and Informal Education (Thailand)
PCD	Personal Competence Document (Norway)
PEC	Public Employment Services
PLA	Prior Learning Assessment (United States of America)
PLAR	Prior Learning Assessment and Recognition (Canada)
PUP	Polytechnic University of the Philippines
QAA	Quality Assurance Agency (Higher Education) (United Kingdom)
QCA	Qualifications and Credit Authority (Scotland)
QCF	Qualifications and Credit Framework (Scotland)
RCC	Recognition of Current Competency (New Zealand)
RNCP	National Directory of Professional Certifications (Répertoire National des Certifications Professionnelles) (France)
RNFIL	Recognition of Non-Formal and Informal Learning (OECD)
RNMER	Norwegian Ministry of Education and Research
RPL	Recognition of Prior Learning
RTOs	Registered Training Organisations (New Zealand)
RVA	Recognition, Validation and Accreditation of the Outcomes of Non-formal and Informal Learning (UNESCO)
RVCC	Recognition, Validation and Certification of Competences (Portugal)
SAQA	South African Qualifications Authority
SCKK	Centre for Development of Human Resources and Quality Management (Denmark)
SCQF	Scottish Credit and Qualifications Framework
SCQFP	Scottish Credit and Qualifications Framework Partnership
SEP	Department of Public Education (Mexico)
SMEs	Small and Medium Enterprises
SLN	De Paul University School for New Learning (United States of America)
SQA	Scottish Qualifications Authority
SVEB	Swiss Federation for Adult Learning

SVQ	Scottish Vocational Qualifications
TESDA	Technical Education and Skills Development Authority (Philippines)
TVET	Technical and Vocational Education and Training
UIL	UNESCO Institute for Lifelong Learning
UN	United Nations
UNHCR	United Nations High Commissioner for Refugees
UNESCO	United Nations Educational, Scientific and Cultural Organisation
UNICEF	United Nations International Children's Education Fund
VAE	Validation des acquis d'experience (France)
VET	Vocational Education and Training
VEU-Râdet	Council for Adult Education and Training (Denmark)
VNFIL	Validation of Non-Formal and Informal Learning (European Union)
Vox	Institute for Adult Learning (Norway)
VPL	Validation of Prior Learning (Denmark and Netherlands)
VUC	General upper secondary subjects (Denmark)
VVU	Continuing post-secondary adult education
Wba	Weiterbildungsakademie (Academy of Continuing Education) (Austria)
WBL	Work-Based Learning
WIA	Workforce Investment Act (United States of America)
WTCS	Wisconsin Technical College System
YFJ	Youth Forum Jeunesse (European Youth Forum)

Chapter 1
Introduction

This study on recognition, validation and accreditation of non-formal and informal learning, in short RVA, seeks to contribute to the vast and growing field of interest in recognition – or making visible and valuing knowledge, skills and competences, and learning that is still largely invisible. While it is widely accepted by educationists, governments and the general public, that learning takes place not only in formal educational or training institutions but also in the workplace and in non-formal and informal activities, not all learning is formally recognised. A number of international organisations – particularly the Organisation for Economic Co-operation and Development (OECD), the International Labour Organisation (ILO) and the European Union (EU) – have conducted studies on the RVA experience across different country contexts. However, those studies have varied greatly in terms of focus, agenda and direction. For this reason, it is important to clarify at the outset the focus of this study and the useful and distinctive contribution it seeks to make to the growing body of knowledge and ideas concerning recognition of non-formal and informal learning.

1.1 Context and Rationale

For the purposes of this study the acronym RVA is used. It was coined by the United Nations Educational, Scientific and Cultural Organisation (UNESCO) and means the *recognition, validation and accreditation of the outcomes of non-formal and informal learning*: a practice that

> renders visible and gives value to the hidden and unrecognised competences that individuals have obtained in various contexts, through various means in different phases of their lives. Valuing and recognising these learning outcomes may significantly improve individuals' self-esteem and well-being, motivate them to further learning and strengthen their labour

© UNESCO Institute for Lifelong Learning 2015

M. Singh, *Global Perspectives on Recognising Non-formal and Informal Learning*, Technical and Vocational Education and Training: Issues, Concerns and Prospects 21, DOI 10.1007/978-3-319-15278-3_1 market opportunities. RVA may help to integrate broader sections of the population into an open and flexible education and training system and to build inclusive societies. (UIL 2012, p. 3)

In the context of non-formal and informal learning the term 'recognition' has several different meanings. In a general sense, it can mean the process of giving official status to competences (or learning outcomes) through the awarding of qualifications, equivalencies, credits, or the issuing of documents such as portfolios of competences. It can also refer to social recognition in terms of the acknowledgement of the value of skills and competences in the labour market or for academic entry or progression – sometimes called currency. It refers to the acceptance of the principle of recognition of non-formal and informal learning by national education, training and employment stakeholders (UIL 2012). Ultimately, it underlines the recognition that learning is a social activity and depends for its value on its embeddedness within a social framework.

This study examines the implementation of RVA and its impact on those who have acquired skills outside the formal education system. For such people recognition is a means of facilitating first-time or renewed participation in formal education and training, or of recognising skills gained in the workplace or through voluntary work. In other words, such recognition has both a personal, individual impact and a social and economic effect upon the collective. This *impact* has many dimensions (from psychological and personal through to the communal), and *transfer value* in the labour market, *progression value* within an education system, as well as *use value* in daily life situations.

To put it more simply, the present study aims to further an understanding of the following:

• How RVA policy and practice contribute, or could contribute further, to improving quality of life and well-being in those countries that need it most;
• How such recognition is crucial to the educational, economic and social development of many countries;
• The features of good practice in RVA processes that can be shared;
• The key factors that influence the use of RVA in different learning environments;
• The main challenges to the practice of RVA; and
• How RVA can be a part of an appropriate policy response to education and training.

1.2   Sharing Learning Across Countries

There is no single, simple way that a country should approach the use of RVA in order to achieve the desired personal, social and economic *impact*. Rather, there are many examples of diverse, successful approaches to RVA that can be shared, discussed and developed in new ways to achieve a country's goals. This study, therefore, considers examples from a variety of countries in the global North and South. The study's distinctive contribution to the RVA discussion is to harness lessons learnt about RVA from many contexts, and to present these as an enabling contribution to RVA policy discourse in less developed countries.

In countries where the large sections of the population have yet to gain access to even the most basic education, the debate on the recognition, validation and accreditation of existing skills, knowledge and competences can seem less crucial. However, it is precisely at the time when countries are developing broader learning reforms – such as the introduction of lifelong learning strategies, competence-based qualifications or national qualifications frameworks – that it is necessary to discuss access to concepts and mechanisms that promote equality and value alternative ways of acquiring knowledge, such as RVA.

The challenge facing governments and other stakeholders is to find ways to harness the benefits of a coherent RVA framework in tandem with broader educational goals such that it promotes substantive equality and inclusiveness for all members of society.

The perspectives of developing and least developed countries where basic education, economic and social systems are facing acute challenges – have much to teach all countries, both developed and developing, about innovation and opportunity in RVA. Those perspectives can also provide crucial information to governments about how to respond to grassroots community developments in educational programmes such as community-school interactions and how to strengthen informal learning in adult and community learning programmes. Although these programmes and centres operate outside the official education system, they provide youth and adults with a foundation for future development and learning. In light of this, the present study emphasises policy dialogue and learning rather than policy borrowing.

Policy dialogue and learning are particularly important in the context of a "politics of knowledge and a politics of competing theories of knowledge" (Visvanathan 2001). In taking issue with Castells' *The Rise of the Network Society* (1996), and calling for Science to open up to the knowledge of the people, Visvanathan (2001, p. 4) criticises Castells' network society as lacking an explicit theory of knowledge or the varieties of knowledge. Citing Richards (1983) on African models of farming, Visvanathan makes a point about varieties.

> As Paul Richards argues, African models of farming might embody different notions of community and science. It is this community of expertise that the official application of development [model of Science] might have destroyed. Within such a framework, African agriculture and systems of healing might be alternative paradigms, elusive and elliptical to current models of science. Viewed in this way, the Fourth World becomes not a void or a black box but an alternative list of diversities, possibilities, epistemologies (Visvanathan 2001, p. 5).

Visvanathan also cites Wes Jackson (1987), a botanist, who observed that though we are in the midst of an informational explosion, few dispute the loss of biological and cultural information. Cultural information is the information that has left the rural area and the kind of information that is the necessary basis for a sustainable agriculture.

For Visvanathan the definition of knowledge is crucial to the debate about what counts as knowledge. To define knowledge solely as formal, abstractable knowledge is to impoverish knowledge and to deny the existence of tacit, embodied and, alternative knowledge. Visvanathan calls such sensitivity to alternative ideas of knowledge the "dialogue of knowledges" or "cognitive justice". Cognitive justice asserts the diversity of knowledges and the equality of knowers. Visvanathan defines cognitive justice "as the right of many forms of knowledge to exist because all knowledges are seen as partial and complementary and because they contain incommensurable insights" and because they are "link[ed] to livelihood, lifestyles and forms of life" (p. 8).

Defending Visvanathan's notion of cognitive justice, against the charge of an "everything goes" relativism, Van der Velden (2006, p 13) argues that Visvanathan is not arguing for romantic, "museumised" or revivalist ideas of a return to indigenous and traditional knowledge and solutions that are unrealistic in the context of a political and economic globalisation (See Visvanathan 2001). Rather the solution, he argues, lies in a political economy based on the following cognitive principles:

> Cognitive justice is first of all a call for making other ways of knowing visible, in particular the knowledge of the defeated and the marginalised. Only on that basis, argues Visvanathan, is it possible to examine the validity of these different ways of knowing. The supposed validity of people's knowledge lies not ... in the fact that there are diverse ways of knowing (the logical fallacy). Their relative validity will be realised through their inclusion in the heuristic dialogue between (conflicting) knowledges. It is in that sense that these different ways of knowing are valid: they should be treated equal in terms of access to and participation in dialogues of knowledges (Van der Velden 2006, p. 14).

A similar dialogic principle is relevant for the so-called "informal economies" where alternative communities of practice and culturally relevant knowledge are important aspects of professional development. In this context, Michelson (2012) suggests that recognition be understood not as a mere technical issue involving the accumulation of skills and the accreditation of informal knowledge hitherto disregarded, but as an engagement with alternative communities of practice, disparate forms of cultural expression, environmental traditions and workplace practices. Recognition, she argues, needs to be understood as a holistic exploration of the knowledge, skills and understandings that exist in individuals and communities. Recognition speaks to the human aspiration to be seen and honoured for what one already knows, and to be given new learning opportunities and to contribute to society through creative and meaningful work. As Michelson (2012) points out, recognition 'is central both to recognising the skills that exist in the workplace, creating learning pathways where gaps exist, and distinguishing a true "skills gap" from what is better understood as a "recognition gap"' (Michelson 2012, pp. 21). Michelson argues that by relocating recognition of non-formal and informal learning within an epistemology of situated knowledge, we can reconfigure it as a dialogue across alternative modalities of knowledge. This, she says, is not a question of epistemological relativism, or of softening of academic "standards". Rather recognition is a way of making the criteria of judgement visible and it can grant visibility to knowledge that is valuable for its divergence from formal ways of knowing. Most importantly, Michelson argues, "RPL [Recognition of Prior Learning] can become an important venue for revising the relationship between authorised and devalued forms of knowledge *precisely because it formalises it."* (Michelson 2006, p 155).

In the so-called "knowledge-based economies", the "dialogue of knowledges" has been described by Livingstone and Guile (2012) in terms of the "interplay" between those responsible for generating the knowledge that constitutes curricula in formal learning on the one hand, and occupational epistemic cultures that arise through the interplay between the desire of experts (knowledge workers) to continue their individual informal on-the-job-learning and the organisations nurturing that desire, on the other.

The development of the knowledge society based on dialogical learning means that non-formal and informal learning is an expanding aspect of adult learning. This is also evident from the evolving informal learning processes and supporting non-formal learning pedagogies and applications in the digital age. Paradigms such as just-in-time learning, constructivism, learner-centred learning and collaborative approaches have emerged and are being supported by technological advancements such as simulations, digital gaming, virtual reality and multi-agents systems (International Association for Development of the Information Society (IADIS) 2012).

In the context of the present study, it will be important to ask how, for example, RVA could promote and build upon the latent capabilities, understandings, values and attitudes, perceptions, creative capacities and resourcefulness which adults have and which they use in the everyday transactions and tasks of their working, learning and community lives? How could this learning potential, these everyday strategies of learning be harnessed to increase employability, promote lifelong learning and reduce poverty?

1.3   The High Relevance of RVA in the UNESCO Context

Since its early days, UNESCO, as the United Nations agency responsible for education, has continuously supported the renewal of educational structures, contents and methods at all levels. UNESCO programmes emphasise both the development of flexible, diversified modes of learning that are adapted to young people's and adults' needs, languages and cultures, and their acquisition of practical skills for active daily life and employment. Another objective UNESCO has promoted as important for sustainable learning is the participation of all interested stakeholders and partners at local, national and international levels in the development and renovation of education systems.

The study deals with issues that are at the top of the policy and research agenda in many countries around the world. It is highly relevant in the UNESCO context since RVA ranks among the possible ways to redress the glaring lack of relevant qualifications in many developing countries and to promote the development of competences and certification procedures which recognise different types of learning, including formal, non-formal and informal learning, everyday knowledge and skills, practical wisdom and indigenous knowledge.

The opening up of learning systems to RVA is a central tenet of the "learning society" as expressed in the Faure Report, *Learning to Be*:

> If learning involves all of one's life, in the sense of both time-span and diversity, and all of society, including its social and economic as well as its educational resources, then we must go even further than the necessary overhaul of "educational systems" until we reach the stage of a learning society. For these are the true proportions of the challenge education will be facing in the future? (Faure et al. 1972, p. xxxiii)

According to this report, a learning society embodies fundamental alternatives to the prevailing concepts and structures of education, which are as pressing today as they were more than 40 years ago, when the Faure Report was first published. They include:

- restoring the "dimension of living experience" to education, focusing not on "the path an individual has followed, but what he [or she] has learnt or acquired" (p. 185); acknowledging and setting up all paths, whether formal, or informal, institutionalised or not, that employ different learning methods;
- providing an "over-all open education system [that] helps learners to move within it, both horizontally and vertically, and widen[ing] the range of choice available to them" (pp. 183, 185, 188);
- giving every worker the right "to re-enter the educational circuit in the course of his [or her] active life" (p. 190);
- changing certification procedures in order to rule out premature selection. Procedures should stress the value of "real competence", aptitude and motivation over and above marks, class ranking or formal credits obtained (p. 190);
- ensuring that "access to different types of education and professional employment depend *only* on each individual's knowledge, capacities and aptitudes" (p. 203, emphasis added).

The Faure Report defines a learning society as one in which learning is valued by all members of society, in which stakeholders invest in recognising and developing human learning potential, and everyone regards people's non-formal and informal learning as a cornerstone of lifelong learning strategies.

The notion of a learning society has far reaching implications not only for the redirection of the formal educational system but also for policies, theories and practices concerned with lifelong learning, which many authors like Hager and Halliday (2009) consider to be unfortunately based on the assumption that such learning should be predominantly formal. This assumption according to them excludes the educative possibilities of informal learning which they consider to be equally worthwhile as formal learning, because informal learning relates to the social circumstances of people, to cultural transmission between generations, and to the "variety of mutually shared interests" (Dewey 1966, p 322). And these aspects are necessary for a democratic and harmonious societal development. According to them, "there is a necessarily a balance to be struck between formal and informal learning and that one is not inherently superior to another" (p. 2). In the same vein, Rogers (2014) argues that lifelong learning should be promoted not only as a learning programme with a purposeful agenda; rather it should take into account the "universal natural learning for the specific". It matters to take this informal learning into account because firstly tacit or implicit knowledge and understandings form the basis for our decisions and actions; secondly informal learning helps to develop skills, which we develop unconsciously in the course of the many tasks we undertake, be they mental skills such as calculations or physical skills such as making a meal; and thirdly it is mainly through informal learning that a whole range of perceptions, feelings and attitudes are developed (pp. 32–41).

1.4   Addressing the Challenges of a Learning Society

The educational challenges UNESCO foresaw several decades ago are not so different from the learning challenges confronting us today. In the context of rapid societal transformation arising from globalisation, the information revolution and the need for sustainable economies, the learning systems of "the North" and "the South" face the same general issues of social inequality. Not everyone has the same opportunities to enter education and attain specified outcomes, be they standard indicators of school attainment or broader parameters, including environmental, health and cultural education. At the same time, there is a growing education-job gap and a widening chasm between the haves and have-nots. One of the principal consequences of such inequality is a major under-utilisation of existing human potential, talents and human resources, which people may have acquired in non-formal and informal learning settings. These settings have long been underexploited and not counted as real learning or with real outcomes. Furthermore, formal education and training systems are finding it increasingly difficult to respond to the full range of individual and social needs and demands in an ever changing world. There is therefore clearly a need to accord sufficient esteem and respect to the unrecognised potential in society and to make better social and economic use of the outcomes of non-formal and informal learning by offering a greater range of avenues for self-improvement and personal fulfilment to all citizens, increasing a country's economic potential and making its political arrangements more socially inclusive.

1.5   Human Capabilities and the Social Dimensions of Learning

The prevalent dependence on formal education in the past meant that social goals such as the promotion of social cohesion and democratic citizenship and the preservation of humanistic values were neglected. By emphasising knowledge, capabilities and competences in all social contexts, a learning society involves all social and cultural groups, irrespective of gender, age, social class, ethnicity, mental health difficulties, etc. People are encouraged to learn throughout their lives – to learn what they like, when they like, and from whomever they like – and to impart their knowledge to those who wish to learn from them (Naik 1977).

Lifelong learning that values all varieties of non-formal and informal learning, seeks to open up the individual learner's prospects within the social context. A wide range of types of learning exist and add social value. Competences acquired in informal and non-formal situations are essential to each individual's performance in the labour market and the education system, as well as in local communities and volunteer work. Central here, then, is the insight that we are always learning everywhere, albeit not always in a conscious or self-chosen learning situation. Likewise, we should be mindful of our non-formal and informal learning achievements and the possibility of building on these acquired competences.

The acquisition of such self-awareness – who we are and how to use our talents – is a precondition for "deployability" and "employability" "Deployability" denotes the potential to increase our general capability as persons in order to enhance our contribution and participation in society. Greater self-awareness through recognition involves not only the differentiation of one's self from others but also the development of self-awareness and self-caring in and through solidarity with humanity and through direct engagement and action in the world (Gibbs and Angelides 2004, p. 336). This point is eloquently elaborated upon by Nobel Laureate Amartya Sen in his influential book *Development as Freedom* (2000). The recognition of the individual's value in order to empower people and provide social opportunities lies at the centre of his book. Sen (2000, p. 31) identifies "social opportunities" as one of the five instrumental freedoms (the others being political freedoms, economic facilities, transparency guarantees, and protective security) that influence our substantive freedom to live better and advance our general capabilities. With adequate social opportunities (such as support for RVA and basic education), we can effectively shape our own destiny and help each other. He observes, "Individual freedom is quintessentially a social product, and there is a two-way relation between (1) social arrangements to expand individual freedoms and (2) the use of individual freedoms not only to improve the respective lives but also to make the social arrangements more appropriate and effective" (p. 31).

Sen argues that, while human capital and labour market integration are important, they form only a part of the picture and require supplementation. Societies need to develop approaches that encompass the notion of human capabilities and the social dimensions of learning (Sen 1993). In the context of the RVA of non-formal and informal learning, Sen's observations suggest that broadening the scope of recognition, validation and accreditation to include all types of learning outside the mainstream mutually reinforces human capabilities in a society and the opportunities that the society offers. The development of individual capabilities is the aim of RVA, and serves as the driving force for social change, development and social progress. As social opportunities and human capabilities are cultivated, substantive freedom is promoted.

Individual freedoms and choices are also principal determinants of individual initiative and social effectiveness. The individual, as an "agent", "acts and brings about change", and his or her "achievements can be judged in terms of his or her own values and objectives, whether or not we assess them in terms of some external criteria as well" (p. 19). Sen's ideas concerning agency can be seen in discussions of RVA in the learning theories of Lave and Wenger (1991). They see learning as a result of participation in "communities of practice" in which learning cannot be reduced to the passive reception of items of knowledge. The individual learner acquires the skill to perform by actually engaging in an on-going process of learning. Learning is not merely reproduction but actually the reformulation and renewal of knowledge and competences (Bjørnåvold 2000). The notion of agency also presupposes social capital, social networks and trust (Coleman 1988, 1994; Schuller and Field 1998). A feature of learning in non-formal and informal settings is the development at the individual level of the capability to mobilise resources (that is, other people/institutions/technologies) in order to address arising challenges (Livingstone and Guile 2012, p. 357).

Similarly, Giddens (1991) and Beck (1992) emphasise "reflexivity", specifically that the learning society requires that individuals and institutions reflect on themselves, the choices they make and their relationships to others. The UNESCO publication *Learning: The Treasure Within* (Delors 1996) – also known as the "Delors Report" – acknowledges that lifelong learning must not only adapt to changes in the nature of work, but must also constitute a continuous process of forming whole beings – their knowledge and aptitudes, as well as the critical faculty and *ability to act*. [RVA has the potential to] enable people to develop awareness of themselves and their environment and encourage them to play their social role at work and in the community. (p. 19). In the context of the Report's "four pillars of education", education is not only about learning to know, but also entails learning *to be, to live together*, and learning *to do*.

Schuller and Field (1998) considered the relationship between social capital and learning not only in respect of high educational attainment but more widely in the context of the learning society. They prefer to see social capital as both internally differentiated and constantly changing. They give the examples of high flows of information and the fostering of mutual approaches to problem solving through membership of close social networks. But they also see social networks as restricting the range of actors from whom information is sought (as with family businesses). Similarly, in the context of globalising tendencies, the link between space and social capital is being uncoupled, so that one may share relations of reciprocity and trust with neighbours and kin, yet engage in the close social networks and institutions which are remote and perhaps even short lived (Beck 1992).

On the issue of measurement and recognition of social capital they consider it to be helpful to think not of alternative and competing sets of measures, but of "nested sets", from the narrowest qualifications-focused to the broadest set of social indicators. At the heart of the learning society they consider the importance of more debate on the precise types of social arrangements and kinds of contexts (voluntary, youth work, sports, leisure) which promote communication, reflexivity and mutual learning over time. Finally, on the relationships between different varieties of knowledge they note: "Rather than accumulating certificates as individual pieces of evidence of human capital, we need to ask what the balance is across portfolios held by individuals and by groups, so that the awards are related to the social units which are to deploy the knowledge and skills" (Schuller and Field, p. 234). They thus raise the issue of balance between human and social capital as an important one facing policy makers and providers, appealing to the pragmatic needs of the employers and learners while retaining the cultural interest and knowledge of those who perceive the value of learning as predominantly a means of personal development and self and community fulfilment (Atkin 2000, p. 263).

1.6   Key Areas for Analysis

A vast amount of information about education, training and learning exists that would be useful in a cross-country conversation about RVA. However, providing an exhaustive and comprehensive survey of each country of interest would not be a practical way to contribute to this dialogue. Such a comprehensive approach would be unwieldy. Instead, we shall focus on a small group of topics that promise to be of strategic value in the on-going discussion about how RVA might best link up with broader objectives of both developed and developing countries. For the purposes of this study the following areas of analysis are highlighted as useful starting points for sharing learning across the North and the South, and between developed and developing countries:

1. The strategic value of RVA (legislation, policy objectives for sustainable development, stakeholder involvement).
2. The features of best practice and of the quality of processes and mechanisms to be employed.
3. The outcomes in view of the challenges a given country faces and the directions in which it aims to move in the future.

1.6.1   The Strategic Value of RVA

We take the strategic value of RVA to be an issue about motivations, overarching strategies, purposes and uses that countries have for implementing recognition and how effective and successful they are in achieving their sustainable development targets. Unless governments think strategically about embracing RVA, grassroots initiatives alone are unlikely to realise the full potential for recognising non-formal and informal learning to the benefit of individuals, communities and economies.

   The question of the strategic-level analysis is a large one. It comprises three sections.

- First, it deals with questions of how high RVA is on a country's political agenda and how it is reflected in legislation and lifelong learning policies and strategies.
- Second, it deals with the status of RVA in the broader country policy objectives of the education and training system and their connection to sustainable development.
- Third, it deals with the interests and motives of the different stakeholders.

Strategic value refers also to the extent to which countries regard RVA as part of broader education and training reforms and as a key element of lifelong learning and sustainable development. In light of this, it is necessary to discuss briefly the theoretical understanding of what 'strategic value' entails.

Although there are few theoretical perspectives on the notion of "strategic value", Downes and Downes' "organic systems theory" (2007), may provide a useful way to understand the notion of "strategic value" from a systemic perspective. They characterize system change in terms of certain structural or transformational indicators,: sustained interventions; a focus on transition difficulties; developing links between different parts of the system and subsystems in a two-way flow; feedback built into systemic responses; promotion of growth rather than focusing on deficits; an organic system is dynamic and changing rather than static and inert; a multileveled focus is needed to bring about system level change. Much like "system change", "strategic value" may be considered to include many of these elements. From a systems perspective, strategic value will involve holistic thinking.

For Bjørnåvold (2000), institutional and political requirements must first be met if genuine value is to be given to the recognition of non-formal and informal learning. "This can be done partly through political decisions securing the legal basis for initiatives but should be supplemented by a process where questions of 'ownership' and 'control' as well as 'usefulness' must be clarified" (p. 22). It is important for enterprises and institutions to trust and accept the results of RVA of non-formal and informal learning. The participation by all stakeholders and the role of information as highlighted by Eriksen (1995) are also important strategic issues. How, for example, are stakeholders involved in RVA and how these stakeholders respond to RVA according to national and local conditions and needs are important issues of strategic value. The future role of systems for RVA cannot therefore be limited to technical questions of methodology, but must consider the role RVA serves in society, the individual, the labour market and the education and training system.

It may also be useful to view the strategic value of RVA in relation to the broader and more diverse sets of goals within the framework for sustainable development identified by governments in the United Nations Decade of Education for Sustainable Development (UNESCO 2005). Education for Sustainable Development (ESD) in which so many governments, authorities and agencies are currently preoccupied, includes education that is based on such principles and values as respect for others, respect for difference and diversity, respect for responsibility, exploration and dialogue. These principles and values deal with all diverse realms of sustainable development – namely environment, society and economy – and promote lifelong learning. ESD should be locally relevant, culturally appropriate and based on local needs, precepts and conditions, but should also acknowledge that fulfilling local needs often has international effects and consequences (UNESCO 2005).

This understanding of ESD provides a useful strategic framework for the analysis of RVA from environmental, educational, economic, social and cultural, and individual perspectives. From an "environmental" perspective, the analysis of RVA's strategic value deals with the enabling policy and legislative environments. From the educational perspective, the analysis considers a country's policy objectives that contribute to avenues for educational progression and qualifications. From an economic perspective, the analysis involves the strategic role of recognition in workforce development and employability. From the social and cultural perspective, the analysis concerns how processes of recognition are helping to address the challenges of equality, inclusiveness and democratic understanding. And finally from the individual perspective, the analysis involves the role of RVA to offer a greater range of avenues for personal empowerment and development and self-improvement. We are aware that these aims of RVA cannot really be separated from one another. There is a close interplay between compulsory and post-compulsory education and training, adult and continuing learning, and informal learning within the community, at home, in the workplace, in social and cultural agencies, and in universities and colleges, for a better workforce and at the same time a better democracy and equitable society and a more fulfilling life.

1.6.2   Best Practice and Quality of RVA Mechanisms and Processes

The analysis of best practice will identify crucial features of the RVA methods and processes, and the factors that contribute to the sustainability of learning processes. RVA concerns almost always specialised advisory, administrative and pedagogic (or mediating) processes, as well as differing types of valid evidence and assessment. The discussion on methods is closely linked to the challenge of interpreting standards, in particular how the concepts of learning outcomes and competences underpinning reference frameworks are understood and applied. The important issue in quality and transparency of assessment and recognition processes relates to developing methodologies for making visible kinds of knowledge that have long been excluded from mainstream curriculum or standards development processes and that have meaning and relevance for individuals, societies and economies. Quality also implies a shift to education and programmes that are more demand-driven rather than supply-driven; where individuals are not mere receivers of education and where motivated individuals have an interest in continuing to learn.

Building upon the UN framework of indicators regarding the international right to health, it will be useful to include "process" indicators in order to study features of best practice and quality of RVA mechanisms. According to Stecher (2005), process indicators provide a better picture of the quality of services and better information for programme improvement. As Downes (2011, p. 133) explains, "If a structural indicator level analyses the presence or absence of a policy or law, a process indicator is focused more on its implementation dimensions." In our study we examine the issue of defining and monitoring quality in recognition processes by documenting examples of recognition practices in different countries and analysing quality more closely with regard to:

- Standards and methods of assessment.
- Delivering RVA and strengthening professionalism.
- Quality assurance mechanisms.

1.6.3 The Challenges and Future Directions in RVA

The third area of analysis of RVA pursued in this study concerns the challenges and future directions in RVA. The recognition, validation and accreditation of non-formal and informal learning is a constantly evolving field, and many countries are poised to implement significant changes in the future that will impact on the on-going RVA dialogue. The challenges will be analysed at three levels: macro, meso and micro. Challenges at the macro level include absence of a legal frameworks, national guidelines and regulatory frameworks for regional coordination and quality. Obstacles to RVA highlighted at the meso and micro levels include institutional attitudinal resistance, convincing providers and enterprises, and lack of communication and delays in processing RVA.

With regard to the future directions in RVA, we believe it is important to view RVA's contribution to lifelong learning as closely linked with the need for countries to learn and define their own RVA values and to make RVA an expression of their efforts to contribute to social, economic and educational development (Keevy et al. 2012). At the same time, given the global context, a common understanding and language are needed in order to promote the continuous exchange of country experiences in RVA. The emphasis, therefore, will be on arriving at common benchmarks which policy makers and practitioners could use to ensure that policies and practice articulate more purposefully with the holistic principles of lifelong learning and sustainable development.

1.7 Methodology

The present study focuses on a sample of countries selected according to strategies that Miles and Huberman (1994) have highlighted, namely "logic of maximum variation" and "criterion". The focus on the logic of maximum variation seeks to identify countries from different regions of the world, while the strategy of criterion identifies the criteria of selection.

From the perspective of maximum variation, the countries from the North and the South were selected in order to have a fair regional representation. The countries from the developed North include the USA and Canada (North America); Australia and New Zealand, Republic of Korea and Japan (Asia and the Pacific); Norway, Portugal, Denmark, Finland, France, Germany, Austria, Scotland and England (Europe); and South Africa (Africa). The countries from the developing South include the Philippines, Thailand, Bangladesh (Asia and the Pacific); Namibia, Mauritius, Burkina Faso and Benin (Africa); and Mexico (Latin America).

The first criterion of selection was that countries have either well-developed policy and practice in RVA, or islands of good practice, or are in the process of developing an RVA system, so that these can be compared and shared for the benefit of countries that have yet to develop RVA systems.

The second criterion was to select countries with distinct approaches to:

1. legislative environment, institutional processes and outcomes;
2. policy objectives with respect to the role of RVA in further learning and qualifications, workforce development, and social inclusion and personal empowerment; and
3. RVA in the context of institutions in the educational sector, workplace, and third-level institutions such as the non-governmental sector and agencies of civil society.

A third criterion was that the countries had participated in studies or international conferences that the UNESCO Institute for Lifelong Learning (UIL) promoted for the sharing of information and mutual learning.[1]

We also use government websites; journals, publications and recent conference papers; as well as publications by relevant international organisations – OECD, EU, CEDEFOP (European Centre for the Development of Vocational Training) and ETF (European Training Foundation).

Information on countries from the various sources was analysed according to the three areas of research (strategic value; best practice and quality of processes, and challenges and future directions). Country examples are used to highlight the diversity of contexts and purposes, as well as the distinct processes and outcomes

---

[1]These include the publication based on the international conference "Linking recognition practices to national qualifications frameworks: International benchmarking of experiences and strategies on the recognition, validation and accreditation of non-formal and informal learning. (Singh and Duvekot 2013); a consultation with Member States to draft the UNESCO Guidelines on the Recognition, Validation and Accreditation of the Outcomes of Non-formal and Informal Learning (UNESCO Institute for Lifelong Learning 2011); reports submitted to the CONFINTEA V on the development and the state of the art of adult learning and education; contributions to 2008 and 2012 Association for the Development of Education in Africa Biennials and Triennials (Singh 2008; Steenekamp and Singh 2012); collaboration with the French National Commission in the context of two international seminars (France National Commission for UNESCO 2005, 2007); and UIL's first international survey of 36 countries (UNESCO Institute for Lifelong Learning 2005).

of RVA in the countries analysed. Developing typologies was a methodology used for comparing countries and arriving at points of divergence and convergence. Since RVA is a relatively new concept in many countries, it will take time before deeper understanding is developed. The study therefore does not aim to make any generalisations. Rather, it seeks to highlight a number of critical factors that are conducive to the implementation of RVA. Again, since RVA is a fast-moving field, the patterns that emerge here reflect the current situation in the countries studied.

Validation of the information was a major methodological element of the study. In most cases the official narrative was used. The strength of the evidence derived from the fact that the examples were taken from accounts by practising experts and officials who themselves have worked in the development of policy and practice of RVA at the national level, in the field of commissioned work for implementing RVA or in national research institutes. It was therefore possible to use information provided by persons with first-hand knowledge of RVA developments and implementation in their countries.

This study has been subject to two limitations. The first concerns the random selection of countries: while patterns, trends, convergences and divergences will be highlighted, generalisations cannot be made across all countries. The second limitation is that some regions (e.g. the Arab States) and some sub-regions (e.g. Central and Eastern Europe) are not represented.

1.8   Structure and the Content of the Chapters

Chapter 2 provides a discussion of the concepts and the choice of terms and definitions used in this study. It includes a clarification of RVA and a presentation of models of RVA – the convergent model and one that encompasses the parallel or divergent model. This chapter underlines the trend towards lifelong learning as a standard. Furthermore, the chapter discusses the reciprocal relationship between lifelong learning and NQF developments: how lifelong learning has inspired learning outcomes-based national qualifications frameworks (NQFs), and how NQFs improve lifelong learning.

The subsequent three chapters deal with the strategic value of RVA in three different ways. Chapter 3 engages with countries' legislative environment. Chapter 4 further explores RVA's contribution to sustainable development (including educational, economic, social and cultural, and personal development), based on country policies and practice selected from a broad cross-section of international experience. Chapter 5 looks at shared responsibility among stakeholders.

Chapter 6 provides insights into features of "best practice" and the quality of RVA processes. It deals first with countries in the North and then countries in the South.

Chapter 7 charts some of the lessons that can be learnt and shared from current in-country practices – lessons that provide a way for countries to view, at a glance, key issues in RVA and that can be used to optimise educational reforms and achieve national development goals. Based on the foregoing analysis and comparison, the chapter aims to push the recognition process forward towards a set of global benchmarks that will serve the continued discussion on RVA.

Chapter 2
Key Concepts, Definitions and Assumptions

This chapter provides an overview of the main components that comprise the conceptual framework of this study. Beginning with a discussion of the key dimensions of lifelong learning, it then clarifies the terms formal, non-formal and informal learning; and system-wide or top-down and individual or bottom-up approaches. The chapter continues with a reflection on the growing awareness of the contingency of lifelong learning upon the establishment of national qualifications frameworks (NQFs) and the use of learning outcomes.

Following this discussion, the study defines the different terms applied in reference to RVA within various countries as well as the different interests, agendas and directions of RVA studies among diverse international organisations, in particular the EU and OECD, before discussing convergent and divergent models of RVA and the notions of formative and summative recognition.

The final section includes a critical reflection on the conceptual variations that may present challenges when comparing policy and practice across developed and developing educational and economic contexts. In particular there are significant divergences in:

1. the nature of non-formal learning across the two;
2. the nature of workplace learning;
3. the positioning of the individual in the recognition debate;
4. the importance of levels of learning below upper secondary schooling;
5. the distinctions between types of non-formal learning;
6. the potential for enhanced informal learning in the South through Information and Communication Technologies (ICTs).

© UNESCO Institute for Lifelong Learning 2015   17
M. Singh, *Global Perspectives on Recognising Non-formal and Informal Learning*,
Technical and Vocational Education and Training: Issues, Concerns and Prospects 21,
DOI 10.1007/978-3-319-15278-3_2

2.1   Lifelong Learning – The Holistic Approach

The notion of lifelong learning, which has risen prominently in recent years to the top of policy agenda in many countries has wide ranging implications for our understanding of the growing importance of RVA. The famous Faure Report *Learning to Be* (Faure et al. 1972) while advocating lifelong education, specified core elements of a learning society embodying fundamental alternatives to the prevailing concepts and structures of education. By the mid-1990s, a clear shift emerged from the term "lifelong education" to "lifelong learning", putting the emphasis on learner needs and individual choice. This trend was reflected in the UNESCO's *Delors Report Learning: The treasure within* (Delors 1996), acknowledging lifelong learning as one of the guiding and organising principles of educational action and reform that underlines the essential role learning plays for both society and individuals.

Despite the fact that the notion of "lifelong learning" has replaced the notion of "lifelong education" proposed in the Faure Report and promoted by UNESCO during the 1970s, many of the objectives and strategies of "lifelong education" are now evident in many countries (McKenzie 1998). The lifelong education proposal tended to place a greater emphasis on programmes for adults. Distance education and open learning, and various combinations of work and learning and now evident, are all consistent with ideas that were first given a high profile under the lifelong education banner. By contrast lifelong learning pays considerable emphasis to strengthening the foundation for effective learning throughout the life span. In practice this entails developing the skills, knowledge and motivation among young people and adults to enable them to be self-directed learners. Lifelong education implies a greater emphasis on learning within formal educational institutions than lifelong learning, which potentially encompasses all forms of learning.

However, just as the concepts of lifelong learning and lifelong education were being introduced in countries' reform processes, there were growing concerns that lifelong learning is driven by demands in the labour market and linked to opportunities for employability. There are also issues around what counts as knowledge in a knowledge society and the growing individualisation. Despite its strong humanistic origins, the concept of lifelong education was trivialised to mean adult and continuing education (Duke 2001, p. 502). The division between countries with a narrow definition of lifelong education as merely adult and continuing education and those that embrace a broader perspective of adult learning has been highlighted in the recent UNESCO *Global Report on Adult Learning and Education (GRALE)* (2013). Some authors like Hager and Halliday (2009) expressed concerns about the lack of importance given to humanitarian values and the ideals of democracy and citizenship education on an individual level in lifelong learning policies. They argue that these latter richer meanings of the learning society as expressed in Faure's report are outside the ken of most policy makers.

Despite these criticisms, we consider lifelong learning as implying a broader concept of education and training. It is used in the present study as a standard and an organising principle to promote learning on a holistic basis, to counter inequalities in educational opportunity, and to raise the quality of learning (see also Germany. Federal Ministry for Economic Co-operation and Development 2012). Lifelong learning implicitly references the links between various learning settings and serves social, economic and personal development goals. Together with Aspin and Chapman (2000), we see lifelong learning as having a multifaceted character with relationships to a broader and more diverse set of economic, social and personal goals. This is a more pragmatic and problem-solving approach than one which accepts the relativism of a maximalist position i.e. a position which sees lifelong education as involving a fundamental transformation of society, so that the whole society becomes a learning resource for each individual (Cropley 1979, p. 105). All three elements – economic, social and personal – interact and cross-fertilise each other.

Lifelong learning is often understood in terms of three principles: the principles of "lifelong"; "life-wide"; and "learning vis-à-vis education" (Schuetze and Casey 2006). "Lifelong" learning implies that people should continue learning throughout their lives, not just through organised learning in formal and non-formal settings but also in informal ways. The notion of lifelong learning entails the question about the transitions and pathways not only between different sectors of the educational system, but between school and work, and conversely between work, and education and training.

The "life-wide" approach emphasises the integration of learning and living – in contexts across family and community settings, in study, work and leisure, and throughout the life of the individual. The life-wide component also recognises the fact that organised learning occurs in a variety of forms and in many different settings, such as in workplaces or in communities.

Schuetze and Casey (2006) highlight the importance of mechanisms of assessment and recognition in a system of "life-wide" learning. They argue that the assessment and recognition of knowledge, skills and competences learned outside the formal educational system is necessary because the mechanisms need to assess and recognise individual knowledge and know-how (i.e. the applied form of knowledge), understandings, values and attitudes, instead of simply formal qualifications, or the reputation and quality of accredited or otherwise recognised formal educational institutions and programmes. Several studies and surveys such as the Adult Literacy Survey (IALS), Schuetze and Casey argue, have highlighted the discrepancies of certified knowledge and actual know-how. The IALS has shown that holders of high school had only minimal levels of literacy. On the other hand those with few formal qualifications demonstrated literacy competences at advanced levels. "Therefore, assessing and recognising knowledge that has not been learned in and certified by the formal education system is a major conceptual as well as a practical problem." (Schuetze and Casey 2006, p. 281). This we argue is because learning in life-wide contexts measures aspects such as the potential of learning rather than a tick-box accreditation against a formal syllabus.

The change from 'education' to 'learning' implies a greater recognition that there is room for flexibility rather than rigidly structured curricula. The change also entails a more learner-centred system in which individuals have to make meaningful choices among the various options open to them (Schuetze and Casey 2006). More importantly learner-centredness means addressing the fundamental issue of learner motivation rather than only being concerned about the level and availability of provision (Atkin 2000, p. 263).

The concepts of formal, non-formal and informal learning have become key terms within the lifelong learning approach. The following definitions of these terms are used in the *UNESCO Guidelines on the Recognition, Validation and Accreditation of the Outcomes of Non-formal and Informal Learning* (UIL 2012).

- Formal learning takes place in education and training institutions, leading to diplomas and other qualifications recognised by relevant national authorities. Formal learning is structured according to educational arrangements such as curricula qualifications and teaching-learning requirements.
- Non-formal learning is learning that is in addition or alternative to formal learning. In some cases, it is also structured according to educational and training arrangements, but in a more flexible manner. It usually takes place in community-based settings, the workplace and through the activities of civil society organisations.
- Informal learning is learning that occurs in daily life, in the family, in the workplace, in communities and through the interests and activities of individuals. In some cases, the term experiential learning is used to refer to informal learning that focuses on learning from experience.

Many authors have argued that formal, non-formal and informal learning must not be seen as dichotomous and discrete categories, but rather as continuous elements within the "learning continuum". As Eraut et al. (2000), Eraut (2004) and Livingstone (2005) point out, informal learning and work take place in all settings. All informal learning and work, whether in formal or informal learning contexts, has to do with "engagement in the world than with internal thought alone"; informal learning is "flexible and inclusive of diverse knowledge"; learning is political, emancipatory and empowering; and there is a need to develop more clearly articulated assessments of learning in all settings (Sawchuk 2009, p. 324).

The clarification made by Colley et al. (2003) in their seminal effort of comparative integration is particularly relevant. There, the authors noted that: "Learning is often thought of as 'formal', 'informal' and 'non-formal'. [To think they are discrete categories] ... is to misunderstand the nature of learning. It is more accurate to conceive 'formality' and 'informality' as attributes present in all circumstances of learning" (2003, ibid.). Furthermore, the two notions are inextricably linked.

Straka (2005) argues that informal and non-formal learning are basically metaphors that have acquired importance in adult education. Using the distinction between "external" and "internal" conditions of learning developed by Gagné (1973), Straka maintains that "formality" can be differentiated according to the "external conditions" of learning, i.e. the degree of educational arrangement, pre-defined learning objectives, and certification approved by public regulation. However, the "internal conditions" of learning are still missing. The "internal conditions" of learning are the conditions that enable a person to act on the basis of her/his qualities like abilities, skills, knowledge, motives, or emotional dispositions. Information, action, motivation and emotion are dimensions of a learning episode. Thus learning is connected with a person acting at the micro level (socio-culturally shaped external environment) leading to durable change of his internal condition.

In contrast to the position taken by Colley, Hodkinson and Malcolm, for Hager and Halliday (2009), "the distinction between formal and informal, is both useful, and in most contexts, easily made" (p. 1). The fact that there are borderline cases does not make a distinction less useful (Wittgenstein 1953). Moreover, these distinctions are important in policy and practical terms in order to strike a balance between formal and informal learning, the incidental and the intentional modes of education. Similarly, according to Straka, since most learning takes place below the surface, there is still much work to be done in order to obtain empirically grounded valid evidence on the learning outcomes in informal and non-formal settings. This needs to be done by investigating the learning potentialities of workplaces and youth organisations by according greater visibility and wider recognition to the learning outcomes.

Rather than simply describing the attributes of formality and informality in all learning situations, Rogers (2014) attempts to see the interfaces between formal, non-formal and informal learning.

With regard to the relationship between formal and non-formal learning, Rogers argues, both share a similar profile, in that both are intentional learning by the learner. Both forms of learning can be treated as learning with a '*participant orientation*', i.e. participation in some programme or course, with non-formal learning being more adaptable to the participants than is formal learning. An important factor causing the change in the balance between formal and non-formal learning is the use of self-directed learning. This change is to be seen not only in terms of the logistics of self-directed programmes but also in terms of the content and materials. New technologies such as mobile phones, digital tools and digital gaming are also changing the balance between formal and non-formal learning and now within the mainstream of formal programmes (IADIS 2012).

As regards the relationship between informal learning and formal learning, the relationship is widely recognised. According to Hager and Halliday (2009) "what is learnt formally is affected by what is learnt informally and vice versa" (p. 87). Informal learning, because it is largely unconscious, is more difficult for the learner to recognise it for what it is and to perceive its relevance to a new learning programme. Whereas formal (and non-formal) learning tend to be more generalised, informal learning is always applied to specific situations and can be applied to real life immediately since the learning comes from application.

Formal learning is not without values of its own. It provides knowledge by which the existing pre-understandings, frames of references, funds of knowledge and social imaginaries can be recognised and changed and developed through critical reflection. It enables the participant to recognise and validate the informal learning and to build it to new learning. Informal learning can never see itself for what it is; it takes formal learning to develop such a perspective (Thompson 2002). According to Rogers, "this unconscious non-agentic learning which equips the learner with their individualised tacit funds of knowledge, pre-understandings, frames of reference and perceptions and attitudes needs to be taken into account, when constructing learning programmes for young people and adults" (2014, p. 49).

Harris (2006) and Michelson (2006) also argue that caution must be exercised in suggesting that there is similarity and continuity between skills, knowledge and competences acquired in different settings as this ignores the *differences* in the "cultures of knowledge" within formal, non-formal, and informal learning settings; there is mounting evidence that they are not the same. Michelson (1998), arguing from a feminist, situated knowledge and postmodernist perspective, positions RPL as a vehicle for recognising and therefore equalising epistemologically unequal cultures of authority based on difference. According to her, all knowledge needs to be seen as a social product and as partial. This, she argues, extends an invitation to RPL to recognise divergent yet complementary knowledge. Spencer et al. (2003, p. 45) writing from labour educator perspectives, note that "(E)xperiental learning is not inferior to formal learning, it is different, there are times when it closely resembles academic learning but there are many occasions when it does not". Harris (2000) draws attention to relationships between different forms of knowledge, arguing that in some educational sites academic knowledge and experiential knowledge may be closer than in others. She argues that those who argue for recognition of prior learning (RPL) based on knowledge transfers from informal into the formal need to question what and whose knowledge is likely to transfer in the most efficacious ways.

It is therefore more accurate to say that given a certain definition of a set of skills, knowledge and competences, the type of setting where they acquired does not matter. This being the case, ideally, a more practical approach is to consider RVA as capturing outcomes from all forms of learning, including formal as well as non-formal and informal learning. As will be shown in later chapters (Chaps. 4 and 6), many forms of non-formal learning can be integrated into the formal education system, depending on the definitions applied. In Germany, non-formal and informal learning are an integral part of the education and training system, particularly within the dual vocational education and training system. Similarly, workplace learning in Australia and New Zealand includes formal, non-formal or informal learning (Arthur 2009). The comparisons show how knowledge transfer occurs between distinctive and different forms of learning from formal, non-formal and informal learning settings. It is quite possible that some non-formal programmes might be recognised as formal learning, depending on the definition applied. In that sense, our understanding of various existing education programmes will always depend on the definitions in play.

2.1.1 Understanding Lifelong Learning from a Multi-level Perspective

The implementation of lifelong learning from a systemic multi-level perspective entails several challenges. The responsibility for tackling inequality in educational opportunities and raising the quality of learning outcomes lies both at the (macro) policy level and at the (meso and micro) institutional and individual level. At the macro-level, a lifelong learning approach calls for a more flexible and integrated educational and training system. In a number of countries national qualification frameworks have been developed to respond to the growing need to recognise learning and knowledge that have been achieved outside the formal education sectors. A national qualifications framework (NQF) classifies and registers learning/skills according to a set of nationally agreed standards/criteria. Qualifications are provided once competences or learning outcomes have been demonstrated based on these set standards. This means that learning can take place anywhere and that the process of gaining a qualification is not bound to a traditional educational setting. The interplay between formal education and training and the recognition of non-formal and informal learning is regarded as a particularly important element of the NQF in several countries, and as a means of redressing past inequalities in the provision of access to formal education, training and employment opportunities.

At the micro-level, recognition practices serve as bottom-up strategies that support individuals by providing the basis for goal-directed development and career planning, tailor-made learning, and the on-going documentation of professional and personal development. This entails attaching special importance to learner participation and developing the capacities of assessors, social partners (employers and employees) and national authorities to utilise portfolios for recognition purposes.

We argue that simultaneously developing and implementing bottom-up and top-down strategies can improve the holistic purposes of education – personal development, community participation, active citizenship, social inclusion, and economic integration and well-being – thus contributing to two important development goals: social equity and sustainable development.

2.2   NQFs and the Different Uses of Learning Outcomes

In spite of their financial constraints, many developing countries have successfully taken an incremental and thus more manageable approach to the growing need to recognise learning and knowledge achieved outside the formal education sector by developing learning outcomes-based or competence-based NQFs. In addition to NQFs, other regional approaches and frameworks are being put in place, such as the European Qualifications Framework (EQF) and other collective initiatives, including the Transnational Qualifications Framework, which operates across Commonwealth of Learning Small States (Commonwealth of Learning 2010).

Since the shift in many countries towards qualifications based on learning outcomes and competences has important implications for RVA it might be useful to examine the subtle variations in the use of the notion of learning outcomes and the manner in which they manifest themselves at different levels (Brockmann et al. 2011a). Learning outcomes in a national qualifications framework include a combination of knowledge, skills and competences an individual has acquired and/or is able to demonstrate after completion of a given learning programme. Competence is the ability to apply learning outcomes adequately in a defined context.

Depending on the discursive context, learning outcomes need to be understood in three possible ways:

- as an overarching aim or vision underpinning curricula or qualifications;
- to describe "intended learning outcomes" in qualifications or curricular frameworks (Depover 2006, p. 23; see also Winch 1996.); or
- in relation to the learning objectives of specific programmes.

Germany and Scotland offer good examples of the application of learning outcomes as overarching objectives which inform curricula and qualifications within NQFs (see Frommberger and Krichewsky 2012). The German concept of *Handlungskompetenz* and the "Outcomes and Experiences" defined in the Scottish Curriculum for Excellence describe the overarching objectives of vocational education in accordance with the different values and specific understanding of competence in those societies. The German *Handlungskompetenz* includes a national understanding of competence which is integrative in that it includes a social, moral and civic dimension. Brockmann et al. (2011b, p. 9) contrast this integrative understanding of competence with the more task-focused notion evident for example in England, which may, but need not, involve the application of underpinning knowledge. In France and the Netherlands, where competence is also held to be task-focused, a multi-dimensional understanding of competences as knowledge, skills and attitude is assumed in practice (Frommberger and Krichewsky 2012).

2.2.1 Use of 'Intended' Learning Outcomes in Qualifications Frameworks

The second use of "learning outcomes" is in qualification frameworks (QFs). In the European Qualifications Framework (EQF) learning outcomes are defined as "statements of what a learner knows, understands and is able to do on completion of a learning process, which are defined as knowledge, skills and competences" (European Parliament and Council of the European Union 2008, Annex 1). However, since they are prescribed a priori, before the beginning of the learning process, they need to be understood as "intended learning outcomes" when speaking of consequences for curriculum (Frommberger and Krichewsky 2012).

In the New Zealand Qualifications Framework (New Zealand Qualifications Authority (NZQA) 2011), learning outcome statements also detail the education or employment pathways available to the learner after completing the qualification. This raises a number of relevant issues with regard to how curricula could promote the interplay between formal, non-formal and informal learning. For instance, do different branches of the curriculum differentiate between different pathways? Is there sufficient choice? Does the outcome statement in the curriculum structure reflect the result of a negotiation process between stakeholders? Does the curriculum envisage learning outcomes from non-institutionalised learning through community activities, use of media or working? Curriculum structure can thus be assessed on its responsiveness to the interplay between formal curricula and outcomes from non-formal and informal learning.

The NQFs developed after 2005 differ in important ways from the first generation of frameworks developed in England, New Zealand and South Africa (in the meantime these have been revised). The early frameworks were based on what may be described as an "outcomes-led" rather than "outcomes-based" approach. The former approaches tended to make a distinction between learning processes and learning outcomes. A number of countries refer to competences within qualification frameworks, particularly in areas where concrete tasks and skills can be identified. Young (2010) argues that such behavioural output measures employed in NVQs (National Vocational Qualifications) in England, in the South African NQF, in the New Zealand Qualifications Framework and, until recently, in the EQF represent an attempt by industry and the labour market to take control of educational outcomes from educational institutions. Within the NVQ, individuals are able to fulfil the requirements of a set of descriptors without necessarily following a prescribed curricular and pedagogic path. There is thus no internal or conceptual link between the assessment of a learning outcome and a particular path of study.

Recent developments in learning outcomes-based NQFs have precipitated change in an increasing number of countries in the developing world (Singh and Duvekot 2013). India, Bhutan, Bangladesh, Namibia, Burkina Faso and Ghana have either developed or are in the process of developing an NQF in the Technical and Vocational Education and Training (TVET) sector. This shift towards learning outcomes reflects the growing perception of the recognition of skills and knowledge as an achievable goal. Learning outcomes expressed in terms of competence-based approaches hold the potential for the immediate recognition, utilisation and further development of existing skills. However, the possibility that curricular and pedagogic processes might be disregarded, with serious repercussions for the quality of the learning, cannot be discounted within this context. As Young and Allais (2011) alert us with respect to the development of qualifications frameworks in developing countries, competence-based approaches must be complemented by inputs, i.e. the knowledge that a learner needs to acquire if he or she is to be enabled to move beyond existing performance levels.

The EQF originally represented an attempt to adopt a transformational approach to qualifications by regimenting national systems in broadly behavioural terms (Raffe 2011). Brockmann et al. (2011b) criticise the manner in which the term "competence" is used in the EQF as a separate category from knowledge and skills, therefore making it potentially non-integrative (p. 9). The EQF concept of broader competences, they argue, is reduced to responsibility and autonomy and excludes the moral and civic dimensions. However, this ambiguity in the concept of competences has been addressed by several countries as reported in the recent European Inventory on NQFs (CEDEFOP 2012), in which it has been shown that several countries have changed and re-phrased the third "competence" column of the EQF, incorporating additional dimensions such as learning competences, and communicative, social and professional competences. In Finland aspects such as entrepreneurship and languages have been added. Germany and the Netherlands use the term "competences" as an overarching concept, reflecting existing national traditions.

2.2.2 Learning Outcomes as Objectives of More Restricted Programmes of Learning

Outcomes do not stop with the frameworks or qualifications – they are also applied to learning objectives for specific learning programmes. These can be related to learning inputs and have a more pedagogical purpose like the English National Curriculum, which has programmes of study (prescribed content) and attainment targets (assessment waypoints which serve as points of reference in the design of targeted assessment instruments). Some countries, such as Scotland and Ireland, make a distinction between learning outcomes – defined and assessed at a national or regional level – and inputs, as defined by education providers. Assessment instruments are devised to ascertain whether and how well a standard has been reached, as is undertaken in the case of learning outcomes. There is thus an internal or conceptual relationship between the prescribed content (which aims to satisfy the learning outcome descriptor) and the assessment of whether the learning outcome has been achieved (Brockmann et al. 2011b, p. 11).

Criticism has been made of the negative impact of learning outcomes approaches in NQFs on programme design. Govers (2010) argues that the NQFs in New Zealand are detrimental to programme design as they separate learning outcomes from pedagogy, programme design from programme delivery, and assessment from teaching and learning (Govers 2010). This is not the case, she argues, when generic outcomes are applied, as these still leave a lot of flexibility in programme design and delivery, and allow a broader range of people with different interests to be involved in the programme approval process and its implementation. Another notable aspect of some NQF programme design processes is the specification of its individual parts prior to the description of the programme as a whole – as seen in modular approaches. Such approaches heighten the risk of insufficient integration, depth of learning and coherence within educational programmes.

Similarly, authors like Hall (1995) and Zepke (1997) point out that the definitions of learner-centred learning employed by NQFs are restricted in their scope and primarily oriented to promoting "access" rather than empowering learners to negotiate their own learning objectives. Learner-centredness, as advocated by adult learning theorists (Brookfield 1986; Knowles 1975), is associated with critical reflection, empowerment, pro-activeness, and self-direction and control over learning. These aspects are a central concern in RVA. Other criticisms relate to the mechanistic approach advocated through qualifications systems, which does not allow a developmental approach to learning, with a focus on post-formal thinking and open-ended learning (Watson, 1996), or the tackling of culturally sensitive issues (Kurtz 2007). Bohlinger (2007–2008) cautions that learning outcome-based approaches in NQFs should not conflict with the wider character-forming processes implied under the concept of lifelong and life-wide learning.

In the case of South Africa, Allais (2011) has examined learning outcomes in terms of their capacity to promote quality in education and training programmes and to enhance transparency between stakeholders. She argues that neither of these goals championed by propagators of the learning outcomes approach has proven attainable in the South African context. One problem specific to this context is the tendency towards over-specification and fragmentation into standard units. An epistemological issue is the tendency in South Africa to map knowledge onto learning outcomes. Knowledge, Allais states, should be considered in its own right.

Nevertheless, more and more countries are exploring approaches based on learning outcomes, and while countries such as the USA and Canada do not yet have learning outcomes-based qualifications frameworks, some institutions have begun to design degree programmes and curricula around learning outcomes or competences rather than college credits. These institutions grant degrees based on student's demonstrated knowledge and abilities. At this time, however, only a small number of US institutions offer competence-based programmes (Ganzglass et al. 2011).

In Portugal, key innovations in learning outcomes-based adult education and training have resulted in flexible but structured curricula that allow for the acquisition of qualifications and awards through the assessment of formally or non-formally acquired competences. The adoption of dual certification (vocational and academic) based on competences together with modular curricular frameworks affords adults opportunities to further their learning while facilitating labour market integration. While modular organisation has been subject to criticism, in the case of Portugal it has allowed for the development of adult education and training curricula that reflect local demands. In France, learning outcomes, while input-related, are used to link adult learning provision to the labour market by referencing occupational profiles describing typical tasks and resources. Some countries, particularly the German-speaking countries, are careful to ensure that, at a conceptual level, outcome orientations are not reduced to narrow task-related skills and basic knowledge, and instead include broad descriptors of knowledge, skills and competences, learning objectives, standards and quality of input (Bohlinger 2007–2008).

In sum, we argue that the understanding of learning outcomes requires attention to the distinction between learning outcomes defined at a national or regional level, and inputs as defined by education and training providers. In addition, learning outcomes approaches should not be used in a narrowly technical manner to refer to just skills, precisely because of the implications this has for education and training (Sultana 2009). It is important to have a holistic understanding of "competences" (See Weinert 2001). They contain cognitive, emotional, motivational and social components, as well as behavioural features, general attitudes, and elements of self-awareness. As competences are focused on goals, intentions and tasks, they manifest themselves in individual actions. Competences therefore can be formulated in educational standards and in learning goals as "outcomes" and their acquisition can be evaluated. If it is clear what is supposed to be learned, content or formal knowledge can be chosen accordingly. Thus the aim of learning outcomes approaches is not to empty education of content or formal knowledge, rather content needs to be chosen on the basis of people's prior knowledge, their motivation, and their local and individual daily experience

2.3   Recognition, Validation and Accreditation

2.3.1   Different Terms Used in Different Countries

The concept of RVA is not new. Its practice spans several decades in some countries, most notably in Australia, New Zealand, the UK and the USA. Different terms are used for RVA in different countries. In some countries such as South Africa, the term *Recognition of Prior Learning* (RPL) is used. This is a process undertaken by learners, for example adults considering a return to "learning", that involves describing their experiences, reflecting on those experiences, identifying the learning associated with those experiences, defining the learning in terms of given statements of skills, knowledge and understanding, and providing evidence of that learning. Within this context learning providers are required to support learners and to manage the recognition process in a clear and consistent manner (Andersson and Harris 2006; Harris et al. 2011).

In the USA, RVA is referred to as *Prior Learning Assessment* (PLA). In the UK, the terms *Accreditation of Prior Learning* (APL), *Accreditation of Prior Experiential Learning* (APEL) and *Accreditation of Prior Certificated Learning (APCL)* are used. On the one hand, APL tends to have a higher education focus and is established as a method of recognising non-formal (experiential) learning for individuals with relevant knowledge and experience who have not gained a qualification through the formal education system. On the other hand, the main characteristics of APEL are that it always and necessarily assesses the individual's competences and skills, and its relation to the economic skills agenda (Pokorny 2011). APCL can be described as a process, through which previously assessed and certificated learning is considered as appropriate and is recognised for academic purposes.

In Scotland, the definition of APEL has been redefined since its introduction in colleges and universities in the late 1980s. The change from the term *accreditation* to *recognition* of prior informal learning has enabled a clear distinction between the separate, but linked, processes of formative and summative recognition (Whittaker 2011). Since 2005 there has been a shift in the way the terms are used, with a growing focus on the extent to which an individual's competences are equivalent to the required learning outcomes, competence outcomes or standards in qualifications of a specific course or study programme.

In Canada, *Prior Learning Assessment and Recognition* (PLAR) emerged through government initiatives to increase and improve the quality of Canadian labour supply through further and accelerated education (Van Kleef 2011) and has been practiced for over two decades. In New Zealand, there are various terms used in reference to RVA, such as RPL and *Recognition of Current Competency* (RCC) as well as APL and *credit transfer* (Keller 2013). In Australia, RPL is subsumed under the overarching term of *credit* and is defined as one of the credit processes (Cameron 2011).

In the Republic of Korea, RVA is an essential element of the Academic Credit Bank System (ACBS). In the Philippines, RVA is exercised through the Equivalency and Accreditation Program of non-formal and informal learning. In most developing countries it is common to use the term RPL.

2.3.2 Different Interests, Agendas and Directions

To date, the Council for Adult and Experiential Learning (CAEL) has been the most prominent proponent of PLA worldwide. In the case of Sweden, Andersson and Fejes (2011) note the influence of PLA on Swedish initiatives in the 1970s to broaden access to higher education through the recognition of general work-life experience and aptitude. The Swedish system of RVA at that time differed however from that of the United States, which focused on specific competences (Abrahamsson 1989).

Among the various international organisations, the OECD and CEDEFOP are the most prominent within the European and OECD contexts in promoting RVA in the field of skills and competence recognition in non-formal and informal settings. Within the OECD the term *Recognition of Non-Formal and Informal Learning* (RNFIL) is applied (OECD 2010). The recognition of learning outcomes refers to "the formal part of the [learning] process and the way to communicate to the rest of the world about the knowledge, skills and competences one has acquired" (Werquin 2008, p. 144).

Within the EU, the report *Making a European Area of Lifelong Learning a Realit* comprises a key political landmark with its finding that learning should be valued as a prerequisite for the area of lifelong learning (European Commission 2001). In the EU, RVA is referred to as *Validation of Non-Formal and Informal Learning* (VNFIL). Validation is defined as the process of identifying, assessing and recognising the wide range of skills and competences that individuals develop throughout their lives in different contexts. Designed by the Council of the European Union and developed further by CEDEFOP, VNFIL has a strong vocational training focus. Identification and validation are seen as key instruments in the transfer and acceptance of learning outcomes across different settings. The identification of non-formal and informal learning records makes visible the individual's learning outcomes (Bjørnåvold 2000). This visibility does not automatically result in the awarding of certificates and diplomas, but may provide the basis for such formal recognition and accreditation. In 2004, the Council of the European Union adopted the conclusions on common European principles for the identification and validation of non-formal and informal learning (Council of the European Union 2004), and in 2009 published the *European Guidelines for Validating Non-formal and Informal Learning* (CEDEFOP 2009).

Developments in the context of the European Qualifications Framework are proving to be a stimulus for European countries to consider how non-formal and informal learning outcomes might be directly embedded within their national qualifications frameworks (NQFs). Within the European Commission, the Cluster on the Recognition of Learning Outcomes – the largest of the eight education and training clusters – supports countries in developing NQFs and systems for VNFIL. The cluster uses peer-learning methods to exchange good practice and channel collective efforts (CEDEFOP 2008). However, there are several challenges to the learning outcomes approach as reflected in the EQF (see Brockmann et al. 2011b; Bohlinger 2011), and while the EQF levels provide a benchmark for any learning recognised in a qualification, the EQF does not directly recognise learning (Bohlinger 2011, p. 134). The development of systems to support this validation varies across the participating countries – some have already established systems, while others are only beginning to develop appropriate instruments. A number of steps have been taken at a European level. An inventory of the validation of non-formal and informal learning is produced and updated regularly on behalf of the Commission and CEDEFOP, with a detailed survey of developments in Member States.

The responses to a recent consultation on the European Guidelines clearly indicate the important role of VNFIL in making visible the skills and competences gained through life and work experience, and underscore the strong support it enjoys from a diverse group of individuals and stakeholders. At the same time, the responses show that existing validation schemes and arrangements are considered to be too limited in coverage and impact. In some countries and sectors – the knowledge, skills and competences acquired outside schools, universities and vocational training establishments remain in many cases invisible and are not appropriately valued. (Council of the European Union 2012). Member States therefore agreed that they:

> [S]hould (. . . .) have in place no later than 2018, in accordance with national circumstances and specificities, and as they demand appropriate, arrangements for validation of non-formal and informal learning which enable individuals to (a) have knowledge, skills and competences acquired through non-formal and informal learning validated (. . . .); (b) obtain a full (. . . .) or partial qualification on the basis of validated non-formal and informal learning (. . . .). (p. 3)

A seminar organised in April 2013, used the above Council Recommendations as an opportunity for actors from all relevant areas to discuss how the European Guidelines can be reviewed, so as to form a common basis for practical European cooperation on validation. At the heart of this seminar were four questions dealing with: how to increase availability and access of validation, how to strengthen professionalism of validation practitioners and clarify the procedures they follow; how to improve the identification, documentation, assessment and certification of non-formal and informal learning; and finally, how to ensure trust in validation through quality assurance of validation (Council of the European Union 2012).

Within the International Labour Organization (ILO), RVA is considered primarily as a skill development pathway and a crucial means of helping individuals maintain their ability to compete in the labour market. The ILO Recommendation R-195 on the framework for recognition and certification of skills (ILO 2004) is an important point of reference. According to this document: "Measures should be adopted in consultation with the social partners and using a national qualification framework, to promote the development, implementation and financing of a transparent mechanism for the assessment, certification and recognition of skills including prior learning and previous experience, irrespective of the countries where they were acquired and whether acquired formally or informally" (p. 6). In order to provide policy advice on the adaptation and application of these recommendations, the ILO's Skills and Employability Department launched its Qualifications Framework Research Project in 2009 to help improve understanding of qualification and the recognition of experiential-based learning in terms of the information conveyed to employers about the expertise of prospective workers. The study (Allais 2010) showed that the frameworks for the recognition of existing skills, knowledge and abilities of workers and potential workers are insufficient in most of the countries considered, and did not provide clear evidence of improvements in international recognition or mobility due to the existence of a qualifications framework (Allais 2010).

2.3.3 Carrying Forward the UNESCO Project

While each of these different agencies aims to focus on a specific aspect of the recognition of non-formal and informal education – be it within the labour market, the TVET and the higher education sectors, its economic imperatives, its relationship to formal qualifications and practice within the European Member States (CEDEFOP) or OECD countries – *Global Perspectives on Non-formal and Informal Learning* is committed to a holistic analysis of RVA in its fullest sense and the promotion of RVA as a means to empower individuals to make meaningful and constructive choices about their lives and to engage in the societies in which they live. As the Faure Report demonstrates, this has been the motivation behind UNESCO's work since the early 1970s.

Since the publication of the Faure Report, UNESCO has formulated its *Guidelines on the Recognition, Validation and Accreditation of the Outcomes of Non-formal and Informal Learning*, and while these are not legally binding, the promotion of lifelong learning for all remains a major commitment. Member States' authorities are expected to make efforts to apply the UNESCO Guidelines and to develop guidelines appropriate to their specific national contexts. The UNESCO

Guidelines were developed in consultation with Member States and with the professional advice of an Experts Group composed of representatives from each of the regions as well as leading international agencies (UIL 2012).

2.3.4   Convergent and Divergent or Parallel Models

Analyses of approaches to RVA commonly reveal a combination of different models of RVA at work within countries. Andersson et al. (2004) have identified two main types of recognition models: recognition which is adapted to the education and training system (convergent), and recognition that is oriented towards changing the system (divergent). Harris (1999) explores RPL practices in the South African higher education context in terms of its application as a mechanism to change the system.

In line with Harris' definition, in the convergent approach, recognition is awarded depending on an individual's capacity to meet goals or criteria that have an equivalency in the existing programme of study. In this sense, validation converges with the standards of the existing programme (Harris 1999). Parallel or divergent models stress the unique quality of informally acquired competences and are based on special procedures of identification and validation which are independent of the institutions of the formal educational system. In order to guarantee the validity of such a system, there has to be consensus in the community between the significant sectors, regional and occupational stakeholders of what constitutes an appropriate set of standards (Harris 1999).

In divergent models, RVA practice seeks to challenge and broaden existing fields of recognised knowledge by building bridges between traditional academia and the kinds of knowledge that are at risk of being excluded from the curriculum and/or standards development processes. RVA has a role to play in making this kind of knowledge visible and available to the curriculum design process. In doing so, RVA bolsters inclusion rather than acting as another device for exclusion (Harris 1999, p. 135).

Although we consider the above two approaches applied by Andersson et al. (2004) and Harris (1999) as relevant for understanding RVA, we argue, however, that convergent and divergent models are not static categories; rather they are evolving. For example, while RPL in South Africa, on the one hand, is highly standardised and centralised through being closely associated with the South African Qualifications Authority (SAQA), on the other hand it recognises the different strategies in implementing RVA for different target groups – "access", "redress" and "credit/qualification attainers" (SAQA 2012b). In Iceland too, RPL displays both convergent and divergent tendencies. On the one hand, it has a highly standardised approach through the issuing of a National Curriculum Guide for upper secondary schools. This guide sets out the principles for the evaluation of prior studies – whether formal or informal – with the objective of establishing whether prior learning is *equivalent* to the standards defined in the curriculum guide and provide the student with the qualification to complete a programme of study. On the other hand, work experience gained by a student prior to the commencement of an apprenticeship may be recognised. In case of doubt, adults may be offered the opportunity to take a test of competence, allowing applicants to demonstrate their knowledge in a specified subject or field (Iceland. Ministry of Education, Culture and Science 2008). In this context, the process centres on recognising the complementary rather than identical nature of the knowledge and skills gained in non-formal and informal learning. Furthermore, in many countries such as Mexico and the Philippines, accreditation processes are expected to stimulate supplementary programmes, with non-formal education routes to formal learning impacting positively on the certified learning standards.

At an individual level, the distinctions between convergent and divergent can be equated with those between summative and formative approaches to recognition. The *summative* mode offers a direct and formal procedure for accrediting the learning experiences of an individual to a qualification and a specific standard within an NQF. Its focus is on certification or qualification where individuals seek this goal. The *formative* mode aims at personal and career development, and formative assessment is a more informal procedure for accrediting learning experiences in relation to a specific active goal in professional and voluntary work, and further learning (Duvekot and Konrad 2007).

While the awarding of specific credit within the context of formal programmes is an important function of summative assessment and recognition, the formative role of RVA in terms of personal growth and development remains equally important. Acknowledging and making explicit key outcomes of formative recognition is important (Whittaker 2011). Thus, while there is a clear distinction between formative and summative assessment (Whittaker 2011), countries must be aware of the linkages and be clear about how assessment in recognition is to be employed for their specific educational and broader policy goals.

At the systems level the distinction between convergent and parallel models may be related to the manner in which countries relate recognition to national reference points. Singh and Duvekot (2013) identify a fundamental division between RVA based on standards defined within NQFs (divergent), and RVA based on education and training curricula (convergent). Examples of the latter case, are equivalency frameworks, which are frameworks that compare non-formal education to standards in formal basic education (convergent), and are to be found in many developing countries with a large non-formal basic education sector.

National Qualification Frameworks vary widely according to whether they are grounded in the TVET system – and more generally the education system – or in the labour market. This distinction impacts too on how learning outcomes are understood and recognised; on the one hand as standards and on the other as workplace performance descriptors. In many developing countries, NQFs are perceived to provide a means to recognise learning that takes place outside the formal education sector, helping those who have dropped out of the academic systemic to receive a more vocationally oriented-training. Recognition of non-formal and informal learning thus becomes a key issue and can be subsumed under the divergent model.

However, depending on the sector concerned (vocational, academic or adult); most countries tend to combine both convergent and parallel systems. Generally, the recognition of labour competences is more easily facilitated in parallel systems as equivalents frequently do not (yet) exist within the formal system of education and training for that learning. In some countries recognition takes place through the educational system (convergent) or against specially designed competence-based vocational qualifications frameworks for adults (Finland).

When referencing qualifications to the EQF, countries in Europe are making great efforts to identify and assess learning outcomes from non-formal and informal learning that do not yet have an equivalent in the formal system. Norway is now debating the merits of accommodating non-formal and informal learning within a distinct NQF (parallel approach), rather than integrating the recognition process within the formal education system (convergent approach).

By orienting practice towards acknowledged qualification standards, processes at a country level can strive to attain parity and equivalence, shifting from a parallel to a convergent model. Convergent and divergent models are therefore not static categories; rather they are evolving.

2.3.5 What Counts as Knowledge, Skills and Competences in RVA

RVA is a process that provides individuals with an opportunity to validate knowledge, skills and competences not recognised to date. The implementation of RVA practices presents numerous challenges however. As suggested by Harris (1999), if only the site of knowledge production is challenged through RVA, and what counts as knowledge is not, then we must question the assumption that RVA is a democratic and inclusive practice. There is need therefore to understand the conditions under which RVA is to be developed. The question of what is it that should be validated, what skills should be recognised is critical to the development of RVA. Is knowledge production only within traditional academia? Or will workplace relevant skills play an increasing role in this phenomenon?

According to one line of thought, the skills and knowledge that need to be recognised depend on the socio-economic change and technological advances that have resulted in different labour market requirements and job profiles (Brockmann 2011). Brockmann points out, for example, internationally recognised individual competences (divergent tendencies) in the field of software engineering are increasingly taking priority over formal VET programmes (convergent models) in determining employability. A common trend towards greater workplace orientation is apparent in many countries such as Germany, the Netherlands, France and England. Brockmann (2011) highlights the following as factors in this trend:

competence-based qualifications, oriented towards situations in the workplace and social competences; work-based learning, as part of both initial VET (for example through apprenticeships) and continuing VET and lifelong learning; a shift away from knowledge-based initial VET to work-based continuing VET. Within the context of fast-changing industries such as software engineering, the ability to perform tasks is increasingly valued over formal qualifications. In such situations, Brockmann argues, it will therefore be critical to recognise outcomes from non-formal and informal learning. Brockmann draws attention to the so-called "specialist" qualification of "Software Developer" in Germany, which constitutes a radical departure from traditional occupational models, relying on the assessment of competences developed through involvement in the professional environment. This assessment process is not tied to a specific curriculum and requires students instead to self-direct their learning according to what they perceive as necessary to solve the tasks at hand.

Similarly, with regard to the nursing profession, Brockmann highlights the tendency towards the inclusion of more "technical tasks". In order to enhance the relevance of qualifications in the workplace, many countries have introduced competence-based approaches, identifying specific clinical competences which then serve as the basis for both VET programmes and job profiles (Brockmann 2011, p. 124). Nursing serves as an example of the potential conflict between broad academic education and workplace-relevant skills. In both England and France, nursing education is integrated or converged with higher education to a greater extent than in Germany and the Netherlands. Both these countries, which have a strong tradition of VET, have sought to safeguard the multi-dimensional concept of competence within the nursing profession. Definitions of knowledge must accordingly take into account the various national perceptions of 'competences'.

Notwithstanding the divergent tendencies resulting from technological change, which give greater importance to work-related competence-based qualifications and to the strengthening of informal learning in enterprises and industrial sectors, it is important that RVA take into account the full range of lifelong learning goals. Striking this balance requires that other domains of informal knowledge be taken into account such as the formal recognition, support and respect for indigenous ways of knowing, traditional knowledge, language, culture and self-determination of indigenous peoples. The work of the International Indigenous RPL Network has shown how recognition of indigenous knowledge and ways of knowing have helped to enhance employability and social mobility both within the mainstream and in indigenous communities (Day and Zakos 2000).

Striking a balance away from a systematisation that is built into an over formalised view of recognition is what Hager and Halliday (2009) regard as valuing internal goods (such as ideals, creativity, the care of animals and environment) vis-à-vis only external goods (such as money, status or power), a distinction they use from the work of Alasdair Macintyre (1981).

The implications of this understanding of recognising internal goods for RVA is that recognition should not over-formalise practice by turning it into something that lacks vital features of actual practice. Furthermore, workplace practice is but one kind of societal practice. Knowledge, skills and competences from contextually sensitive societal practices such as hobbies, crafts, sports and other recreational activities; activities preparing for work, for continuing vocational development or for coping with survival (Hager and Halliday, 2009, p. 235) should also be taken into account in RVA. All these societal practices involve various internal and external goods which need to be taken into account when recognising outcomes from non-formal and informal learning.

2.4   Challenges of Sharing Learning Across Developed and Developing Country Contexts

Sharing learning across the North-South divide can be challenging. Putting aside the issues of terminology – a hurdle already well documented in previous studies, especially from the OECD (Werquin 2007) – there are conceptual variations that present difficulties when comparing policy and practice across developed and developing educational and economic contexts. There are also differences in the size of the non-formal/informal learning sector, with much larger non-formal education and informal economic sectors in the South than in the North (see Singh 2011, 2012) on traditional non-formal learning in informal economies of the South; and Hoppers (2006) on non-formal education in developing countries). More explicitly, it is worth noting that there are key differences between contexts in developed and developing countries with respect to:

- the line between non-formal and formal
- the nature of non-formal learning
- workplace learning
- the way that the individual is positioned in the recognition debate
- levels of learning below upper secondary schooling
- the distinctions between types of non-formal learning
- the enhanced potential of informal learning in the South through ICTs.

2.4.1   The Line Between Non-formal and Formal Learning

Non-formal learning in contexts located in the South requires further examination due to its role in delivering basic education and vocational skills and life skills learning to the majority of the population in these countries, and in filling the substantial gap left by weak or inadequate and poor-quality mainstream basic education and training provision. Often, the line between non-formal and formal learning systems is not so sharply drawn. In some countries, such as Bangladesh (Us-Sabur 2008) and Mali (Diarra Keita 2006), non-formal education (NFE) programmes can be highly organised and national, provide the bulk of education services to the population and can even be based on consistently described and assessed learning outcomes. Similarly, the Kenyan adult and continuing education system – now in its fourth decade – has been operating as a secondary service without a nationally recognised or validated qualifications framework, even though adults must undergo the same the examinations as those directed towards children leaving primary school (Westman 2005). In other countries, such as South Africa, Botswana and Namibia, non-formal basic education is considered a better, more future-oriented option by many participants who feel stigmatised and excluded from formal education (McKay and Romm 2006). In many cases, their non-formal status is more a matter of definition than fact. Often NFE programmes are non-formal only in that there is little or no framework to "accredit" them against rather than because they are "outside" in any sense (Hoppers 2005, 2006).

In contrast to the cases outlined above, in developed nations drawing a line between non-formal and formal education systems is a centrally important notion in discussions of RVA due to the key role that RVA plays in creating visibility for skills and knowledge. In countries of the North with highly developed education and training systems, the line between "outside" – non-accredited learning programmes – is effectively drawn by what is "inside" – accredited courses and programmes. As Werquin (2007, p. 4) succinctly notes, non-formal learning happens only in relation to formal learning – "it happens only if and where there is formal learning". In the North, formal accreditation processes stimulate supplementary non-formal programmes that are work-oriented and often combined with social and pedagogical remedial support, giving the individual the opportunity of reintegration into the formal system and transition into the workforce (Singh 2008).

2.4.2   The Nature of Non-formal Learning

In the North, the term "non-formal learning sector" is generally used in reference to non-formal work-related continuing vocational education and training (CVET), while deficits in basic education are largely addressed within the formal sector through remedial initiatives. In Germany and Austria, for example, the demand for non-formal learning at the basic level of the kind described above in the case of developing nations (as a parallel system to the formal basic education system) has so far played a limited role. The comprehensive nature of education and training systems in these countries has resulted in comparatively low levels of demand for the recognition of competences acquired in the non-formal education sector. The fact that the dual system rests upon a combination of school- and work-based learning makes explicit the inclusion of experiential learning within the official models, reducing the need to assess non-formal education acquired outside the formal system (Straka 2005). Within these two countries the formal system is informed by *Berufsprofile* (vocational profiles) representing a clearly defined set of qualifications, competences and profiles, indicating both learning content and where learning is to occur. *Berufsprofile* are the standards or the benchmarks of this system, and can to a certain degree be seen as "input oriented". At a conceptual level, the individual *Beruf* (profession) is linked to a specific approach to training and is also tied to specific wage levels and rules defining the rights and responsibilities of practitioners. All of these factors contribute to the high value afforded to the formal system. Alternatives such as non-formal education face significant obstacles in systems in which each step is planned in relation to other social partners, etc. (Straka 2005).

There has been a notable increase in non-formal work-related CVET in countries of the North. Evidence from Germany (Germany. Federal Ministry of Education and Science 2008) indicates that non-formal CVET rose from 52 % in 1994 to 72 % in 1997 – up from 67 % in 2000 – with two out of three employees engaging in non-formal continuing vocational education and training. The level of participation in eastern Germany was somewhat higher than in western Germany. Analysis by gender and age reveals that women value non-formal learning more than their male counterparts and that both the younger and older age groups consider it to be more important than those in the middle age group. More generally, the data suggests that across the board, individuals who change professions or place of employment more frequently tend to make greater use of non-formal learning to expand their range of competences. In order to broaden the available data on the use of recognition programmes, the development of a database to record skills is under consideration (Germany. Federal Ministry of Education and Science (BMBF) 2008).

Self-assessments of continuing learning by adults suggest that learning takes place more often in non-formal "lessons" and informal settings than in formal courses. It is possible that the certification and documentation of informal learning increasingly favoured in many countries such as Germany, could contribute towards encouraging individuals with less access to formal and remedial learning to make (even) better use of the potential of this form of learning in future (Germany. Federal Ministry of Education and Science (BMBF) 2008).

While, non-formal learning, especially of adults and young people, does not necessarily stand in opposition to formal learning, nevertheless, the main character-istics of non-formal learning have developed as alternative and complementary to the formal. These distinctive characteristics render strength to non-formal learning (Chisholm and Hoskin 2005). Further distinctive features of non-formal learning are highlighted by Rogers (2014). Non-formal learning includes active, participatory, democratic, responsible, reflexive, critical and inter-cultural elements. Non-formal skills tend to be similar to everyday life skills, or at least, to be a means by which individuals can cope with their lives in different contexts. Non-formal competences could be specified in terms of acting as a bridge between formal knowledge on the one hand and informal aspirations, wishes and perceptions on the other. They constitute prerequisites for participating in life as a whole – professionally, socially and personally. Employers increasingly demand non-formal competences alongside formal qualifications. They offer an additional way to differentiate between potential employees in a situation where more and more young are well-qualified in formal terms. Non-formal competences are most visible and best recognised when people take part in some activity or programme. Nevertheless, there is still need to render non-formally acquired social and personal skills more explicit and more visible than has been the case until now and with greater assurance that all young people and adults benefit fairly.

2.4.3 Workplace Learning

There are significant differences in workplace learning between the North and the South. In the developed North, workplace learning is formal, non-formal and informal (for New Zealand, see Keller 2013). In developing countries such as Bangladesh (Arthur 2009) however, most informal and non-formal workplace learning has not met some quality assurance requirement such as accreditation and is not recognised through any credit transfer arrangement. This situation is in contrast with that in Australia, for example, where credit transfer arrangements exist even for workplace learning. In other words, until such time as formal education and training and qualifications in developing countries includes RVA for all forms of learning, it will focus primarily on recognition in the context of non-formal and informal learning, without being related to the formal system (Arthur 2009).

Workplace learning is a powerful tool to enhance capabilities and competences, and to lower some of the barriers to obtaining qualifications or becoming qualified. In many countries efforts are therefore being made to put systems in place to ensure that informal workplace learning is encouraged, formalised and recognised. Lave and Wenger (1991), put forward the communities of practice approach based on the notion that better learning takes place in groups, which can share and diffuse tacit knowledge within an organisation. Wenger (1998), has extended the concept of workplace learning to encompass learning that involves the whole person rather than learning which occurs in relation to specific economic or productive activities.

According to Taylor and Evans (2009) and Livingstone (2001) workplace informal learning is not simply self-directed learning such as independent mastery of work procedures, but encompasses the relationships among workers and employees, context and opportunities. For example, informal learning can also result from coaching or mentoring as well as participating in focused workplace discussions or committees. This type of work-related learning is a complex process that involves the interplay of employee agency, workplace relationship and interdependencies of the wider environment and the affordances of the wider environment (Taylor and Evans 2009; Livingstone 2001). It takes into account workers' existing skills and competences, and tailors them to the actual demands of the workplace. It provides appropriate encouragement to them to expand their capacities in ways that can benefit their workplaces and themselves and their families (ibid.).

Unfortunately, the notion of "work" continues to be understood as what people do for a wage. Livingstone (e.g. 1998, 2005; Livingstone and Sawchuk 2004), however, has most persistently argued that this approach is inadequate for fully understanding both the creation of value that human beings add to organisations and society.

Livingstone argues that in the same way informal learning has emerged to challenge the hegemony of "formalised education" so too must an expanded notion of work which includes domestic (without pay) and community volunteer work challenge the hegemony of paid employment as constituting work-based learning. It has been shown that family work teaches us work-relevant skills. The action-oriented learning, direct, personal and emotional, and the responsible nature of the family as a learning place has a stronger and sustainable effect on skills development (Gerzer-Sass 2001). Similarly, gaining personal satisfaction or receiving social esteem and approval for investing time and energy on behalf of the community should by no means be excluded from worthwhile and useful "work".

2.4.4   The Positioning of the Individual in the RVA Debate

Another issue relating to the differentiation of non-formal learning is the position of the individual within recognition systems. In the North, RVA systems in highly developed countries often place a significant emphasis on individuals' motivations to acquire certification and the manner in which information on acquiring certification is accessed. In the Netherlands, for instance, it is usually framed in terms of the lifelong learning of the 'enterprising individual who is working to develop himself or herself continuously' (Duvekot et al. 2003, p. 3). Individual responsibility is incorporated into recognition processes.

The motivation theories deployed in the North are grounded in an individualistic perspective, in which access to education and upward mobility is defined as an individual problem amenable to individual solutions, thus marginalising both community and collective values and, frequently enough, female learners. To some extent this emphasis assumes not only the existence of a strong formal sector, but also some individual resistance to engaging in the sector which must be overcome. As Gomes et al. (2007) point out, within this context a lack of motivation might potentially be viewed as an individual deficit rather than as a problem that is relational, leading to the stigmatisation of those, for example, who do not wish to continue their studies.

The context in the South can differ markedly. The barriers there are not only dispositional, but primarily situational and structural (Singh 2009). Where populations are engaging effectively with non-formal and informal learning, for example, it is collective activities such as systemic recognition (e.g. through effective and transparent equivalence or actively embedding the existing programme into an NQF) and policy coordination that are foremost in RVA reform efforts. It is in this sense that the several international humanitarian organisations in the area of internally displaced persons make a strong case for all children, young people and adults to have the right to a record of what they have learned. Another area of focus is the right of access to examination or assessment processes that are validated by relevant authorities or educational institutions, enabling learners to resume, continue and complete schooling and access further learning opportunities and employment (Kirk 2009).

In the North, a focus on individuals is important when tackling persons within target groups such as minorities, migrants, second-chance learners; in the South, however, the sheer number and proportion of the population for whom non-formal learning is the only available pathway has a significant impact on policy. The recognition of non-formal learning in countries of the South is more a societal project than one focused on individual access to lifelong learning. Faced with millions of women and men who lack access to educational learning opportunities, education systems invariably seek to reach numbers rather than addressing the multiple learning needs of individuals.

Thus while developed countries emphasise the exercise of individual choice and preference as central motivations, this perspective is yet to be explored in developing countries – a state of affairs which is due in part to the high levels of functional illiteracy, and the need to continue to focus on access to basic education.

2.4.5   Levels of Learning Below Upper Secondary Schooling

A further issue that distinguishes discussions about RVA across developed and developing nations is the place of basic and post-primary levels of education and training in overcoming issues of progression to and through formal education and the labour market. In the so-called "Western world" recognition and validation are particularly relevant to higher education and vocational education (Bohlinger and Münchhausen 2011). Overarching national frameworks frequently identify upper secondary schooling or baccalaureate programmes as an initial transition point towards further education and –directly or indirectly –labour market opportunities. In developing countries, on the other hand, areas of education below this are frequently bundled together as "literacy and basic education". This is perhaps appropriate where well-functioning education at the primary and early secondary level is in place and second-chance education at these basic levels is accessed by a relatively small minority of the population.

In many developing countries where the Millennium Development Goals for universal primary education and the Education for All goals for universal basic education are yet to be reached, greater proportions of the adult and out-of-school youth population need a more fine-grained approach to levels within this sector of education and training in order to create meaningful bridges and pathways to opportunity. In these cases, levels must not only be fine-grained, there is also a need for different conceptual elements. The term "levels" implies a process of progression from one element to the next. In fact, these elements should encompass qualitatively different learning, especially for adults, who require an entirely different pedagogical approach to school pupils.

The identification of levels, exit, and re-entry points within this subsector is critical to providing the variety of programmes required. RVA is an important mechanism for ensuring that individuals are undertaking meaningful programmes that will move them on to further opportunity. For example, Ethiopia (Ethiopia.

Ministry of Education 2006) has identified the eighth grade as an important "qualification" level where a successful transition to development work or health agent training and practice can be made. Recognition of differentiated adult basic and even literacy programmes, as well as the skill levels of the individuals accessing them, is an issue of much greater significance in many countries of the South than is evident in the approaches in the North.

In considering points of reference for recognition and their frameworks together with their correlation to broader mobility systems it is therefore important to consider that levels *within* basic education may be as important to contexts in the South as levels beyond it. Basic education and literacy programmes must ensure that initial diagnosis (a form of RVA) facilitates appropriate placement of individuals to maximise learning.

The growing interest in post-primary education found in learning programmes is mirrored in the need for RVA at this level – again to ensure that individuals are indeed afforded relevant opportunities to learn new skills. When considering the RVA of post-primary education, the reputation and social/employer standing of the formal system by which skills are benchmarked will also play a critical role in determining the value of and progression to work and further education and training which stems from core effective practice in this area.

2.4.6   Distinctions Between Types of Non-formal Learning

Clarifying the distinctions between the various types of non-formal learning will enable readers to fully appreciate the implications of RVA for non-formal learning. Three major types of non-formal learning programmes are modelled below, showing that RVA implementation can be complicated both by the absence of frameworks of integrated education and training, and through policy approaches which fail to consider life skills, work skills, and education and training within an integrated and holistic perspective.

Non-formal education and training (schooling and TVET) that is not defined in an NQF but is standardised through a curriculum with equivalence to formal education. This includes general education and training programmes that are assessed against the same curriculum as school qualifications and are accordingly recognised as equivalent to formal school qualifications. However, as any recognition is based on the curriculum rather than the learning achievement, equivalence is achieved through the same examinations utilised in schools (which are not necessarily appropriate for adults), making recognition of wider learning in labour market or community contexts less visible than in the case of the previous category. Ecuador gives high priority to the relationship between non-formal and formal education through its high school certificate (*Bachillerato*). In the Maldives, the principle of equivalency applies to primary and secondary education; but it also applies to literacy programmes entailing 3 years of study, leading to a certificate equivalent to the completion of the sixth grade in basic education which qualifies adult learners to join the seventh grade. Those who cannot continue their education in the formal system can choose to join any of the various adult education courses available. An important mode in which equivalency programmes are offered is through distance learning, e.g. the Open and Distance Learning (ODL) programmes of the Institute of Adult Education in the Maldives (Maldives. Centre for Continuing Education 2009). Equivalency programmes also exist at a basic level in various developed nations, but RVA is more frequently an integral component. In Norway, recognition is deployed for the purpose of matching the learning of individuals to the national curriculum and thereby shortening the period required to complete school certification (Norway. Ministry of Education and Research 2007). RVA serves to recognise the complementary rather than the identical nature of learning programmes.

Non-formal education and training that is defined in an NQF or formal standard and assessed against learning outcomes. General education or training programmes that are assessed against learning outcomes described within either NQFs or the defined outcomes of other recognised programmes. The outcomes help establish the achievements that are included in the certification, which can be meaningful for both education/training and labour market progression. The relationship established between the programme and the level helps the student to progress to further levels of formal education. Adult Basic Education and Training (ABET) in South Africa, for example, has more than one level, enabling this equivalence to be understood across a number of levels of the NQF. It is the existence of the NQF as well as the linkage to it that makes such programmes better able to provide access and progression to formal education and can also enhance their meaning in the labour market, because standards would include work skills and life skills in addition to the formal criteria of general education (McKay and Romm 2006).

Non-formal learning programmes with a developmental focus rather than overtly educational focus. Such programmes, although sometimes considered to be part of the non-formal learning sector, are generally uncertified, or if certified have meaning only in terms of the social/work learning (rather than being seen as also educational). However, the wide range of social, interpersonal and life skills imparted in such programmes imply a strong transferability to education or vocational learning and thus these non-formal programmes have a greater potential of recognition within formal systems than is currently being exploited. In post-conflict countries these programmes focus on civic and peace education, environmental improvement, HIV/AIDS and community reconstruction. In Bangladesh, non-formal education programmes include literacy programmes in various development spheres (agriculture, health, universities, and distance learning) as well as vocational skills and income-generation skills that build on the informal learning of disadvantaged people, facilitating lifelong learning and enhancing earning capabilities with the objective of reducing poverty (Bangladesh. Ministry of Primary and Mass Education (MoPME) 2008). However, there is no standard mechanism or system that has been instituted for the recognition of these skills.

By contrast, in other countries, such as New Zealand, non-formal adult and community education frameworks have been established for literacy and adult community development. The primary areas of focus include: personal development (e.g. parenting skills, computing skills, music, foreign languages, arts and crafts, recreation and fitness activities); community development (e.g. capacity-building for community groups, training community volunteer workers); civil society development (e.g. workshops on the Treaty of Waitangi and participation in governmental submission processes).

The European Youth Forum is soon to have a Quality Assurance Framework for its non-formal education programmes so that they are sufficiently recognised within society and within youth organisations themselves. NFE in youth organisations in the European context fosters active citizenship and the transmission of values, e.g. human rights and freedom; democracy; respect, diversity; peace and prosperity; sustainable development; social justice; solidarity; and gender equality. Youth organisations select needs that they themselves identify, or that are articulated by young people. Quality of the NFE provider takes learning outcomes into account and compares them with the learning quality learning objectives agreed to by all stakeholders. In addition, each learner is expected to evaluate for himself whether the learning objectives have been met. Recognition through reflection and self-assessment makes visible the learning outcomes. Youth organisations need to be aware of how all their individual learners perceive their learning experience. The YFJ sees peer-feedback and the establishment of indicators as a good starting point for building confidence in the quality of NFE and enhancing its recognition and its parity of esteem with formal education (Youth Forum Jeunesse 2008).

2.4.7 The Potential for Enhanced Informal Learning in the South Through ICTs

While there is an emphasis on formal and non-formal learning, informal learning and non-institutionalised learning through media was previously neglected in the South. More recently, interest has grown in enhanced informal learning via satellite television, telecommunications, mobile networks, and through Massive Open Online Courses (MOOCs) etc. Some open universities in developing countries, such as Indira Gandhi National Open University (IGNOU) in India, have a wide basket of media and technologies including non-formal distance learning programmes (Panda 2011). The work of Mitra (see Mitra et al. 2005) on computer-based informal learning highlights potential even in situations where basic education levels are low. Since 1999, Mitra has convincingly demonstrated that groups of children – irrespective of their location or background – are able to use computers and the Internet on their own using public computers in open spaces such as roads and playgrounds. The transferability of these informal computer skills to education and training needs to be further exploited.

2.5 Summary

Lifelong learning has been described as a standard that promotes learning on a *holistic basis*, counters inequalities in educational opportunities and raises the quality of learning. Lifelong learning implies the linkages between various learning settings and serves social, policy and economic purposes. However, the implementation of lifelong learning presents several challenges. The responsibility for tackling the problem of inequality of educational opportunity and raising the quality of learning outcomes is located at both a systemic and an individual level. Several Member States have developed national objectives to move towards a lifelong learning society.

The definition of non-formal and informal learning remains a subject of discussion in the field of RVA. For many it is more helpful to speak of a formal-non-formal-informal continuum, recognising that different combinations of features occupy different positions along the continuum. For many others, drawing a firm line between non-formal and informal on the one hand and formal education and training on the other is seen as both essential and desirable. For these authors non-formal and informal learning are distinctive and positive alternatives to formal learning and need to be valorised. For the latter group, RVA is a way to rectify the distorted balance between formal learning vis-à-vis non-formal and informal learning.

The adoption of the lifelong learning approach gives rise to the need for a more flexible and integrated system of qualifications. In a number of countries learning outcomes-based NQFs have been developed in response to the growing need to recognise learning and knowledge that has been achieved outside the formal education sector. However, the aims, objectives and purposes of establishing NQFs varies, and there seems to be a general agreement among countries adopting NQFs that the formal education system does not cater fully to the learning needs of the population.

RVA is a process that would provide individuals with an opportunity to validate unrecognised skills and competences. There is a need to understand the conditions in the field in which RVA is to be developed. Two models of RVA are presented – the convergent and the parallel model. We argue that both of these models overlap. On the one hand, RVA interacts by necessity with predefined categories (convergence). At the same time, it challenges normative classifications of knowledge. While summative recognition leading to predefined categories in the formal system is important, formative recognition plays an equally important role in personal growth and development. Acknowledging and making explicit key outcomes of formative recognition is important. In other words, while there is a clear distinction between formative and summative assessment, and convergent and parallel models, they are linked and evolving processes.

Finally, sharing learning across North and South has brought to the fore the disparate issues relating to RVA in the North and South. There is a clear difference in the subsector focus on RVA activity between the North and the South. Countries with well-developed education and training systems focus much of their recognition implementation efforts on non-formal continuing vocational education and training and workplace learning, attempting to make informal learning more visible and facilitating direct access to accredited and non-accredited programmes. In the countries of the South, where basic education is delivered extensively through the non-formal education sector, there is a greater focus on equivalency and improving links between non-formal programmes and their formal counterparts (often school certification) with the aim of facilitating access to further opportunities in education and training. There is clear evidence that enhancing alignment to qualifications through RVA in the literacy and adult basic education sectors can lead to important innovations in linkages and pathways.

Chapter 3
Policy and Legislative Environment

The strategic value of RVA comprises the first of three analytical categories identified in Chap. 1. This chapter offers an analysis of a cross-section of international experience in the area of policy and legislation on RVA and lifelong learning.

Policies and legislation that endorse the recognition, validation and accreditation of non-formal and informal learning, whether as part of educational reforms or the establishment of NQFs, are powerful tools and drivers of the RVA of non-formal and informal learning. Countries as diverse as the Scandinavian nations, the Czech Republic, Latvia, Mexico, Cambodia, Thailand, and Trinidad and Tobago all have policies backed by legislation that reinforce efforts to value and recognise non-formal and informal learning. Legislation of this kind not only improves the likelihood that competences will be recognised in formal education and/or training systems, it also bolsters efforts to garner support for recognition processes across a number of areas. This effect is most pronounced in the political sphere, but also extends to social partners and other ministries. Moreover, legislative acts are important if countries are to draw on both public and private investment in the development of new qualifications and competency systems. These factors have made legislation a popular means of advancing the case for recognition across a variety of countries with disparate national goals.

Within this context, Werquin's classification of countries in terms of models and "best practices" (Werquin and Wihak 2011 p. 164) offers a useful point of reference. Werquin highlights key differences among OECD countries in a format that identifies countries as possessing a fully developed "system", a "quasi-system", a "consistent set of practices", a "fragmented set of practices", "some practices", an "initial stage", or "nothing". Two of Werquin's categories (Werquin and Wihak 2011, p. 164) for the description of models and "best practice" are of interest here; namely the distinction between a fully developed "system" and a "quasi-system" of RVA. Werquin defines the two in the following manner:

© UNESCO Institute for Lifelong Learning 2015
M. Singh, *Global Perspectives on Recognising Non-formal and Informal Learning*,
Technical and Vocational Education and Training: Issues, Concerns and Prospects 21,
DOI 10.1007/978-3-319-15278-3_3

- "System: inclusive policy, a vision, a culture of Recognition of Non-formal and Informal Learning (RNFIL), and a global system. In detail: a legal framework or political consensus, practice, all groups or individuals, financial provision, quality assurance, all levels and sectors of education and training, high level of acceptance by the society, evaluation of the system (data, research . . . .).
- Quasi-system: inclusive policy, a vision, and a global system. In detail: a legal framework or political consensus, all groups or individuals, financial provision, quality assurance, all levels and sectors of education and training" (See Werquin and Wihak 2011, p. 164).

What is interesting here is the importance given to the role of policy and legal frameworks as key elements in the development of a "system" or "quasi-system" of RVA. According to Werquin's classification, none of the countries included within the OECD study possess a fully developed RVA system. Only Ireland, the Netherlands, Denmark and Norway can be described as possessing a quasi-system of RVA.

3.1 Policy and Legislation Relating Specifically to RVA

In line with Werquin's distinction between countries with fully-developed systems of RVA and those with quasi-systems, a distinction can also be made between those countries with uniform legal frameworks for RVA – such as Norway, Finland and Denmark (countries which display quasi- systemic characteristics) – and those countries in which policies and legislation relating to RVA are located within the context of education and training systems (i.e. countries that have not yet developed systems or quasi-systems of RVA). However, a third group of countries, which includes the USA, is particularly notable for its high levels of RVA activity combined with a lack of RVA-related government policy or legislation. This is because policies and RVA processes in the latter countries are institutional.

3.1.1 A Uniform Legal Framework for RVA

Legislation is a distinctive feature of RVA in the European context. Its formulation is guided by the European Council Resolution on Lifelong Learning (Council of the European Union 2004), which stresses that lifelong learning includes all learning from pre-school age through to post-retirement, including the entire spectrum of formal, non-formal and informal learning. The Resolution also reaffirms the effective validation and recognition of formal qualifications as well as non-formal and informal learning across countries and educational sectors, through increased transparency and better quality assurance. EU Member States are invited to encourage co-operation and the establishment of effective measures to validate learning outcomes, both as a crucial means to building bridges between formal, non-formal and informal learning and as prerequisites for the creation of a European area of lifelong learning.

Most countries in the European Union have explicit laws and regulations that provide a general framework for RVA within various sectors of education. In Norway, the Competence Reform (*Realkompetanse*) of 1999 guarantees the right of individuals – particularly adults – to primary, secondary and higher education services that are adapted to their needs and circumstances. Accordingly, laws and regulations exist which describe a general framework for this form of validation at every level of education. Another objective of this reform was to establish a national system for documenting and validating the non-formal and informal learning of adults that would be acknowledged in workplaces and within the education system. These principles are now anchored in legislation and have been reflected in the successive introduction of various elements which together comprise a national lifelong learning policy package (Christensen 2013).

At a strategic level, there has been a trend towards policies aimed at creating broad, differentiated opportunities for competence development. In the Strategy for Lifelong Learning 2007 (Norway. Ministry of Education and Research 2007), the validation of informal and non-formal learning was identified as a central priority. The government's Initiative on Lifelong Learning 2009 urged the promotion of a system for the validation of prior learning. The principles underpinning this validation system apply across all sectors and specify, among other provisions, that the validation process should be voluntary and beneficial to the individual. The opportunities, rights, and benefits relating to this validation process are promoted by various stakeholders at a local and national level.

Other Scandinavian countries – Finland and Denmark – present a similar situation. In the case of Finland, policy relating to learning outside the formal system is included in the country's Development Plan and is defined primarily in recent education legislation which provides for the recognition of non-formal and informal learning in the various education sectors, including comprehensive schools, upper secondary schools, post-comprehensive vocational institutions and adult vocational education (Blomqvist and Louko 2013). In Denmark, Act No. 556 of 6 June 2007 allows for the recognition of non-formal and informal learning by adults within the education and training system within the context of a comprehensive adult education and training system. The Act covers the following programmes for adults: subjects within general adult education (at primary or lower secondary levels) at Adult Education Centres; general upper secondary subjects at (also called higher preparatory single subjects); adult vocational training programmes; adult vocational basic education programmes; short-cycle post-secondary adult education; medium-cycle post-secondary adult education (diploma degrees); Adults are entitled to have competences previously acquired in non-formal and informal learning settings assessed by educational institutions (Andersen and Aagaard 2013). The Act has met with a high level of support, resulting in both public and private investment in the development of new qualifications and competences. In addition to this, Denmark has promulgated legislation for vocational education and training (VET) which includes the general principle of individual competence assessments as a basis for the preparation of personal education plans (Denmark. Ministry of Education (Undervisingsministeriet) 2008). The evaluation of legislation as a means to facilitate discussion of its outcomes and necessary future actions is an on-going process in some countries. In 2010 and 2011, the Danish Ministry of Education evaluated Act No. 556 (Denmark. Institute for Evaluation (EVA) 2010) with the aim of developing a new RVA action plan. The results of this evaluation were discussed by the Council for Adult Education and Training (VEU-Râdet).

In France, a key driver of RVA has been the validation of acquired experience (VAE) through the Social Modernisation Law of 2002, (France. Ministry of Employment and Solidarity, 17 January §133-146) together with two decrees, a general decree (No. 2002-615) and a specific one for higher education (decree No. 2002-590). This law made it possible to award full official qualifications on the basis of personal and professional experience if the candidate has been involved in paid, unpaid or voluntary employment or activity for at least three years. This legal framework extended the procedure to all educational institutions awarding qualifications registered in the Qualifications Register.

According to Werquin (2012), France has several coexisting laws, serving a range of specific purposes, such as the Bilan de Compétences (1991) which serves the specific purpose of providing workers with reskilling opportunities, particularly in the use of new Information and Communication Technologies (ICTs), which are having a big impact on the content of trades and occupations. Another specific feature of the French legislation is that none of the new laws have totally replaced previous ones in the same field. The VAPP 85 that established the principle of Validation of Occupational and Personal Learning Outcomes is used together with the Social Modernisation Law of 2002 to gain access to universities. In fact, it has been a tradition in the tertiary education system to use validation of occupational experience for access since the 1930s. Since the adoption of Validation of Acquired Experience (VAE) in the Social Modernisation Law of 2002 a significant investment has been made in the adult or continuing vocational education and training (CVET). While the Ministry of labour is in charge of lifelong learning in general, and of adult learning in particular, public policy concerning CVET has been highly decentralised and is overseen – and funded – by the regions. Companies must allocate a training budget equivalent of at least 1.6 % of their payroll to training employees.

Mexico has granted legal status to RVA through Agreement 286, which is designed to give learners access to all levels of the education system by offering an alternative pathway to that provided by the formal system. This Act also allows equivalences of competence certificates with credits of formal education programmes at the vocational and professional levels. The Mexican approach eschews adding new levels to the accreditation system, and instead distinguishes between separate pathways to the same educational or qualification outcome. The informal and non-formal pathways, though outside the traditional institutional structures, are nevertheless considered significant enough to be deemed equivalent pathways to a qualification (Campero Cuenca et al. 2008).

3.1.2   RVA Policy and Legislation Set in the Education and Training System

Germany, Austria, the Czech Republic, France, Republic of Korea, Canada and Mexico have located RVA policy and legislation within their respective education and training systems. In contrast to the Scandinavian countries, Austria does not have a uniform legal framework or an explicit RVA national strategy that includes *all* sectors, but it does have relevant legal acts and regulations set in the formal system of education allowing ministries and institutions to develop a variety of mechanisms and arrangements for RVA (Austria. Federal Ministry of Education Arts and Culture 2011). In Germany, RVA is an institutionalised part of the education system and, above all, the dual system of vocational education and training. The Vocational Training Reform Act, which came into force on 1 April 2005, reformed and amalgamated the Vocational Training Act and the Vocational Training Promotion Act with the policy objective of dismantling barriers between education and vocational training (including work experience), and facilitating the translation of such recognition into both qualifications and employment benefits where possible (Germany. Federal Ministry of Education and Science (BMBF) 2008).

In the Czech Republic, the legislative framework for RVA is outlined in Act No. 179/2006 Coll., on the Verification and Recognition of Further Education Results, implemented on 1 September 2007. This legislation provides a definition of the term 'qualification' (full or partial) and establishes a national qualifications register. In accordance with Act No. 179/2006, any individual over the age of 18 years who has completed (as a minimum) basic education can request the assessment of their learning outcomes in view of achieving a partial qualification (Stárek 2013).

Staying in Europe, but in contrast to these broader aims, Latvian policy and legislation focuses on particular sections of the education system. The Education Law, which forms the basis of education policy in Latvia, stipulates that teachers in the education sector (except in higher education institutions) are entitled to receive pedagogical training through self-directed or further education programmes (Šiliņa 2008). This initiative, comprising a one-year process of diverse training modules, begins with a procedure to validate participants' prior experience, skills and relevant activities in the field.

In the Republic of Korea, the Academic Credit Bank System (ACBS) has a strong statutory foundation. The Act on the Recognition of Credits etc. of 1999 recognises non-formal and informal learning. Degrees conferred through ACBS are recognised as equivalent to those of a university or college under the Higher Education Act. No legal discrimination is made between university graduates and ACBS degree holders (Baik 2013). Indeed, in 1990, prior to the implementation of the ACBS Act, the Korean government had already established a legal basis for the attainment of bachelor's degrees through self-education programmes comprised of self-directed learning systems. Credits are also awarded within the ACBS through job-training institutions accredited by the Ministry of Labour. These institutions rely on the Act on the Establishment and Operation of Private Teaching Institutes and Extracurricular Lessons and on lifelong education centres associated with universities (Republic of Korea. Ministry of Education, Science and Technology 2009).

In the Philippines, Executive Order No. 330 allows individuals who have acquired work experience and expertise through non-formal and informal training to be awarded appropriate academic degrees in higher education institutions by the Commission on Higher Education. This executive order was adopted by the Expanded Tertiary Education Equivalency and Accreditation Programme (ETEEAP) as an integral part of the educational system, and designated CHED as the authority responsible for its implementation. In addition to this, under Executive Order 358, the Technical Education and Skills Development Authority (TESDA) and CHED are jointly charged with the promotion of the Ladderised Education Programme. Under the existing model, TVET qualifications are embedded in the curriculum of the degree programme. This allows the individual free entry and exit. There are also schools equipped with open learning systems which factor in the experiences of learners, although not necessarily in the form of accreditation. Other RVA tracks include accreditation programmes, such as the Non-Traditional Studies Programme of the Polytechnic University of the Philippines (PUP), which assesses 72 units of college education and accreditation of prior learning; the open distance learning courses operated by the PUP and the University of the Philippines; and per unit study options leading to college courses at the PUP and the Far Eastern University. Beyond these accreditation programmes, the Philippines Commission for UNESCO reports that the Philippines has yet to put in place a national RVA system (Philippines. National Commission for UNESCO 2011).

3.1.3 Policies Are Institutional

In comparison to countries in Europe and developed Oceania (Australia and New Zealand), it is interesting to note that the USA achieves high levels of RVA activity without undertaking government initiatives. Policies and processes for RVA (or Prior Learning Assessment, as it is known in the USA) are institutional. The governing structure of higher education is locally controlled within each individual state, although financial support is delivered through a combination of individual, local, state and federal funding. Secondly, there are no federal curricular standards that all institutions of higher education must follow. Although some rules and regulations exist for institutions receiving federal support, these do not regulate the particulars of curricular decisions. Some states (e.g., Minnesota, Oklahoma, Pennsylvania and Vermont) have created state-wide systems for supporting and evaluating Prior Learning Assessment (PLA). The Pennsylvania Department of Education has developed the Pennsylvania Prior Learning Assessment Consortium, which is comprised of institutions that have agreed to follow the consortium's guidelines. In Vermont, PLA is conducted through an office within the Vermont

State College System and credits are transferable to each of the state colleges by agreement. Educational institutions and workplaces are responsible for the quality of their own PLA assessments and services. A federal initiative directed towards PLA does not exist as there are no regulations to monitor enforcement. However, the USA does possess a national system of accreditation for colleges and universities with the power to influence their PLA processes. The six regional commissions are voluntary, non-governmental membership associations that define, maintain and promote excellence across institutions by accrediting whole institutions.

The Middle States Commission on Higher Education and the North Central Association of Colleges and Schools Higher Education Commission are two examples of commissions that set out principles, standards and guidelines for awarding credit for experiential learning through PLA. Regional accreditation bodies also set PLA guidelines for institutions; the philosophy, policy and practice for accepting PLA credits, established by individual institutions, must reflect local faculty agreement. Consequently, departmental policies and the practices of individual faculty members govern the actual practices of credit. PLA policies and processes in the USA are established within educational institutions and workplaces on an entirely individual basis. Accordingly, with respect to matters of accreditation and quality assurance, educational institutions and workplaces are responsible for the quality of their own PLA assessments and services (Travers 2011).

3.1.4 RVA Legislation in Working Life

The involvement of social partners (including professional associations) is a key feature of RVA legislation. In Norway, the new basic agreement for 2010–2013 between the Confederation of Norwegian Enterprise (NHO) and the Norwegian Confederation of Trade Unions (LO) emphasises the importance of making prior learning visible, stating in § 16-4 of the Documentation of actual competence (i.e., informal learning): "It is important that the enterprise has a system for documenting the individual's experience, courses and practice related to the employment relationship." (Norway. LO and NHO 2009, p. 42). For many adults who may have worked in a trade for years with little schooling and without any professional qualification, the desire to obtain formal trade certification is a key driver of RVA. Experience so far shows that validation is often geared to obtaining a trade certificate (Christensen 2013).

In France the Social Modernisation Law of 2002 was consolidated in the law of 4 May 2004, ratifying the social partners' unanimous agreement of 2003. Further legislation (including the Decentralisation Act of 2004) extended the scope for RVA, along with numerous inter-professional agreements encompassing various professional sectors and companies (Paulet 2013). The Law on Lifelong Vocational Training and Social Dialogue, which enables employees to access training outside working hours, is another important legislative instrument, as it gave employers an important role in RVA. The main purpose of this reform was to empower employees to take charge of qualification and skills development in order to strengthen the link between vocational training and career progression, and to overcome the divide between employer-driven training pathways focussed on specific workplaces and self-motivated training undertaken by individuals. There has been significant growth in the number of professional training contracts in the wake of these reforms and 100,000 professional training contracts had already been ratified by 2005. These professional training contracts serve to construct on-going courses for employees and are designed to stabilise them in their jobs and to enable them to advance in their careers. Moreover, RVA measures enable many individuals to obtain an annual certification of their skills and acknowledge the formative nature of work (or of another activity) (Paulet 2013). Awareness of the right of employees to training is growing and all employees now have a capital of acquired rights. RVA is fully integrated in enterprise skills development strategies and has met with a favourable reception in public opinion.

In Germany, the inclusion in collective agreements of arrangements for the recognition of experience-based non-formal and informal learning is particularly conducive to the development of RVA. A legal basis for the recognition of employees' skills and qualifications in collective agreements is provided by Article 9 Section 3 of the Basic Law, in which freedom of association is defined as a fundamental right; and the Collective Agreements Act, which asserts the principle of the autonomy of collective bargaining. Pursuant to these, employers and employees are free to agree on working conditions in companies with no regulatory intervention by the state. In addition to defining pay and working hours, this includes arrangements for training and continuing education (Germany. Federal Ministry of Education and Science (BMBF) 2008, p. 50).

While the general institutional framework for recognising non-formal and informal learning in Mexico is governed by the Ministry of Education Agreement 286 (Acuerdo 286 de la SEP; issued on 30 October 2000), labour competences are equivalent to full or partial formal programmes, at technical and/or professional levels of the national education system.

3.1.5 Laws to Improve the Recognition of Foreign Professional Qualifications

The German federal government passed the draft of the Law to Improve the Assessment and Recognition of Foreign Professional Qualifications (Recognition Act) in March 2011. This draft included a new federal law, the so-called Professional Qualifications Assessment Act along with amendments to existing regulations relating to the recognition of vocational and professional qualifications across roughly 60 occupational and professional laws and ordinances at a federal level. The federal states have announced changes in regulations within their jurisdiction to improve procedures for the recognition of teachers, pre-school teachers and engineers. Previously, relatively few professionals entering Germany were able to have their vocational qualifications assessed. The new federal law will greatly extend the entitlement to an assessment of foreign vocational qualifications (Germany. Federal Ministry of Education and Science (BMBF) 2012).

3.2   RVA Subsumed Under NQFs and Their Regulatory Bodies

France, Australia, New Zealand, Mauritius, Portugal, Namibia, Scotland, England, and South Africa have all subsumed RVA within legislation regulating NQFs and their regulatory bodies. In Australia, RVA was introduced in the early 1990s as part of a larger national training reform agenda that included the Australian Qualifications Framework (AQF). As Cameron (2011) notes, RVA is standard and a requirement of any accredited training delivered within the AQF. Every qualification in the AQF is categorised according to the educational sector responsible for its accreditation. Likewise, in New Zealand, the standards for qualifications in relevant schools and in tertiary education dominate the discourse on recognition. Under section 246A (1) of the Education Act 1989 (New Zealand Government 1989), the functions of the New Zealand Qualifications Authority (NZQA) include mechanisms for the recognition of learning (for example the recognition of learning through qualifications gained and standards met). The New Zealand Qualifications Framework (NZQF) is designed to optimise the recognition of educational achievement and its contribution to New Zealand's economic, social and cultural success (Keller 2013).

Education and qualifications in Scotland and Wales are the responsibility of the Scottish Government and Welsh Government and their agencies. In Scotland, for example, the Scottish Qualifications Authority is the responsible body. RVA is driven by the Scottish Credit and Qualifications Framework (SCQF). Formally launched in 2001, the SCQF has generated renewed enthusiasm and momentum for RVA since 2005, increasingly driven by a workforce development agenda linked to employability and skills development. The SCQF is a descriptive rather than a regulatory framework, and "facilitates the awarding of credit and supports credit transfer and progression routes within the Scottish system" (SCQF 2005). It provides a model capable of integrating learning from different contexts, both formal and informal. In addition to the SCQF, this renewed interest in RVA at a national level is driven by government policy, as set out in *Skills for Scotland*: A Lifelong Skills Strategy (Scottish Government 2007a) and *The Government Economic Strategy* (Scottish Government 2007b). Efforts to harmonise the separate systems across the UK through a national qualifications framework have been in progress since the mid-1990s (Hawley 2010).

In Wales, the Credit and Qualifications Framework for Wales (CQFW) has, since 2002, been developed (Welsh Assembly Government 2010). It is intended to facilitate "parity in the recognition of achievement for learners of all ages, whether they are learning in the workplace, community, at school, college, university." The framework comprises three pillars, including frameworks for regulated general and vocational learning (the NQF and QCF), the Framework for Higher Education Qualifications (FHEQ), and Quality Assured Lifelong Learning (QALL). QUALL encompasses learning which takes place outside regulated qualifications. It may include adult and community learning, company training, non-formal and informal training.

The NQF models implemented in England, Wales and Northern Ireland draw substantially from the Scottish model. In England and Northern Ireland the Qualifications and Curriculum Authority (QCA) is the responsible body and has recently completed a major project to establish and implement the Qualifications and Credit Framework (QCF), which replaced the National Qualifications Framework in September 2010. According to the QCF, qualifications are broken down into units comprising a number of credits each. Within the QCF all units of learning accrue value as credits within the education and training system, enabling learners to transfer learning from one context to another, steadily building upon previous experiences. Credits accrued by learners can ultimately lead to the award of a qualification. At present, over 1,300 approved qualifications fall within the framework and, as of March 2009, there were over 650 providers of relevant courses (Schuller and Watson 2009, p. 148). This framework is still in its initial stages and must be given time to fully develop, but these are positive early signs.

The South African Qualifications Act of the South African Qualifications Authority (SAQA) was promulgated in 1995 and provides the context for RVA in the post-apartheid era. This was replaced by a new NQF Act promulgated in 2008 and implemented from 1 June 2009 (Samuels 2013). Its key objectives remain unchanged and reinforce the importance of the underlying principles of mobility and progression, quality of education and training, and the redress of historical discrimination. The NQF Act in South Africa is an enabling piece of legislation for RVA. Through implementing all aspects of the Act, RPL could enter into the mainstream to become one of the ways in which learners can gain access to learning opportunities, achieve credit towards a formal qualification or be awarded a qualification should they meet all the quality assurance criteria of a specific qualification (Lloyd 2012). All three sub-frameworks of the Quality Council also speak to RPL. There are some challenges in the implementation of RPL: Two current statutory regulations are inhibiting the development and implementation of RPL: matriculation with endorsement as an entry requirement into higher education; and the 50 % residency clause. The endorsement requirements indicate certain subject combinations and particular grades at which these must be studied: At present there is no formal systemic funding for RPL in South Africa; A limited number of assessment centres focusing on RPL have been established based on local needs, in contrast to the priority given to RPL in national policy; and finally RPL should be an integrated feature of assessment policies of ETQAs and their constituent providers (Ibid.)

In Portugal, a legal regulation allows the New Opportunities Initiative to be linked to the NQF. The Decree Law of December 31, 2007 concerning the NQF

(Administrative Rule no. 370/2008) is also the basis for the regulation of various components of the adult education and training system (Gomes 2013). As a result, a comprehensive legal basis for the entire adult education and training system has been developed. The existence of this wide-ranging and comprehensive framework assists those institutions that are responsible for ensuring that Portugal's policies on adult education and RVA meet EU recommendations (European Commission 2004, 2008).

In Namibia, one of the objects of the Namibia Qualifications Authority (NQA), as stated in the NQA Act, Section 4(g) is to evaluate and recognise competences acquired outside formal education. The Act was promulgated in 1996 and, as a result, the recognition of non-formal and informal learning is legally provided for and is thus mandatory in Namibia. The challenges relate more to the implementation of this mandate. The NQA, together with the Namibia Training Authority, recently developed a national policy on RVA which was approved, in principle, by the Minister of Education. Once formal approval has been granted, this policy will be implemented.

In Mauritius, the Mauritius Qualifications Authority (MQA), the regulatory body of the TVET sector, introduced the concept of RPL "to recognise and validate competences for the purpose of certification obtained outside the formal education and training systems", that is both non-formal and informal learning, with the intention of bringing people back into the training system and/or enabling them to upgrade and sustain skills previously acquired through work and life experience (Allgoo 2013).

3.3 Lifelong Learning Policies and Legislation

There is a growing trend towards a perception of RVA as a key pillar of lifelong learning policies, legislation and strategies. RVA legislation in most European countries forms part of an overarching lifelong learning strategy for broader reforms in the education system and in society. Since the publication of the landmark European Commission report *Making a European Area of Lifelong Learning a Reality*, lifelong learning has been on the political agenda (European Commission 2001). The key elements of the lifelong learning strategy in Norway include (in addition to RVA legislation): rights-based basic education (13 years); building "bridges" between different types of education and training; avoiding dead ends the right to (unpaid) study leave for employees; career guidance; the right and obligation to Norwegian language training and social studies for immigrants/refugees; the general availability of a variety of further and continuing education and training opportunities; and finally, the development of appropriate and adequate financing arrangements for education providers and beneficiaries, including companies and individual learners (Norway. Ministry of Education and Research (RNMER) 2007).

Strengthening adult education services across the country, including those located outside the school system in local communities targeting job-seekers and prison inmates has been the focus of the Norwegian government's 2007 Strategy for Lifelong Learning. The subsequent 2009 Initiative on Lifelong Learning states that RVA will be important to counteract the rising drop-out rate in secondary education and the problem posed by the large number of unemployed persons who have not completed upper secondary education (45 % of all unemployed). The development of a flexible system with the capacity to address the widespread need to reconcile education and training with work and family life was highlighted accordingly in a 2009 white paper (Christensen 2013).

Recognition and permeability are among the seven strategic goals of the Czech Republic government's lifelong learning strategy (Stárek 2013). In Denmark, the national strategy for lifelong learning is based substantially on 'Education and Lifelong Skills Upgrading for All', a report compiled for the European Commission in April 2007 (Denmark. Ministry of Education 2007). The strategy promotes participation in adult education and continuing training, and aims to improve opportunities for adults in the labour market (Andersen and Aagaard 2013). In France, the lifelong learning policy is closely linked to vocational training and social dialogue enabling employees to access training outside working hours (Paulet 2013). In New Zealand, the thrust of lifelong learning policy is centred on enabling flexibility in learning pathways through the New Zealand Qualifications Framework (Keller 2013).

In Japan, the Lifelong Learning Promotion Act was formulated in 1990. In addition to this, a commitment to the philosophy of lifelong learning was clearly expressed in the Revised Basic Act on Education (enacted 2006). Moreover, the Social Education Act makes reference to activities organised through libraries and museums. Home education is prescribed under the Basic Act on Education, while the Act on the Open University of Japan aims to provide the general public with a wide range of opportunities to access university education services through the effective utilisation of broadcasting media such as television and radio. The Human Resources Development Promotion Law is underpinned by the understanding that enabling workers to effectively demonstrate their abilities throughout their entire working lives will enhance both their status and job security. Accordingly, employers are encouraged to promote the development of their employees' vocational skills by providing access to necessary professional training services and affording employees the assistance necessary to secure opportunities to undertake job training relating to their work (Japan. Ministry of Education, Culture, Sports, Science and Technology (MEXT) 2008).

A growing number of developing countries have established lifelong learning policies and legislation. The Republic of Korea's Third National Lifelong Learning Promotion Plan runs from 2013 to 2017 (Republic of Korea. Ministry of Education, Science and Technology 2013). In Thailand, the National Education Act (1999) and the Amended Act (2002) state that educational management must be centred on a lifelong and continuing process of learning that identifies lifelong education as the integration of formal, non-formal and informal education. Chapter 3, Section 15 of the Act clearly defined three modes of education: formal, non-formal and informal (Thailand. Ministry of Education, Office of the Non-Formal and Informal Education (ONIE) 2011). Special laws promote non-formal education in Thailand. The Promotion of Non-Formal and Informal Education Act (2008) states that all sectors of society shall participate in the provision of education.

In Cambodia, the Non-Formal Learning Act 2001 has facilitated several alternative learning pathways to ensure equal access to education opportunities, taking into account human development outcomes, programmes for those with disabilities, re-entry programmes, accelerated learning, functional literacy, and learning in community learning centres. The more recent Education Law further helps to strengthen governance and accountability, while the Expanded Basic Education Programme 2006–2010 promotes development outcomes that integrate life skills and aims to achieve equitable access to quality basic education by 2015, thereby meeting commitments under the United Nations' Millennium Development Goals (Cambodia. Ministry of Education, Youth and Sport 2008, p. 3). In Indonesia, the Act of the Republic of Indonesia No. 20 of 2003 on the National Education System provided the impetus to support educational reform. The Act clearly states the equivalency of the formal and informal (UNESCO Bangkok Office 2006).

In the Philippines, two parallel basic education systems exist: the school-based, formal basic learning system and the community-based Alternative Learning System (ALS). The ALS provides a Non-formal Education Accreditation and Equivalency (NFE A&E) Programme outside the school system to address the learning needs of those who wish to acquire basic literacy skills as well as functional literacy skills equivalent to both elementary and secondary levels (Philippines. National Commission for UNESCO 2011).

While legal provisions promoting the right to education of all citizens in countries such as Thailand and Indonesia have facilitated the implementation of equivalency programmes, there still continues to be a stigma attached to non-formal or alternative modes of learning. A report on the Joint UNESCO and UNICEF Regional Workshop on *Equivalency programmes and alternative certified learning* states that the low value attached to non-formal education "can be removed only when Equivalency Programmes provide the same level of quality education as that acquired through formal education and produce results that are comparable within which countries strive to develop programmes, whether formal or non-formal. Introducing alternative delivery models in formal systems may also serve to augment the social value of such programmes and the resources available for reaching the marginalised." (UNESCO Bangkok Office and UNICEF 2011, p. 27).

3.4 Summary

This section on RVA legislation has examined whether countries have developed an overarching legal framework specifically for RVA, as is the case in Norway, Finland and Denmark, or whether a range of relevant legal acts and regulations set in the formal education and training systems exist, allowing institutions and government departments to develop a variety of mechanisms and practical arrangements for RVA, depending on the diversity of purposes of RVA and different interests at stake, as in Germany and Austria.

Not all RVA activity is necessarily linked to governmental policy and legislative activity. A significant level of RVA activity is undertaken in the USA, for instance, despite a lack of relevant government policies or legislation.

Countries with NQFs, particularly the first generation developers of NQFs, have institutionalised RVA as a standard and a requirement of any accredited training within the NQF. This is the case in countries such as Australia, New Zealand, Scotland, the UK and South Africa. But this is also a growing trend in many developing countries, where, in fact, NQFs are being developed to make RVA happen. In Mauritius and Namibia, governments expect to mainstream RVA within their education and training system through legislation establishing NQFs.

The classification of legislation and policies outlined in the chapter will however need further interrogation and research, particularly in relation to the question of whether countries with a uniform policy and legislation on RVA are more likely to develop systems of RVA than is the case where such legislation is absent. Another issue to probe could be whether policy discourses on funding, quality assurance, assessment, and the nature of educational practices are fragmentary or consistent.

Another question of importance would be whether NQF legislation alone is able to ensure that RVA is taken on board; or, whether other legislations specific to RVA are needed to enlighten users about the vision of the processes such as assessment, financing and guidance and counselling as is done in France. Werquin (2012) has highlighted that in the French case there are several other laws, such as the Law of Decentralisation accompanying the Modernisation Law of 2002, which have given stakeholders and providers the power to implement RVA (Werquin 2012).

Legislation is an important aspect of RVA in European countries. Werquin (2012) has highlighted some of the typical characteristics of RVA legislation in France that could also apply to most Western and Northern European countries. In France the purpose of legislation is to give every individual the right to apply for RVA. Legislation targets specific groups, such as adults lacking secondary education (France, Norway), i.e. adults, who may benefit from participating in a process of recognition of non-formal and informal learning. Another feature is the wide involvement of several stakeholders at both national and local levels (e.g., role of regional authorities in France), and end-users (e.g., employers), in both preparatory work and in work concerning the formalities of the law. This ensures societal recognition, acceptance and ownership in the RVA process. Moreover, legislation comes from the involvement of stakeholders both from the world of work (including community and volunteering "work") and the world of education. Finally, legislation is considered a way to communicate to the wider world the value of the RVA process (Werquin 2012).

In contrast to the context in the developed North outlined above, most countries in the developing South, with the notable exception of Mexico and the Republic of Korea, still lack specific legislation(s) on RVA. Namibia has developed a set of Guidelines on RPL, but Guidelines and RPL policies, as Werquin (2012) points out, do not have the same currency as law.

In many European countries RVA legislation forms part of an overarching lifelong learning strategy for broader reforms in the education system, with far-reaching implications for the management, delivery and design of programmes. Although there has been a growing interest in the development of lifelong learning strategies and legislation in the South, these strategies deliver *access* to non-formal *provision* for early school-leavers as a second chance to enter the education system, rather than making RVA a right through the *assessment and validation* of the competences and learning that adults and youth already possess. Despite this shortcoming, many governments in developing countries are currently making efforts to make RVA integral to NQFs. Through linking RVA to NQFs, RVA could enter into the mainstream to become one of the ways in which learners can gain access to learning opportunities, achieve credit towards a formal qualification or be awarded a qualification should they meet all the quality assurance criteria of a specific qualification.

Chapter 4
RVA's Role in Education, Working Life and Society

The recognition of all forms of learning is one of the many proposed solutions to the biggest socio-economic challenges including poverty reduction, economic development, the enhancement of employability, social inclusion and cohesion, personal and professional development as well as democratic citizenship in society. Unfortunately, countries frequently focus on particular aspects of RVA as discrete fields or prioritise a single particular aspect. In contrast, this chapter aims to understand RVA in terms of the broader and overarching notions of education for sustainable development and lifelong learning. Both perspectives imply an integrative approach with the potential to draw together the various sectors and purposes of personal, social and economic development. Moreover, both concepts are underpinned by values of self-respect and responsibility, respect for difference, solidarity, dialogue and exploration. Using empirical evidence from a number of countries, this chapter examines RVA's contribution to:

- paving pathways to education, training and qualifications;
- promoting workforce development and participation in the labour market;
- social inclusion and democratic citizenship;
- personal and professional empowerment.

4.1 Paving Pathways to Education, Training and Qualifications

4.1.1 RVA as a Policy Tool Targeting Education and Training Reforms

RVA is gradually becoming an accepted feature of educational reforms in the developed world. Stimulated not least of all by the efforts of the EU in this area, many European countries recognise the importance of qualifications in the economy

© UNESCO Institute for Lifelong Learning 2015   63
M. Singh, *Global Perspectives on Recognising Non-formal and Informal Learning*,
Technical and Vocational Education and Training: Issues, Concerns and Prospects 21,
DOI 10.1007/978-3-319-15278-3_4

and society at large. RVA is regarded as a policy tool that, in combination with other measures, targets more broadly the education and training system. In Austria, RVA is part of a recently published lifelong learning strategy (Republik Österreich 2011) designed with the objective of:

- enhancing transparency throughout the education system;
- providing certification for knowledge, skills and competences acquired outside traditional educational institutions via allocation in the NQF;
- strengthening learning-outcome orientation;
- establishing mutual recognition of qualifications across institutions and sectors as a foundation of the whole educational system;
- implementing the present validation strategy;
- raising national and international mobility, especially for persons with low formal qualifications.

A key factor influencing RVA implementation in Austria is the structural integration of the business sector with the education and training system. The practical nature of the so-called "dual education" system that is already aligned to skills development in the workplace allows the links between experiential workplace learning and institutional learning content to be acknowledged (Austria. Federal Ministry of Education, the Arts and Culture 2011).

In France, the system of recognition known as the Validation des acquis de l'éxpérience (VAE) have contributed to debate on a professional hierarchy which is based to a large degree on degrees and diplomas. By taking into account acquired experience, VAE is believed to open up possibilities to limit the negative social and economic impacts of dropping out of school, or otherwise 'failing' within the formal education sector. The system of recognition is also having significant effects on the university system. The recognition of skills and competences irrespective of how they were learned requires a revision of university programmes. Universities must focus not on the inputs and duration of programmes, but on what students are able to do and what they know at the end of the learning process. In achieving this, the French system puts great stress on the role of guidance from the point of admission to the point of qualification.

Reforms in US higher education in terms of curricular structures – flexibility, modularisation or elective options of American institutions – have facilitated the development of RVA. Flexible pathways – horizontal, vertical and diagonal – between levels of post-secondary education are an important feature of the US higher education system and allow for other flexibilities. RVA, in its turn, has facilitated further innovations, such as for-credit-RPL workshops, in which RPL portfolios are constructed and submitted; alternative introductory courses that take field experience into account; and "trade-offs" between extra needed work (in English-language academic development, for example) and knowledge informally acquired (other languages or relevant field experience) that are considered as vital to graduate outcomes (Michelson 2012).

The approach to RPL has been quite successful in the United States, with developments in RVA tracking reforms in the higher education sector. Factors contributing to this success story include: a desire on the part of some institutions to attract adult learners; the willingness to offer many degree programmes to students studying part-time; the establishment in the late 1960s and early 1970 of a number of experimental baccalaureate-granting liberal arts colleges, technical and professional colleges, and universities; a single system that spans community colleges, baccalaureate-granting liberal arts colleges, technical and professional colleges, and universities; a relatively large number of elective courses that are not necessarily tied to a particular year of study (Michelson 2012). RPL has resulted in a critical mass of what are termed "adult learner friendly institutions", whose policies and procedures are widely recognised.

In South Africa, RVA is closely tied to post-apartheid education and training reforms. Within the education and training system, RVA has emerged as a key tool in efforts to improve education levels among the black population in particular, operating within the wider context of various formal and informal initiatives. This goal continues to provide the current rationale for RVA in South Africa. Despite the high level of macro-stability achieved, the levels of inequality remain high. Though no longer solely based on racial divisions, high levels of unemployment exist, particularly in the under-30 age group (49 % in 2002), and are higher for women than for men. For all the above reasons, 'redress for past and present discriminatory practices' is still a key purpose of RVA, as is "contributing to a better educated, more skilled and more efficient workforce" (SAQA 2012a, pp. 1–9). One of the specific objectives of RVA is to increase craft and related trades, and take black African employees beyond their current elementary occupations to more advanced levels (Samuels 2013). Much attention is therefore being paid to recognising alternative traditions of knowledge and skills based on the ethnicity or craft. There is also much sustained scholarship to make RVA an effective pedagogical device to create bridges between work-related and academic knowledge (Michelson 2012).

Creating a diversified education and training system that captures the full significance of alternative learning pathways is regarded as an important contribution of RVA in Mauritius, Botswana, the Seychelles, and Namibia (Steenekamp and Singh 2012). Within these contexts, RVA has been implemented with a view to promoting equity of access and fair chances for all learners. In Mauritius, RVA is used as a means of reforming the education and training system, encouraging those people who have been left out of the system to further develop skills and knowledge acquired outside the formal education system and to provide pathways to formal qualification. In the Seychelles, too, RVA is used to facilitate access, transfer and award of credits leading to certification of qualifications within the NQF. In Botswana, the acute shortage of tertiary institutions is forcing a change in attitudes towards the recognition of non-traditional modes of learning. There, RVA is used by individuals in employment to access ODL for personal academic and professional development (Steenekamp and Singh 2012).

4.1.2   Further Education and Training: A New Site for RVA Linked to Higher Education

Germany has several RVA pathways to higher education via education and training: (1) Individuals with previous work experience are able to sit an examination at the conclusion of a vocational apprenticeship comprised of alternating work and training segments. Admission to this examination is granted by competent bodies solely on the basis of documentary evidence; (2) Within the higher education system itself, applicants with vocational qualifications are admitted to universities, contributing to the strengthening of educational mobility in Germany (Lohmar and Eckhardt 2011); (3) Adults with work experience can gain general school certificates constituting an entrance qualification to higher education at a later stage via the second educational pathway; (4) A credit point system to shorten study periods has been developed. The practice of awarding credits for vocational competences towards higher education study programmes (ANKOM) has been implemented at individual institutions of higher education and study programmes (Germany. Federal Ministry of Education and Science (BMBF) 2008, p. 24); (5) Efforts are underway to develop a reference framework for the accreditation of vocational competences towards higher education admission qualifications and the development of recommended action plans for institutions of higher education and education as well as educational policies (Germany. Federal Ministry of Education and Science (BMBF) 2008, p. 47).

In the USA, there has been a growing focus on the development and implementation of RVA (known as Prior Learning Assessment (PLA)) policies and processes for adult learners in higher education institutions over the last 40 years (see Bamford-Rees 2008; in Travers 2011). There, RVA is located almost exclusively in higher education, where it is utilised not as a means to facilitate access, but in the allocation of academic credit to learners who have been admitted through other means. Opportunities for PLA exist in: (1) degree completion institutions – where students can transfer credits earned from a variety of accredited institutions from different states, including PLA credits. (2) Credit transfer support services – organisations which offer information on institutional credit transfer policies and provide students/adults with a "passport" in the form of a web-based platform, enabling individuals to consolidate their academic histories into a single location. Challenges remain however; PLA is not universally available, the acceptance and utilisation of credits may be restricted, and PLA credits are often not transferable between institutions (Ganzglass et al. 2011).

In the Republic of Korea, the Academic Credit Bank System (ACBS) facilitates the recognition of non-formal and informal learning, allowing individuals to obtain academic degrees and vocational certificates on the basis of credits. Entry through the ACBS is predominantly sought by those who wish to acquire a bachelor's or associate's degree, or at least achieve credits towards that end. A range of stakeholders are involved in the ACBS and specialists from industry are on the evaluation committee. One of the most important components in the system is the National Institute for Lifelong Education (NILE). This body accredits educational institutes as well as managing and operating the system as a whole (Baik 2013).

In Japan, access to higher education institutions such as universities, specialised training colleges and vocational schools can be gained through a national high school equivalency examination and certification system established under the 2007 School Education Act. This system is open to individuals educated primarily in informal or non-formal settings, and who lack secondary school qualifications.

Denmark's approach to RVA is based on its long tradition of individual competence evaluation. Starting in 2004, an increased focus was placed on the validation of non-formal and informal learning, and in August 2007 the educational fields covered by relevant legislation were expanded to include vocational training, general adult education and general upper secondary education, adult basic education, VET programmes, and VVU (continuing adult education) degrees and diploma degrees. In Denmark, RVA features in reforms aiming to consolidate adult and continuing education into a single coherent system which allows adults to use RVA at all levels of the adult education system. There is support for those seeking recognition through: bridging or supplementary courses and adult vocational training courses; recognition of workplace learning; reference points that serve the educational objectives of an education and training programme; competence development within enterprises; and capacity-building of teaching and guidance staff of the country's educational institutions. In the voluntary sector, Denmark is particularly well equipped for recognition (e.g. the documentation tool My Competence Folder) (Andersen and Aagaard 2013).

In Finland, RVA is linked to vocationally-oriented competence-based qualifications. It ensures access of adults to further study at all levels of education and provides a flexible method for updating skills through competence tests with a focus on vocational competences. Many adults acquire non-formal preparatory training where they are provided with personalised learning programmes (Blomqvist and Louko 2013).

In the Philippines, adult education and training comprise three programmes, disaggregated into the "tri-focalised" education system: the functional literacy programmes of the Department of Education's Bureau of Alternative Learning System (BALS); the technical and vocational education and training (TVET) of TESDA; and CHED's higher education (Soliven and Reyes 2008). There is a move towards identifying standards to measure the quality of learning outcomes for application in the areas of accreditation and equivalency, literacy, and technical and vocational training among others (Philippines. National Commission for UNESCO 2011).

4.2   Working Life

Providing certification pathways, promoting training in vocational skills and facilitating knowledge development are important aspects of RVA. TVET, up-skilling, informal on-the-job training and a range of other similar types of labour-sector learning fall within this field of action. The challenge for RVA programmes is to function coherently within the education system and to align with the needs of stakeholders, particularly those sectors of the labour market for which training programmes are designed. This is a matter of creating synergies within the education and training system, and facilitating mobility for those who aspire to progress through it. This section explores the following themes:

- RVA at the interface of VET and industry;
- interfaces with social sectors – health, social services and adult education ;
- skills recognition and labour mobility across national borders;
- employability and human resource allocation;
- RVA for skilled immigrants and the recognition of foreign qualifications;
- impacts for employers and organisations;
- Family skills as a potential source of human resource development;
- industry-responsive National Competency-Based Frameworks
- development of competence standards by companies;
- RVA and skills development for the informal sector.

4.2.1   RVA at the Interface of VET and Industry

Workplace-based RVA has been dependent on reforms in vocational training which have promoted stronger integration between industry and the education and training system. In France, historically, there has been a strong degree of structural integration of industry with the education and training system. The term "qualifications" refers to a person's ability to fulfil the requirements of a particular position. This is reflected in many ways: qualifications are linked to specific occupations and are referred to as descriptions of occupations in collective agreements; the training system in France is decentralised and public policy concerning vocational education is overseen – and funded – by regional agencies for youth and jobseekers; and companies are expected to allocate a training budget equivalent to at least 1.6 % of their overall payroll (Paulet 2013).

Germany provides an impressive array of examples of recognition of informal learning in the work domain. The close links between qualification and rehabilitation courses administered through the country's employment agencies have proven conducive to the development of RVA, with close collaborative ties between the qualification system and continuing training providers in particular industries. RVA in continuing training has provided professionals in the field of ICTs with opportunities for further development. RVA also features in collective agreements, giving greater security to individuals who have acquired skills through informal and non-formal learning in recognised apprenticeship trades. Similarly, provisions exist within the German public sector for scaled remuneration on the basis of work experience and length of service. Individuals can enrol in training programmes provided that they have a minimum of practical experience, with industry training agencies providing leadership in the design and development of RVA processes.

The recognition of competences in informal settings in Germany is very important for low-skilled workers, who often lack any formal certification. Low-skilled workers are often unaware of their specific competences and have difficulty identifying and articulating these. It is important that RVA provides opportunities to this target group to make competences visible and to improve employability (Beinke and Spilittstößer 2011).

In South Africa, the SAQA Guidelines on RVA stress the need for policies and procedures that indicate the purpose of RVA to support workforce development within industry sectors. Firms within the formal sector pay a training levy that is administered by the Sector Education and Training Authorities and is used for RVA (Samuels 2013). Despite various successes, the labour market remains concerned about the relevance of the schooling curriculum and of higher education; this is currently being addressed through various initiatives, such as the establishment of a qualifications sub-framework for the occupational sector by the Quality Council for Trades and Occupations. South Africa has developed and is implementing a form of industry-based training known as learnerships. Here, RVA takes place in the workplace. Learnerships are a response to current declines in apprenticeship commencements in South Africa. By 2010 more than 182,000 learnerships had been awarded and over 7,067,688 certificates awarded for skills development activities (Dyson and Keating 2005).

Many countries see the challenge of RVA in the need to align with the needs of stakeholders, such as industry, as a means to enhance the economic capacity of the workforce. Employers are encouraged to invest in the training of those with very low skills, who need to be brought into the productive economy. Mauritius is making concerted efforts through the Mauritius Qualifications Authority (MQA) to implement RVA to support workforce development in certain industry sectors (specifically tourism, financial services, real estate, information and communication technology (ICT) and seafood). Employers understand the role of RVA in supporting a highly skilled workforce and they contribute to the MQA's fees for this exercise. Moreover, well-established companies are also sponsoring RVA candidates. Currently, 19 Industry Training Advisory Committees are generating NQF qualifications in all TVET sectors of the Mauritian economy. While such qualifications are offered by both public and private providers, there is a centralised awarding body that awards the NQF qualifications. In Mauritius, RVA and the NQF co-exist in a symbiotic relationship, where the former is directly linked to the outcomes of NQF qualifications and a smooth transition of many learners is possible to the NQF (Allgoo 2013).

4.2.2 Interfaces with Social Sectors – Health, Social Services and Adult Education

The certification of professional experience on the part of adult educators is gaining in popularity in Austria. The Academy of Continuing Education (*Weiter-bildungsakademie, Wba*) administers the most elaborate framework for certifying and issuing degrees to adult educators according to defined standards. Trainees are required to document a specified period of professional experience as a precondition for obtaining certification as adult educators. Such qualifications are increasingly required of employees at Austrian adult education institutions. These qualifications also provide access to higher education: graduates of the advanced *Wba-Diplom* can attend selected university courses at master's level (Austria. Federal Ministry of Education, the Arts and Culture 2011).

In Scotland, the social services sector has led the way in developing RVA to support workforce development within the context of the Scottish Credit and Qualifications Framework (SCQF) (Whittaker 2011). In Scotland a project was conducted (2005–2008) in the context of the Recognition of Prior Informal Learning (RPL) for workforce development, commissioned by the Scottish Social Services Council. This follows legislative requirements for the registration of staff in sectors such as social services and health requiring the development of a mechanism that will support experienced but unqualified staff to gain necessary qualifications. The project had clear aims: to engage social services workers who lack the confidence to undertake formal learning; to speed up and streamline the process of RVA for credit towards qualifications; and to integrate RVA into existing organisation systems of workforce development from the recruitment and induction stage onwards, and within systems for SVQ assessment. Requiring employees to repeat training that does not take into account their prior learning is both demotivating for the employee and an inefficient use of the employer's resources (Whittaker 2011).

4.2.3 Skills Recognition and Labour Mobility Across National Borders

RVA has been shown to play a role in helping youth and adults to create new employment opportunities abroad. In the Philippines, given that the majority of workers going abroad come from poor families, certifications provided by the Technical Education and Skills Development Authority (TESDA) enable individuals to find employment abroad and provide remittance incomes to their families. The National Certificate (NC) and the Certificate of Competency (CoC) awarded by TESDA to TVET graduates and workers are recognised locally and abroad as proof of competences. Foreign employers, in particular, look for this document among their applicants. NC/CoC holders encounter less difficulty in finding employment, making these qualifications passports to employment (Philippines. National Commission for UNESCO 2011).

4.2.4 Employability and Human Resource Allocation

In the labour market, the RVA of competences can result in improved opportunities for matching competences demanded by labour markets to the competence profiles of jobseekers. In Austria, validation and recognition are used in order to attain more comprehensive and efficient use of human capital within enterprises, raising productivity and raising qualification levels of the country's population (Austria. Federal Ministry of Education, the Arts and Culture 2011).

4.2.5 RVA of Skilled Immigrants and Recognition of Foreign Qualifications

In many countries that depend on attracting immigrants to fill labour gaps, RVA is to a large extent driven by economic and demographic imperatives.

Canada's per-capital immigration rate is one of the highest in the world. Roughly 250,000 immigrants arrive each year. The Canadian government has noted that more effective processes of Prior Learning Assessment and Recognition (PLAR) need to be instituted in order to recognise the qualifications of skilled immigrants. Therefore, although PLAR explicitly states that it is focused on all areas of learning, it has a strong vocational and labour market focus. Progression through access to formal qualifications still remains the key aspect of PLAR, and opening up access and progress in skilled and professional occupations in the labour market is now reported as the key issue across Canada (OECD 2008, p. 14). The location of PLAR at the interface between economic policy and the labour market is evident in the work of the 23 national sector councils which represent economic activities within the economy and play an important role in looking at and improving education and training (OECD 2008, p. 14). Employment and Social Development Canada (ESDC) and, in particular, its foreign credential programme is involved with activities associated with assessment and RPL.

In the area of recognition of foreign vocational qualifications, Germany has introduced a legal entitlement for roughly 350 vocational qualifications that are not regulated (occupations that require formal training in the dual system and skilled crafts and trades). This represents a milestone for the incorporation of RVA in the assessment of foreign qualifications. The new Professional Qualifications Assessment Act creates for the first time a general entitlement for EU citizens and third-country nationals to an individual assessment of equivalence, which so far existed only for recent repatriates. The question of whether the qualification of an applicant is equivalent will be judged by consistent criteria in a consistent procedure. If the equivalence assessment indicates that significant differences exist between the foreign and the comparable German qualification, evidence of professional experience may be taken into account to possibly compensate for the differences. The new procedures create transparency for applicants, employers and responsible authorities (Germany. Federal Ministry of Education and Science (BMBF) 2012).

The decision to emphasise the content and quality of professional qualifications over applicants' citizenship or origin has also influenced recognition procedures in Germany. Decisions with respect to the equivalence of qualifications must be issued within three months from the submission of all relevant documents.

4.2.6   Impacts for Employers and Organisations

There are many benefits of RVA for employers and organisations. In New Zealand RVA has been shown to make employees more competent, confident, reflective and analytical, improving their performance as team members and their communication skills. Employees experience onsite, work-relevant learning and show higher motivation, resulting in gains in overall productivity. RVA of existing competences may lead to an increased willingness among employees to take part in workplace training or learning. RVA procedures may motivate individuals to look upon learning not only in a lifelong sense, but also as a life-wide opportunity. It may also encourage the individual to start new learning experiences (Keller 2013). In Norway, RVA contributes to greater flexibility in working life, enabling employees to more easily move from one position or profession to another. It facilitates access to higher education, and can lead to an improved standing in the job market. RVA can lead to more interesting tasks and better wages, but also to improved social integration through better access to the labour market for those previously excluded (Christensen 2013).

RVA can also help to identify the overall stock of competences and qualifications in an organisation, thus making it easier for organisations to invest in the training of their employees. The training becomes more profitable to invest in for the organisation when it is expressed in terms of national qualifications or industry-sector standards, which employers and employees regard as relevant in the changing world of work. Also, in the case of people who become redundant, RVA can help in finding jobs that are suited to their current competences. Furthermore, RVA provides valuable feedback to educational providers to the content and methods of both formal and non-formal/informal learning. More and more flexible and customised training courses are being offered by private and public sector institutions by using RVA to gauge the existing skills levels of individuals.

4.2.7 Family Skills as a Potential Source of Human Resource Development

In Germany, there have been some attempts in the context of corporate human resource development (HRD) to recognise family work and informal skills gained outside the workplace. A growing number of staff in charge of human resource development in companies see the family as a setting where important skills are learned. A project "Family skills as a potential source of innovative HRD" (Gerzer-Sass 2001, 2005) aims at documenting and assessing social skills gained through family work. The tool "skills balance" is developed to make family skills easily visible to employers. This tool utilises a dialogue-type of assessment for documenting personal skills profiles. An information brochure on this tool has been developed for staff in charge of human resource development in companies (Gerzer-Sass 2001, 2005).

According to Gerzer-Sass (2001), unfortunately, employers and staff associated with human resource development seem to value mobility through work more than parenthood and raising children. Nevertheless, she argues, the tool "skills balance" needs to be seen against broader issues of promoting equal opportunities for women in workplaces as well as encouraging men to gain more skills in family settings. A further benefit highlighted is the gradual acceptance of including "family-related part-time work" in a professional biography, under the section on training. Finally, the "skills balance" is also likely to enhance acceptance among employers and public and private sector organisations of employees' desires to combine family life with work. In a changing world of work, social skills and life-wide and lifelong learning skills are gaining in importance. Whether countries will be economically competitive will depend increasingly on valorising the role of the family in safeguarding human potential.

4.2.8 Industry-responsive National Competency-Based Frameworks

In the USA one of the aims of RVA is to develop a standardised method for assessing the value of occupational education and training that takes place outside or at the margins of post-secondary institutions and their applicability to post-secondary education. To this end education agencies are seeking to develop a national competency-based framework for post-secondary education that includes certificate-level workforce education and training. In the long term, this will enable authorities to scale up the practice of awarding educational credit for what is currently considered to be non-credit education. At the same time, these changes are driving the higher education system towards more industry-responsive curricula, potentially improving employment and career outcomes for students. Currently, there are a wide variety of credentials, but without common metrics or quality assurance mechanisms, they are not portable and their value is not clear to employers, educators, or students. There are also plans to link data systems to create a more comprehensive picture of learning outcomes (Ganzglass et al. 2011).

There have been some industry-driven efforts to support the National Competency-Based Industry Standard Curricula Assessment Credentials. The Department of Labour's Employment and Training Administration, National Association of Manufacturers (NAM) and other associations developed the Advanced Manufacturing Competency Model, which details the development of professional knowledge, skills and abilities for successful performance. The model consists of nine tiers divided across entry level manufacturing foundational employment, and specific manufacturing occupations (Ganzglass et al. 2011).

4.2.9 Development of Competence Standards by Companies

In many countries, companies develop competence standards for the purposes of job classification, succession planning, and assessment and professional development. Concrete examples include the Competency-Based Training Framework (Bristol-Aerospace, Manitoba, Canada) and the Boeing Competency Identification (Manitoba, Canada). In Canada, RVA is regarded as a resource to support recruitment. Countries like Germany and Switzerland, with collective bargaining agreements, often reference employees' length of service as a measure of knowledge, skills and competences extending beyond the qualifications obtained through initial education and training. Recognition is a natural counterpart to this approach. RVA is also used by companies to satisfy regulatory requirements in areas such as food, tendering for contracts, consumer protection. The RVA of non-formal and informal learning may make it easier for employers to motivate employees to embark on courses leading to a certified qualification in these areas (see Werquin 2010).

4.2.10 Skills Development for the Informal Sector

In many countries with a high proportion of persons employed in the informal economy, the focus is shifting from academic pathways to an emphasis on skills development pathways with closer cooperation with stakeholders in the labour market and industry. RVA in Benin's informal economy takes place in the context of training programmes for craftsmen, who acquire vocational qualifications that are specified in the Directory of Training and Professional Qualifications. Another development is the transition from traditional forms of apprenticeship to a regulated dual training system (combining the Vocational Skills Certificate (CQF) and the

Occupational Skills Certificate (CQM)). Master craftsmen who have gained the Vocational Skills Certificate through the recognition of their traditional non-formal apprenticeship are able to train their apprentices up to the level of the Occupational Skills Certificate (Savadogo and Walther 2013).

RVA can be a powerful tool to support and enhance formal learning and can provide a platform for further and on-going formal learning. It can provide a mechanism to bring people with unrecognised skills into a system that recognises their informally acquired skills and knowledge in a formal sense. RVA, by leading to a better matching of skills with labour market demands, could also address skills shortages (Arthur 2009).

4.3 Social Inclusion and Empowerment

RVA is seen to have an ability to contribute constructively to the reduction of social inequality. Tackling inequality can be done through a variety of means, some of which attack the problem indirectly, whereas others are more direct in their targeting of inequality. Direct policies, on the one hand, tend to be aimed explicitly at reducing social inequality. They are framed as matters of social justice and are often targeted at those in the community who need assistance (minorities, migrants, low-skilled, etc.). Indirect policies, on the other hand, result in lowering of inequalities, both social and educational, but are not necessarily framed in the language of social justice. Instead, they are often directed at pragmatic outcomes, such as increasing access to higher education or vocational courses for the sake of driving the economy. In these instances, the issue of equality sits at arm's length from the explicit policy aims, but is nonetheless essential to the setting in which the policies are introduced. As is the case throughout the country examples, one education system can employ a range of methods to achieve the same goal, which means they appear at various points along the indirect to direct spectrum. The two ends of this spectrum are referred to by Amartya Sen in his distinction between human capital and social opportunities, where the former lines up with indirect policy and the latter with direct (Sen 2000). Both types of policy are useful, particularly when policy-makers ultimately value equality.

In line with Amartya Sen's distinction between human capital and social opportunities, direct and indirect policy relating to RVA across a range of countries, both developed and developing, is focused on achieving three particular goals:

- increasing numbers with higher qualifications;
- RVA linked to re-entry into formal school education;
- increasing further learning opportunities in the light of improved literacy;
- targeting socio-cultural and educational inequalities as well as poverty directly.

4.3.1   Increasing Numbers with Higher Qualifications

Raising the number of people with higher education certificates is one way to promote equality in education, but one that is only available to countries with an established, articulated and well-functioning education system. It is a policy pursued by both Australia and Finland, among others. Starting with Australia, in 2008, the Council of Australian Governments adopted a resolution to halve the number of Australians aged between 20 and 64 without Certificate III qualifications by 2020. This body also set a goal of doubling the number of higher qualification completions, such as diplomas or advanced diplomas, over the same period (Australia. Department of Education, Employment and Workplace Relations (DEEWR) 2008). The recognition of non-formal and informal learning plays an important part in these efforts, particularly because the increases in certification will serve the aim of ensuring that learners have better access to higher education, better integrating vocational education and training into higher education and collaborating with key stakeholders to encourage improved transition to work arrangements.

Similarly, Finland is using recognition to raise the level of education among the Finnish population and increase the number of post-compulsory qualifications. The efforts there are directed at the 10 % of the labour force aged between 25 and 34 that lack qualifications at that level (Finland. Ministry of Education 2008). The Finnish government has undertaken reforms of education law, introducing the Act on Liberal Education (632/1998) and the Act on Vocational Education (630/1998), which both aim at achieving these objectives.

RVA in Portugal is closely associated with efforts to reverse the historical trend of an increasingly poorly educated workforce. The Portuguese situation is unique in terms of its per capita qualification levels and educational performance compared with the majority of other EU and OECD countries. This can be attributed to the low commitment to education registered over many decades, as a result of an array of factors, including almost fifty years of dictatorial rule and the regime's opposition to universal access to education (Gomes 2013). Seeking to overcome this situation, stakeholders in Portugal have initiated a major drive for investment in adult education and training courses, including the establishment of the RVCC and a national qualifications framework.

4.3.2   RVA Linked to Re-entry into Formal School Education

With traditional formal schools unable to meet the learning needs of all children and youth in most developing countries, Equivalency Programmes (EPs) offer critical, and often the only, opportunities for learning, particularly for marginalised groups. EPs are alternative educational programmes that provide learning that is supposed to be equivalent to the formal system, and provide skills and competences that are recognised as being equivalent to those acquired through the formal system. EPs are often delivered through non-formal education (NFE) systems separate from formal education system. Creation of synergies between formal and non-formal education is an important element of these programmes, if progression through levels of education, and transfer between formal and non-formal programmes is to take place. In the Philippines, performance in the Accreditation and Equivalency Programmes is assessed through the Accreditation and Equivalency Test at elementary/secondary level. Successful candidates are recognised as elementary/high school graduates. As such these individuals are able to enrol at technical/vocational and higher education institutions as regular students. In Thailand, four programmes exist to provide citizens with opportunities to engage in learning continuously throughout their lives: (1) basic education; (2) occupational development; (3) education for life skills development; and (4) education for community and society. Most importantly, in Thailand, the credits accumulated by learners from these programmes are transferable within the same type or between different types of education, regardless of whether credits are gained at a single or multiple educational institutions, including learning from non-formal or informal education, vocational training or work experience (Thailand. Ministry of Education, Office of the Non-Formal and Informal Education (ONIE) 2011).

However EPs have been criticised. The Final Report of the Regional Workshop on Equivalency Programmes for Promoting Lifelong Learning (UNESCO Bangkok Office 2006) has listed the following challenges. EPs still suffer from: inadequate funding; low status and low pay of grassroots-level workers; high dropout rates as well as low achievement. The Report identified the need for substantive data to show what adults learn, their levels of achievement, and the utility of such programmes in improving the quality of life of members of disadvantaged groups. Furthermore, there is a need to equip learners with the skills required in a competitive global knowledge economy, with an emphasis on the creation, application, analysis, and synthesis of knowledge as well as collaborative learning (Ibid., pp. 24–25).

4.3.3 Increasing Further Learning Opportunities in the Light of Improved Literacy

For many countries without established basic levels of education among their population, equality of educational opportunities must be tackled at a foundational level. To this effect, many developing countries are turning their attention to recognition policy with the aim of increasing the size of the continuing studies sector in light of vast improvements in their literacy rates. Countries in this category, which includes Ecuador and Botswana, now have a predominantly literate society that is ready to enter further education. Strategies of recognition of non-formal and informal education are being designed to fill the new demand. Over the last 60 years, Ecuador's illiteracy rate has decreased from 44 to 9 % (Ecuador. Ministerio de Educacion 2008). This can be attributed to the diverse campaigns and programmes focusing on literacy and post-literacy implemented over this period. The country is now turning its attention to expanding its processes of non-formal and informal education. Another country that has taken giant leaps forward with its literacy rates is Botswana, which has managed to improve literacy from a level of 69 % in 1969 to 83 % in 2007 (UNICEF 2010). Unemployment has also fallen over the past decade, but remains at high 17.6 % (Ecuador. Ministerio de Educacion 2008). This rise in literacy in Botswana is coupled with the country's programme of universal primary education. Not only is the national government able to offer schemes of further learning to cater for the more literate society that now exists in Botswana, but it can also do so to break the traditional barriers that keep various categories of clients from participating in further education programmes. In this sense, recognition is able to play a role in Botswana to entrench the gains made by increased literacy levels and to facilitate equality of educational opportunities.

The incorporation of the Adult Basic Education and Training (ABET) system into the South African NQF has allowed adults successful in the mass literacy campaign level to participate in the ABET system. While fewer than 9 % of adults between 15 and 64 years of age are illiterate, more than 500,000 adult learners are in Level 1 of the NQF, which incorporates the four sub-levels of adult basic education. The four ABET sub-levels are recorded on the National Learners' Records Database. Qualifications, unit standards, modules and short courses can be registered on the NQF. Qualifications and unit standards have been defined as learning outcomes and assessment criteria. If non-formal and informal education lead to registered standards on the NQF and the providers are accredited, then the learning can be formally recognised. The SAQA RPL policy also allows candidates to achieve qualifications in part or in full through RVA (McKay and Romm 2006).

The growing importance assigned to embedded and integrated literacy in work-place settings in Australia and New Zealand is seen in programmes that aim to shape training around the particular task undertaken by employees (Australia. Department of Education Employment and Workplace Relations (DEEWR) 2008; New Zealand Ministry of Education 2008). RVA in these contexts entails valuing and making visible the very experience of adult learning as a means of raising self-esteem, making adults aware of their broader personal knowledge skills and competences, and consequently removing a significant barrier to more formal learning. Rapid economic and societal changes actually increase the importance of personal development, while reducing the importance of task-specific and narrowly defined instrumental knowledge and skills (New Zealand). In Canada, literacy and basic skills are a stepping stone to lifelong learning. Literacy is essential for participation in general adult education. Adult literacy programmes in the context of adult continuing education and training programmes (as part of lifelong learning) help to bridge the gap between literacy and higher education levels. In Canada, data shows that individuals at higher literacy levels are more likely to participate in further education and learning.

4.3.4 Targeting Socio-cultural and Educational Inequalities as well as Poverty Directly

The potential contribution of RVA in closing the gap that exists between the education opportunities of a diverse range of groups in society is another theme that occurs in policy and practice in both developing and developed countries. In many developing countries, where qualifications and certificates are highly valued, tackling educational disparity is an important element in seeking to redress broader structural and economic inequality. In developed countries, too, recognition plays an important role in closing the gap between different sections of the community, particularly immigrant groups, indigenous populations, rural groups and those trapped in the poverty cycle.

In the context of post-conflict societies, the UN Refugee Agency UNHCR (Kirk 2009) sees RVA as an essential tool for displaced persons and refugees – children, young people and adults – to record what they have learned or their prior learning and results obtained. UNHCR calls for the right of access to examination or assessment processes that are validated by the relevant authority or educational institution, for displaced persons and refugees to continue, resume and complete schooling, as well as to attain access to further learning opportunities and employment opportunities (Kirk 2009).

In South Africa, one of the purposes of RVA specifically promoted by trade unions is redress for past and present discriminatory practices. This policy objective is reflected in the country's skills development agenda, which aims to contribute to a better educated, more skilled and more efficient workforce, and development for workers (SAQA 2012a). RVA helps to identify skills gaps that may be compensated for by education and training (Samuels 2013).

In the Philippines, clients of the non-formal/informal education programme are mostly illiterates and school leavers from elementary and secondary schools. They come from marginalised and depressed communities in both rural and urban areas, penal and rehabilitation institutions, remote and otherwise inaccessible regions, areas of armed conflict, and indigenous communities, etc. This group represents 45 % of the Philippine population, or some 40 million persons. Some ALS clients are of school-age (6–15 years) but most are older (15+). They generally want to participate in the programmes and consider ALS as a "second chance" education. The support for learners in the above programmes includes: recognition/certification of learning by NGOs and community centres; CD modules and workbooks; a tracking system (for NFE A&E learners); livelihood projects and microfinance; leadership training; and a referral system for graduates/completers operated by NGOs.

Mexico is a culturally and linguistically diverse nation (the country has 62 ethnic Mesoamerican language groups). It is a country with low completion rates at the basic education level as well as low literacy levels. In Mexico there are over 34 million people over the age of fifteen years who have not completed their basic education (Castro Mussot and de Anda 2007). Demographic features such as a relatively young population, combined with low birth rates and high life expectancy, mean that Mexico will face the problem of an ageing population over the coming decades. Already, young people are under pressure to enter the workforce without completing their formal education and this trend is set to continue. It is for these reasons that the recognition of non-formal and informal education is central to Mexico's education policy and broader social planning. Through accreditation, Mexico is aiming to encourage the development of small enterprises. Accreditation programmes also stand to assist in reducing the damaging effects of migration from Mexico to the USA of working-age family members.

Mauritius has a programme to support the training of low-qualified workers from the sugar and textile industries for work in the tourism industry by taking into account their prior learning. Candidates develop a portfolio based on the unit standards and qualifications defined by the MQA with the help of RPL facilitators. In addition, the MQA is working on an RPL project with the Mauritius Prisons Service for the reintegration of detainees through RVA by assessing their skills (Allgoo 2013).

In Chile recognition of informal learning is a powerful tool for the promotion of inclusion. It is a country where almost 50 % of the adult population do not finish school and where there are many unemployed young people with very low levels of training (UIL 2011). A reform of the adult education system (2003–2009) was initiated in response to the need of many youngsters and adults to catch up with their school studies.

Closing the gap between educational opportunities for different groups in society is an important goal for many developed countries. In New Zealand, for example, the Tertiary Education Strategy 2002–2007 includes RVA to improve foundation skills in general, including particularly those of Maoris in order to bring Maori learners into tertiary education and higher education levels (New Zealand. Ministry of Education 2008).

The Australian government is working through the Council of Australian Governments to reduce indigenous disadvantages (Australia. DEEWR 2008). The government's Social Inclusion Agenda seeks to skill potential workers who can and want to work or are currently excluded from the labour force (see Australian Government, Social Inclusion Unit 2009). In Canada, RVA has been a promising approach among indigenous populations. Research conducted in Saskatchewan firms shows that Aboriginal people value most experiential lifelong learning, which includes, spiritual, emotional, physical and intellectual learning. By comparison, the Western formal learning approach tends to focus primarily on intellectual learning (see Werquin 2010).

In Scotland, RVA and NQFs are linked to career guidance for "young leavers at risk"– youth who have no positive destination in terms of education, training or employment. Whittaker (2011) describes a project undertaken by Skills Development Scotland, which includes Careers Scotland, to integrate the SCQF into careers guidance, specifically through the use of RVA. The majority of participating pupils were leavers at risk with no "positive destination". RVA allowed the candidates to benchmark their attainments and achievement to the SCQF to facilitate participation and workforce development. Learning and skills gained through informal learning were mapped against the appropriate level of the SCQF. In doing so, the project explored whether young people could gain a better idea of the types of job they could seek, or the types of the learning or training programmes open to them. The project showed that young people do understand the role of RVA in their career development.

In Norway, efforts are made to assist marginalised groups by providing RVA at the level of public employment services. As an alternative pathway to formal qualifications, it can help marginalised persons/groups to document their competences and provide access to both employment and further education. For immigrants and refugees without formal proof of qualification, identifying and validating competences can speed up integration and prevent racism and discrimination. Unemployed persons with a right to complete upper secondary education can have an assessment of their non-formal and informal learning paid for by the employment office as part of an approved jobseeker's agreement. Validation has been successful, especially among unqualified women working in the health sector, leading to more secure jobs and higher wages. One important effect of this is the greater availability of more formally qualified employees in the health sector, an issue that has had priority during recent years. In order to shape the validation system as intended by the Public Employment Services (PES), a training programme has been developed for individuals working in this sector. To function effectively this has required close cooperation and coordination between the public education system and the employment service at county level (Christensen 2013).

Germany faces a set of issues of its own. While the country's unemployment rate has declined as a result of greater buoyancy in the labour market, there are nevertheless concerns related to qualifications and unemployment, particularly as affecting specific groups such as migrants and youth (Germany. Federal Ministry of Education and Science (BMBF) 2008). The recognition of migrants' prior learning and experiential learning is expected to become an important integration policy issue in the coming years. Germany is committed to implementing more formalised recognition systems and has stated that its aim in doing so is to engage more people in social and economic participation by emphasising recognition of the skills and knowledge needed in the labour market. This is directed primarily at the integration of low-skilled workers, raising occupational mobility and increasing the number of persons entitled to enter higher education (Germany. Federal Ministry of Education and Science (BMBF) 2008). A focus on economic and social participation is a priority with respect to education policy, though an emphasis on less formal pathways has been gaining ground over the last decade. The current emphasis on recognition in Germany is driven by the combined objectives of providing equal access and utilising existing potential skills in the economy (Germany. Federal Ministry of Education and Science (BMBF) 2008).

In Austria, recognition of non-formal and informal learning can enhance the integration of marginalised groups such as migrants, elderly persons or the unemployed by giving them a "second chance". The process of recognition can influence people's awareness of their knowledge, skills and competences, strengthen their self-perception, enhance their careers and raise their motivation for further education (Austria. Federal Ministry of Education, the Arts and Culture 2011). However, experience from Austria shows that data on the impact of RVA on the integration and empowerment of marginalised groups and individuals is not available. While a small number of studies exist describing the benefits of single mechanisms for individuals, none of this data refers explicitly to marginalised groups. Benefits from the recognition process mostly refer to higher self-confidence, increased problem-solving competences or stress-coping strategies. Knowing and formulating one's own competences has helped many participants in portfolio initiatives to find a (new) job. However, there are always a larger number of factors that need to be taken into consideration when it comes to evaluating the impact on marginalised groups. The Austrian experience demonstrates that the integration and empowerment of marginalised groups are very complex processes which are connected with a wide range of factors and cannot easily be observed or "measured". Accordingly, it is difficult to attribute changes in these respects to RVA only (Austria. Federal Ministry of Education Arts and Culture 2011).

In the US, the Workforce Investment Act (WIA) of 1998 (Public Law 105–220) was instrumental in establishing a fund for Adult Basic Education (ABE) services, which encourages the development of RVA pathways for low-skilled adults to increase their educational attainment and obtain higher skilled jobs. The fund targets at-risk youth, under-educated and/or unemployed/underemployed adults, youth and adults with disabilities, and English language learners (ELL). Progression pathways in the US are called "certification crosswalks". These include: College Credit for What You Already Know: a project developed by CAEL designed to bring prior learning assessments to scale, and increase the number of adults who would benefit from access to these programmes; LearningCounts utilises faculty experts nationwide to teach online portfolio development courses and review student portfolios. The latter sends credit-recommendation transcripts to colleges and refers students to training-program evaluation and standardised-exam services. The users may be unaffiliated students, military personnel and veterans, low-income and unemployed, individual employers and industry groups, unions, and the public workforce system. These services are not intended to replace existing PLA programs offered by individual institutions, but rather to augment services at institutions or provide the resources for institutions that have not developed these programs (Ganzglass et al. 2011).

There are pathways between work and education. The Ivy Tech Community College uses a certification crosswalk to award a consistent amount of educational credit for a wide range of industry certifications and apprenticeships. The Ivy Tech campuses reached an agreement on how to develop a common portfolio assessment. Wisconsin Technical College System (WTCS) provides apprenticeship-related instruction as approved academic programming with full program status. Ohio's Career-Technical Credit Transfer (CT) is an initiative which helps to ensure that workers can earn educational credit for technical instruction. This initiative awards educational credit for occupational and technical instruction is provided through the state's Adult Career Centers. Stakeholders determine which types of occupational and technical instruction merit educational credit (Ganzglass et al. 2011).

4.3.5 Research on Equity Issues and Equity Groups

Research evidence from Australia is critical of governments' perceptions and assumptions regarding the contribution of recognition to access and social inclusion agendas. (Maher et al. 2010) identified little research on equity issues and equity groups (indigenous, non-English-speaking background, women returning to the workforce) showing that these candidates are less likely to access and complete education than other groups. The dominant model of recognition in Australia is the credentialing model. Butterworth (1992) and Cameron (2004) found that recognition is neither relevant nor appropriate to the needs of disadvantaged and disengaged groups of learners. According to Cameron, it is those with 'significant accumulated educational capital who are familiar with formal learning systems and the associated discourse who are more likely to utilise the RPL processes' (Cameron 2006, p. 119).

In Australia, the number of students with one or more subjects gained through RVA as a proportion of the student population rose from 2.4 % in 1995 to roughly 4.0 % in 2001. Age is an important factor with regard to RPL take-up. These results emerged from a study on uptake by Bowman et al. (2003) commissioned by the Australian National Training Authority (ANTA)[1] and published by the National Centre for Vocational Education Research (NCVER). RPL take-up was greatest for students in the 25–39 age bracket. Students in the 40–65 age bracket were the next highest, and those up to 19 years of age had the lowest RPL rates. In many cases, equity group members had lower uptake than students overall. Hargreaves (2006, in Cameron 2011) argues that this is because equity group members are more likely to participate in training than to seek recognition of existing skills. A similar picture presents itself in Sweden, where females in the workplace context are recommended further training, whereas male competences are readily recognised as such.

Summing up the available research on this aspect, Cameron (2011) concludes that uptake remains low although VET sector services are required to offer RPL to any student enrolling on an accredited course. These formal arrangements apply in the adult and continuing education sector. However, Cameron argues that due to limitations of secondary data and on account of the fact that only "up front" enrolment-recorded RPL is counted, the dataset does not account for RPL that occurs through forms of early progression, accelerated learning or challenge testing after enrolment (Bowman et al. 2003; Bateman 2006; Hargreaves 2006). These

---

[1]In 2005 functions of ANTA were transferred to the Department of Education, Science and Training (DEST).

authors also note that these forms of RPL are more effective than the "traditional methodology of RPL assessment conducted up-front and prior to training" (Bowman et al. 2003, p. 47).

4.4   External and Internal Dimensions of Personal Development

In many North countries, RVA is framed in terms of an individualistic perspective that is rooted in the traditions of citizenship and the right of the individual to education. This approach is enshrined in the principles of the European Guidelines for the Validation of Non-formal and Informal Learning, which places the individual at the centre of the validation process (CEDEFOP 2009). Accordingly, many of these countries address the purposes of recognition in terms of its benefits for individuals and learners. These purposes can be described in terms of "external dimensions" or in terms of "internal dimensions" of personal development.

According to a review of studies from Australia addressing the purposes of recognition in terms of its benefits for *individuals/learners* (Cameron 2011), a primary driver for RVA uptake is the opportunity it presents to gain a qualification either for its own sake or for work requirements. Not having to repeat skills and knowledge training has been identified as another significant factor (Bowman et al. 2003, p. 13). RVA could motivate individuals to continue along the path of further education and skills training. Recognition of one's own capacity to learn induces an on-going desire to seek further learning. This applies across a range of individuals, including those who have had limited access to, or low achievement in, formal education and training; those who learnt skills predominantly in non-formal institutions and the workplace; and those who are or have been disadvantaged in further learning and training and have had trouble securing employment that adequately reflects their skills and previous experience. Helping these people to get their competences formally recognised gives them evidence of their personal capital, which in turn assists them in improving their employment and career prospects. Other benefits include: reducing individuals' study time or fast-tracking qualifications (Miller 2009); and gaining assistance with career planning (Cameron 2009).

The recognition of competences in the labour market is a major driver for *individuals*. From Austria, positive effects include: better opportunities for matching competences demanded on the labour market to competence profiles of employment-seeking persons; enhanced opportunities for access to educational programmes; possibilities for receiving credits for parts of programmes; enhanced integration of marginalised groups through second-chance opportunities for migrants, elderly persons or the unemployed; greater awareness of knowledge, skills and competences, greater self-perception, and enhanced careers and strengthened motivation for further education (Prokopp 2010).

In Scotland the value of the RVA process in terms of increasing learners' confidence and motivation to undertake further learning and development was confirmed through project evaluation. RVA promoted a positive view of learning, based on an enhancement rather than a deficit model. The peer-group approach to developing learner self-awareness of skills prior to embarking on a formal programme, and to the development of reflective skills and writing skills, was seen as streamlining and accelerating the process of completing a qualification. As a result of formative RVA, learners embarked on a formal qualification pathway with greater self-confidence and greater understanding of how they learn, and how to express and demonstrate their learning (Whittaker 2011).

In the Republic of Korea, RVA has been shown to protect learning rights by providing learning opportunities anytime and anywhere (Baik 2013). The benefits of RPL for *individuals* include formal acknowledgement and certification of skills, improved access and equity in vocational education and training, self-assessment allowing individuals to identify skill deficits, and the building of confidence, self-esteem and motivation. It relieves learners of the obligation to repeat training to learn skills which they are already applying in the workplace. RPL ensures each learner's right to choose diverse learning options and promotes self-directed learning management. In addition to this, learning results can be linked to general and vocational certification schemes. The Lifelong Learning Account System Lifelong Learning Account System enables *learners* to plan their learning process systematically (Baik 2013).

In New Zealand, RVA has been shown to improve personal reflection. The impacts of a qualifications framework that recognises prior learning for learners are personally meaningful and reflective. They enable learners to integrate understanding from experience, providing peer insight and support. It is of relevance to the learner's current career, provides increased confidence and enhances the *individual's* ability to contribute to business (Keller 2013).

Several recent studies on RPL criticise the overemphasis on the external dimensions of personal development to the neglect of the "internal dimensions" such as self-esteem, confidence and motivation, greater self-awareness, improving personal reflection, increased confidence and self-directed learning management. Singh (2009) argues that institutional and systemic, as well as individual perspectives on recognition, need to be united so as to open the way to a more holistic and integrated approach that would result in: (a) creating greater self-awareness; (b) understanding what counts and is valued as knowledge in our vision of the world; (making sense of the world by acting consciously); and (d) promoting sensitivity to the cultural context of the individual and different forms of knowing (cognitive justice) (pp. 2598–2600). In a recent exploratory study, Armsby (2013) for example, argues that RPL could be promoted through an ontological focus in higher education, where RPL affects ways of being rather than or as well as ways of knowing.

4.5 Summary

It is clear from this chapter that there is considerable variation in the purposes of RVA across countries. While countries tend to concentrate on one or the other purposes depending upon the contexts and circumstances, it is important to keep in mind the entire range of social, economic, cultural and personal purposes – particularly those relating to social inclusion, equity, and personal self-esteem and self-awareness – as expressed in the goals of lifelong learning and education for sustainable development.

On the basis of empirical evidence gathered from various countries, a number of criteria – educational, economic and social and personal development – can be identified to improve countries' contribution to education for sustainable development and lifelong learning.

In the educational context we found that the formal education sector is in the forefront of RVA. Many countries are committed to developing RVA as a policy tool alongside other measures with the aim of enhancing the transparency and sustainability of the education and broader learning system (Austria, Mauritius, Botswana, Namibia); promoting a diversified lifelong learning system; granting flexible access opportunities; establishing synergies between formal and non-formal basic education (Philippines and Thailand); promoting permeability and educational mobility between subsystems of the education and training system; and acknowledging the importance of work experience and vocational skills for achieving qualifications in higher education (Germany).

Besides providers in the formal context, non-formal and individual education and training providers also exist, such as community-based adult learning centres and non-governmental organisations that implement the recognition of non-formal basic education and training programmes as well as adult and continuing education. This applies particularly in developing countries. More and more providers in the field of continuing vocational education and training (CVET) (particularly in the developed countries) are delivering support services which enable adults to use RVA at all levels of the formal education and training system (Denmark and Finland) in addition to providing certified qualifications.

A range of themes relating to RVA's role in workforce development were highlighted: RVA is used in rehabilitation courses administered through employment agencies, with close collaborative ties between qualification systems/frameworks and CVET providers. RVA is also used by training providers in particular industries. It is a feature of collective agreements in the private and public sector. It is used for linking non-credit workforce programmes to educational credit. RVA's importance has also been highlighted in matching labour market competence requirements to the competence profiles of employment seekers. In many counties RVA is used for attracting migrants to fill labour gaps. RVA has been shown to meet part of new qualification requirements in different sectors (e.g., for adult educators; construction, or social services). RVA has supported workers in the private and public sector organisations to complete primary and upper secondary education (Denmark). In the informal economy, RVA helps in the acquisition of vocational and occupational certificates based on previous work experience and informal apprenticeships. The integration of academic credit with non-credit workforce programmes is driving governments to develop national competency-based reference frameworks, learning outcomes-based approaches to curricula and learner databases.

Drawing on Amartya Sen's distinction between human capital and social opportunities, this chapter also highlighted how in some country contexts social-justice related policies are used to tackle inequality, while other countries use indirect policies to deal with increasing equality in educational opportunity. Depending on the particular contexts and circumstances, both policy types have benefits. While in some countries RVA is a tool to increase the number of persons with higher education, in other countries RVA efforts are more targeted and are designed either to entrench the gains made by increased literacy levels (Botswana, South Africa) or to close the gap between different sections of the community, particularly immigrant groups (Norway), indigenous populations (New Zealand), rural groups, low-qualified workers (Mauritius) 'young leavers at risk' (Scotland) and those trapped in the poverty cycle. In the latter approach, recognition is an important tool for the promotion of inclusion.

The chapter also highlighted research evidence showing low-uptake of RVA among equity groups such as women. This finding is related to the lack of familiarity with formal learning discourses. Instead, equity groups are more likely to participate in training than to seek recognition of existing skills.

The use of RVA to promote equality of access and participation in education is often driven by wider policy frameworks or contexts. In Portugal, the high number of under-qualified young people entering the labour market is a major driver of RVA (Gomes 2013); in Scotland, recognition became a means of recognising the skills of learning and qualifications of migrant workers and refugees. In the Netherlands, validation is applied as a tool to tackle the economic crisis and targets young unemployed persons lacking Level 2 vocational qualifications, those who are at risk of losing their jobs, or those who need to achieve mobility on the labour market. In Botswana and South Africa recognition serves to allow adults to participate in adult basic education and training (ABET) upon becoming literate; in post-conflict societies international organisations like the UNHCR are promoting policies so that children, young people and adults record what they have learnt. In many countries, recognition is a part of skills development agendas. In Canada, recognition is an important policy for recognising the experiential learning of indigenous populations; in New Zealand recognition is a part of the Tertiary Education Strategy to close the gap between Maori and the rest of the population. In Australia, recognition forms part of the social inclusion agenda.

RVA benefits individuals by improving career and employment prospects and creating pathways to further learning and qualification opportunities. Beyond the bounds of these external dimensions of personal development, RVA contributes to self-esteem, confidence and motivation, greater awareness, improving personal reflection, increased confidence and self-directed learning management.

This chapter has shown that a diversity of approaches exists to the recognition of competences and outcomes from non-formal and informal learning, as well as a diversity of options to access education, training and qualifications. This multiplicity of forms of recognition systems across sectors, and addressing a broad range of purposes (personal, social, cultural and economic), is a prerequisite for the realisation of lifelong learning within an integrative perspective.

Chapter 5
Coordination and Stakeholder Interests and Motives

The successful implementation of RVA is dependent on the extent to which various partnerships drive the coordination of the RVA process. Information gathered from numerous countries on their policies and practices indicates that partnerships with various stakeholders differ significantly. Four models of implementation and coordination emerge from these country cases:

- Shared responsibility
- NQFs coordinating RVA
- The industry model of shared responsibility
- Stakeholders in the Adult and Community Learning Sector

5.1 Shared Responsibility

5.1.1 The Growing Role of National Bodies, Agencies and Knowledge Centres

In a number of countries, multiple social partners and stakeholders treat recognition as a shared responsibility, coordinating their work in accordance with laws, regulations and guidelines. This ensures legitimacy within a decentralised education system.

In Australia and New Zealand, a legislative basis establishes new *bodies or agencies* at different levels, sometimes according to the subsectors of the education and training system. These bodies operate within the context of a vision for the recognition of all learning, often in line with the broad national and regional policies for promoting lifelong learning. These agencies are fully or partly funded by governments, but are given considerable independence in the way they operate.

© UNESCO Institute for Lifelong Learning 2015
M. Singh, *Global Perspectives on Recognising Non-formal and Informal Learning*,
Technical and Vocational Education and Training: Issues, Concerns and Prospects 21,
DOI 10.1007/978-3-319-15278-3_5

In South Africa, key players in the recognition of non-formal and informal learning include the Department of Higher Education and Training (DHET), Department of Basic Education (DBE), the South African Qualifications Authority (SAQA), the three Quality Councils responsible for the sub-frameworks for higher education, further and general and training, and occupations; professional bodies and councils, and the National Skills Authority. While all Quality Councils (QCs) have developed recognition of prior learning (RPL) policies in order to comply with SAQA requirements, implementation plans and projects have been developed in only a few sectors.

In France legislation has been helpful in defining the roles and responsibilities of stakeholders (Werquin 2012) in a shared system that entrenches the role of stakeholders in processes of validation.

- Information and orientation services are the responsibility of all regions.
- The Ministry of Education, which has jurisdiction over secondary vocational education, organises the implementation of VAE in secondary vocational schools, defines processes and trains staff.
- In higher education and continuing training, individual institutions, organisations and bodies are responsible for defining the process and methodology.
- Where institutions award state qualifications, the procedures are defined by the relevant ministries, which develop a validation action plan, introducing validation regulations, assessment procedures and application forms and tools, and procedures for training professionals. However, it is the individual education and training providers and education and training institutions that are responsible for the validation procedures, and have to learn how to implement VAE for the qualifications of the certifying ministries.
- Researchers and experts help with the development of quality processes.
- An inter-ministerial committee, created by the government, is responsible for harmonising policy and practice.
- At the level of adult learning, it is the national or state bodies that are responsible for quality control and procedures (Feutrie 2008).

In Norway, the Ministry of Education and Research has regulatory responsibility for all levels of education. Employers' bodies and trade unions are important stakeholders nationally and regionally, with both setting policy goals and realising practice (e.g. supporting adults in VET schemes by offering apprenticeships and other training schemes in enterprises locally). It is the responsibility of county authorities to realise the individual right to validation of prior learning and assure quality of the process. Funding is delegated to the 19 counties, and regional centres provide information and guidance. They are also responsible for the quality of the validation process and for training assessors. At the upper secondary level, the practice of RVA is usually carried out within the regional education system. Often, upper secondary schools also function as assessment centres. In order to give the same opportunity to job-seekers who want their competence validated, projects are initiated to improve co-operation between the education system and the Labour and Welfare Administration.

National institutes such as Vox in Norway, NILE in the Republic of Korea, or the Knowledge Centre in the Netherlands, are established under their respective ministries of education, which in turn co-operate with trade unions, enterprises, national labour agencies, national educational associations, organisations, universities and colleges, public and private educators, and social partners. Vox, the National Institute for Lifelong Learning, has a particular responsibility for non-formal education and for improving the participation rate in adult learning, specifically with programmes focused on basic skills training. Vox is active in the recognition of immigrant competences, and works in co-operation with other relevant stakeholders. Vox also has special competence within the fields of adults' legal rights and validation of prior learning (VPL). In addition to activities and responsibilities governed by the formal education system, Vox works in close cooperation with NGOs and social partners to further adult learning in working life. In the case of NILE, the institute provides an accreditation system for non-formal and informal learning that accommodates the full range of legitimate stakeholders.

One distinctive feature of stakeholder participation in the Netherlands is the voluntary character of engagement on the part of employers, employees and educational institutions. This reflects the choice of the Dutch government to favour a bottom-up method for the stimulation and implementation of RVA, putting the initiative in the hands of sectors, regions and individuals. This system relies almost entirely on local initiatives and decentralised policies. Within this approach, stakeholders have an active role in supporting individual learning process; ensuring the relevance of the system of recognition to the individual; and raising awareness of its importance nationwide. In additional to this, stakeholders are responsible for activities such as planning, administration, management and evaluation at different levels of the educational system.

In the Netherlands, the EVC (Erkenning van Verworven Competenties) Knowledge Centre and its partners aim for a "common understanding" among all stakeholders, and promote transparent and ethical practice. The Knowledge Centre works in cooperation with a network of RPL regional offices. These regional offices serve as one-stop offices where individuals can walk in and access multiple services appropriate to their specific needs. This bottom-up approach is facilitated through a history and tradition of dialogue and cooperation between the government, the private sector and civil society. The Dutch government has provided a substantive amount of monetary support for RPL. The current infrastructure was developed with the help of 40 million Euros between 2005 and 2007 alone, and RPL continues to have the support from the Ministries of Education, Culture and Science and of Social Affairs and Employment (Maes 2008, p. 3). In 2006, stakeholders agreed to a quality framework for RPL that while voluntary, promotes transparency and articulates minimum standards (Maes 2008). The quality code is voluntary (Maes 2008). Individuals working through the available RPL structures are granted a Certificate of Experience to submit to educational institutions. The certificate has the status of an advisory document and the "autonomous institutions decide for themselves how to use the results of EVC procedures" (Duvekot 2010).

In the USA (Travers 2011), Prior Learning Assessment (PLA) is not governed by legislation. However, some of the six regional accreditation commissions located across the country have issued policies on PLA. These commissions are responsible for monitoring the quality of higher education in the USA through a formal accreditation process. PLA is driven by several stakeholders. RVA is conducted by many colleges and universities as well as employers. Development has been facilitated by the *American Council on Education (ACE)* and the *Council for Adult and Experiential Learning (CAEL)*. ACE is the national body responsible for coordinating higher education institutions across the country. CAEL is a national, non-profit organisation that works with educational institutions, employers, labour organisations and other stakeholders to promote creative, effective adult learning strategies. Networks and structures like CAEL aim to bring greater coherence to RVA at the level of higher education.

In the majority of the developing countries, ministries of education and, in particular, departments of non-formal education are assuming a new role, evolving from mere providers of services into bodies that supervise the coordination of stakeholders. Where this is happening, as is the case in the Philippines and Thailand, public authorities are the main initiators in promoting the issue of recognition. The role of social partnerships with civil society organisations is increasingly being recognised, although governments have approached the topic of decentralisation with caution thus far. This is because many of these countries lack a formal legislative or policy framework for RVA. Skills are assessed and certified on an individual basis by education providers. While this way of conducting validation appears to be quite flexible, it actually exposes the learner to the arbitrariness of the assessing institution. In such cases, we argue, it is important to ensure that individual education and training providers have access to the right tools, content and funding to develop RVA at their level.

5.1.2 Dividing the Recognition Procedures Between Levels of Federal/Provincial/Territorial Authority and Other Stakeholders

In Canada, PLAR is a highly decentralised process with the responsibility for assessment and validation distributed across the various provincial/territorial governments, educational institutions and professional bodies. Both policy development and the way that PLAR is used in practice vary in different parts of Canada. This is because the ten Canadian provinces have full responsibility for educational matters, while education and training providers and other local agencies at the provincial and territorial levels have a strong measure of operational autonomy. While a bottom-up decentralised and provincial approach has served well in Canada to date, strategic direction at the country level could help to facilitate cooperation and comparisons across provinces and territories (Singh and Barot 2012). Although Human Resources and Skills Development Canada (HRSDC) and Citizenship and

Immigration Canada (CIC) are undertaking several supportive activities alongside CMEC (Council of Ministers of Education, Canada: the mechanism whereby provinces and territories liaise with each other on education policies) they have no regular arrangement on PLAR.

However, at the national level, it is important to highlight that the CMEC has responsibility for the Canadian Information Centre for International Credentials which provides information on formal credentials assessment services, provincial/territorial education systems, post-secondary institutions, regulated and unregulated occupations and how to connect with provincial/territorial regulatory bodies that have responsibility for issuing licences to practice in each jurisdiction. In addition, stakeholder engagement at the national level includes CAPLA's yearly conference that attracts a wide range of RPL stakeholders from across Canada and abroad. A Strategic Advisory Panel on RPL involving representatives from Canada's provinces and territories, has been hosted by CAPLA since 2009 for purpose of sharing innovative ideas and initiatives. The Canadian Network of National Associations of Regulators hosts events for regulatory authorities that have responsibility for protection of the public, and competency assessment is discussed frequently.

Across Europe the tendency is to divide recognition procedures between levels of state authority, private stakeholders, community organisations and agencies of civil society. In 2005, Switzerland launched its RVA system (Validation des Acquis), which is overseen by the Federal Office for Professional Education and Technology and the State Secretariat for Economic Affairs. The system is based on close cooperation between the federal government, cantonal governments and social partners and voluntary associations. In this way, Swiss recognition is founded on a model of shared responsibility. These partners are engaged in the process of developing a common framework revolving around the inclusion of different levels of recognition, the roles of the different agents, the inclusion of quality assurance and the training of experts (Switzerland. Office fédéral de la formation professionnelle et de la technologie (OFFT) 2008). Like Switzerland, Austria is well equipped to operate a system of shared responsibility in recognition policy (Schneeberger et al. 2008). It divides its recognition procedures between levels of state authority, private stakeholders and agencies of civil society. The responsibilities for the regulation, provision, financing and support of learning activities are divided between the national and provincial levels.

In Germany, there is neither a central institution nor a standardised institutional framework in place for validation. Instead, a variety of approaches exist. The chambers of crafts, industry, commerce and agriculture regulate admission to the external students' examination. With respect to access to higher education, the German Rectors' Conference has defined a framework for recognition, but specific regulations and procedures are established by the respective university. The ProfilPASS system is managed by a national service centre which supports 55 local dialogue centres (Otero et al. 2010). The responsibility for continuing education falls across a number of areas. Continuing education in Germany experiences less regulation at the national level than other areas of education and as a result it features a high degree of pluralism and competition among providers. Voluntary participation in continuing education is one of the guiding principles (Germany. Federal Ministry of Education and Science (BMBF) 2008).

5.2 NQFs Coordinating RVA

In Finland, arriving at a broad consensus on RVA at the level of policy development has been critical, particularly with respect to the incorporation of RVA within the NQF. Several working groups for different qualification levels have worked to promote this approach. Today, the stakeholders have reached a broad consensus on RVA at policy level. This has led to the inclusion of RVA within national legislation for all levels of education.

Steps towards the implementation of RVA have also been taken by further specifying the policies for each educational sector. National working groups for upper secondary and higher education are currently preparing policies and procedures for RPL for the respective levels of education. The national working group on RVA in higher education institutions has issued recommendations concerning, for example, the devising of subsector-specific recognition systems and the involvement of the Ministry of Education in this process (Blomqvist and Louko 2013). Finland has a clear division of responsibilities at different levels. The responsibilities for competence-based qualifications relevant here, such as the development of the qualifications, quality assurance, and the actual provision of examinations and training are divided among various actors:

- The Ministry of Education and Culture decides which qualifications are admitted to the national qualification structure.
- The Finnish National Board of Education draws up qualification requirements for each competence-based qualification.
- Sector-specific Qualification Committees supervise the organisation of competence tests and issue the qualification certificates.
- Education providers that have signed agreements with the respective sector-specific Qualification Committees arrange competence tests and provide preparatory training for candidates.
- A Qualification Committee is appointed for each qualification. The Qualification Committees consist of representatives of employers and employees, teachers and sometimes also entrepreneurs. The committees oversee the implementation of competence-based qualifications, ensure the consistent quality of qualifications, and issue the certificates to successful candidates. If necessary, certificates can also be awarded for individual modules, for instance if the candidate does not intend to complete the whole qualification (Blomqvist and Louko 2013).

In Norway too, consensus building around RVA has been important. Political parties recognise the benefits of validation, as can be seen in the wide range of policy documents. Here too, social partners are important stakeholders in policy-making in this field.

In South Africa, a Ministerial Task Team on RPL established at the end of 2011 has proposed that the South African Qualifications Authority (SAQA) be tasked to set up a national coordinating mechanism for RPL. This possibility is explored in a discussion paper prepared within the SAQA RPL Project Team (Keevy 2012). The discussion paper puts forth several factors that would make it possible for SAQA to take up the responsibility of coordinating RPL, not only in the narrow sense of linking RVA to formal learning and qualifications, but also in the sense of addressing broader objectives of RPL such as access, career guidance and labour markets, and professional development. Firstly, the NQF Act of 2008 assigns very specific RPL-related responsibilities to SAQA, notably to develop RPL policy and criteria for assessment and Credit Accumulation and Transfer (CAT). Secondly, SAQA has over the past few years been able to successfully take up complex projects, such as the national Career Advice Service (CAS), which falls within its mandate. Thirdly, SAQA's involvement with professional bodies also creates an opportunity for SAQA to support the professional development of RPL practitioners. There is thus a strong possibility that SAQA will be asked to perform the role of coordinating mechanism at least for an initial period (Keevy 2012). However, this consensus is not necessarily shared by a SAQA initiated research by prominent experts (SAQA 2012b).

Werquin (2012) for example, suggests an inter-ministerial agency as another option, enabling more focus on RPL outside NQF rather than on RPL which associated primarily with the "formalisation" of learning in an NQF (Keevy 2012).

5.3 The Industry Model of Shared Responsibility

Although most countries have at least some aspects of shared responsibility in their recognition policies, in some cases it is industry which is the driving force in a shared system. In these cases, responsibility for validation is shared between the education system and the labour market. This model also involves the government at some point, frequently in an oversight and assessment capacity. An example of this model can be found in Trinidad and Tobago. There, the government involves local industry in the process of validation. Employers in the country's industrial sector define the standards for the assessment of individual learners' skills. The recognition and certification of vocational competences, however, is conducted by the National Training Agency Awarding Unit, which is also responsible for the distribution of information regarding APL and PLAR (Trinidad and Tobago. National Training Agency Trinidad and Tobago (NTATT), n.d).

In Japan, job training and the development of vocational skills through public sector training targets displaced workers. There, public sector job training is expected to compensate for the small number of private sector education and training organisations in the manufacturing sector. The Japanese government also supports skills recognition in small and medium enterprises (SMEs). Under this programme, highly skilled workers and 1st Grade certified skilled workers are registered as personnel to support skills transmission and recognition at SMEs and to train young skilled workers by providing hands-on guidance.

5.3.1   The Role of Industry Bodies and Training Organisations in Designing RVA Processes in the Workplace

One key factor in the implementation of RVA in Australia and New Zealand is the role of industry bodies and registered training organisations (RTOs) in designing and driving the RVA process. In Australia, RVA is offered by registered training organisations (RTOs) and state training authorities in accordance with the standards laid out in the Australian Quality Training Framework (Bowman et al. 2003). The RTOs are also responsible for assessments that lead to qualifications (DEEWR 2008). RVA processes for workers are tailored to their needs and to the needs of the enterprises, and while partnerships with educational institutions are not excluded from these RVA processes, they are not central to it. Nevertheless, the Australian government takes the lead role in ensuring that the system of recognition functions reliably and transparently; the Australian system relies on the active participation of the state and territory governments and other stakeholders.

In South Africa, the industry Sector Education and Training Authorities have designed RVA processes for workers. In Canada, the certification bodies for regulated professions have developed RVA practices for their jurisdictions and the Canadian Sector Councils have sponsored a range of initiatives to promote RVA at the workplace.

5.3.2   The Involvement of Social Partners (Employers, Employees and Trade Unions)

The involvement of social partners, including trade unions and professional associations, is a key feature in RVA that gives genuine value to employers and employees. In Lithuania, the Ministry of Education and Science oversees the procedure for qualification examinations, including the validation of non-formal and informal learning. Vocational schools and labour market vocational training institutions are responsible for providing the necessary support to applicants who are seeking to validate the knowledge and skills they have acquired outside formal education through final qualification examinations. Social partners are responsible for the assessment of the qualification for those who decide to legitimate non-formal and informal learning achievements in vocational schools. Chambers of Industry, Commerce and Crafts and the Chamber of Agriculture are charged with the organisation of the final examinations, including the design of tasks, identification of relevant members of examination commissions and granting qualifications. Regional Chambers approve requests from those wishing to validate their knowledge in vocational schools.

In France, while vocational diplomas developed in close cooperation with social partners are of genuine value to employers and employees in professional contexts (external efficiency), they also have an internal value in the education system for the individual. Although they were initially created to facilitate direct integration into the workforce, vocational diplomas, like general diplomas, open the way to further studies. The respective proportion of the training programme that focuses on general, technological and vocational content is determined through compromise, and these compromises are regularly examined in order to take account of changing needs in both spheres where such diplomas are of value, whether in the productive or educational sector. In this sense, vocational qualifications in the French system are aligned to academic opportunities that further an individual's possibilities for further learning.

Although promoted and regulated by government, the National System of Competency Standards (NSCS) in Mexico is driven by *employers* and *workers.* The government has the role of evaluating, recognising and certifying students' competences for both vocational and professional education, and provides financial resources for the operation of CONOCER. The Secretariat of Public Education has identified 12 major sectors of Mexico's economy as targets, which are already being addressed by CONOCER. In the area of adult basic education, a national programme operates under the auspices of the National Institute for Adult Education (INEA), accredited by CONOCER, to evaluate and certificate the labour competences of adults. *Social partners* (employers, trade unions and the voluntary sector) participate in the design and development of competence standards through sectoral committees responsible for the evaluation and certification of workers in their sectors. CONOCER issues the certificates for the workers based on the competence standards agreed by employers and/or trade unions in the sector (García-Bullé 2013).

Trade unions and other workers' associations widely view the recognition of non-formal and informal learning outcomes as offering their members the possibility to achieve a particular level of qualification and thus to claim the associated benefits, such as higher wages or promotions. At the same time, RVA is also able to satisfy the future needs of various industry and social sectors (like health and care services) more effectively. In South Africa employers and trade unions play an important role. They are active participants in the education sector and training authorities. Direct input is made regarding the legislation, policies and practices of RVA. Employers have also recently provided some funding for the RVA process, particularly with regard to RPL for their workers. The government is responsible for creating the legislative and policy environment and also provides funding.

5.4 Stakeholders in the Adult and Community Learning Sector

5.4.1 The Role of Communities of Practice

A unique feature of the adult learning sector has been the role of community adult educators and umbrella organisations including adult education associations involved in RVA. In Canada, adult educators have been at the forefront of RVA.

It was the community of Canadian adult educators who became acquainted with the work of CAEL in the USA and began to promote RVA in Canadian post-secondary education, as highlighted in an article by Joy Van Kleef (2011). Their reasons for promoting RVA lay in the nature of adult education, which is that adult education is community-based and encourages the development of knowledge and skills within a framework of lifelong learning. Three groups of adult educators – institutional practitioners, community-based practitioners and academic researchers – have been the primary sources of PLAR research in Canada. Most prominent were the college-based adult education practitioners who developed training resources using the works of Knowles (1970), Brundage and Mackeracher (1980), Bloom (1984) and Kolb (1984) to introduce the principle of adult learning to the uninitiated. However, as Van Kleef (2011) points out, due to policy priorities being focused on economic rather than educational drivers, the emphasis has been on temporary limited funding and short-term projects. Notwithstanding the role of adult educators, progression through access to formal qualifications and opening up access and progress in skilled and professional occupations in the labour market still remains the key aspect of RVA.

The Canadian Association for Prior Learning Assessment (CAPLA) has been the national voice for prior learning assessment and recognition (PLAR) for many years. Beginning in Belleville, Ontario, CAPLA was nurtured by First Nations Technical Institute (FNTI) and continues to benefit from the legacy of its founders. Since the early 1990s, those interested in the recognition of adult learning have come together to share practices connected to experiential learning and how it can be articulated against academic or industry standards. CAPLA has been operating since 1994 and was incorporated in 1997 as a non-profit organisation. Its members are comprised of adult learners, PLAR practitioners, researchers, unions, businesses, academic institutions, equity groups, occupational bodies, sectors and non-governmental organisations. CAPLA continues to host yearly conferences and workshops on a range of PLAR programmes, practices, policies, projects and research with local, provincial/territorial, national and international emphasis. It has provided the expertise, advocacy and support for the development of PLAR in Canada. The existence of PLAR, the communities understanding and use of it, and adult learners' awareness and access to it are key to removing barriers to recognition, regardless of the end uses of the recognition process. CAPLA's online community of practice (www.recognitionforlearning.ca) has become an important resource for online discussions, webcasting and information.

In England, the development of RVA derives largely from the adult education movement of the 1980s, and from concerns about social justice and the need to widen adult participation, including the development of "Access to Higher Education", the developer of APEL. In response to widespread concern in the 1980s that traditional school-based qualifications used for higher education entry might be inappropriate for mature applicants, an access course movement emerged, led by adult educators. They developed special courses designed for adult learners, usually with an emphasis on using learners' life experience, and organised in more flexible ways than traditional programmes. These are now formally recognised as an alternative route into higher education for mature learners. Courses are validated by local, authorised validating agencies (currently 24 in England and Wales in 2005) approved by the Quality Assurance Agency for Higher Education (QAA), and some of these are also Open College Networks (OCNs). In 2005, there were 1,200 access courses in England and Wales. Since 1983, OCNs have been leading the way in credit-based accreditation and qualifications.

The QAA has traditionally offered centres the flexibility they need, through a credit-based system, to develop learner-centred provision and recognise learner achievement in small steps. This approach has enabled thousands of learners to receive certificates for their achievements, often for the first time in their lives. OCN London Region offers approved National Open College Network qualifications, which are eligible for funding through the Skills Funding Agency and the Young People's Learning Agency. These qualifications range from entry level to Level 3 (Level 4 qualifications are also available in teacher training) and cover a diverse range of curriculum and vocational areas. However, Pokorny (2011, p. 11) laments that APEL priorities and practices in England have changed from a broader access agenda to one that is suited to a global economic skills development agenda: "Although some adult educators originally saw potential in APEL to open up higher levels of learning beyond the traditional values and interest of academic institutions, governments, professions and employer organisations, this has largely been unrealised in English higher education." (Pokorny 2011, p. 11).

Closely related to adult education, is the increasing demand in the field of youth work, in which a number of national NGOs are taking the lead. As a result of this demand, there are growing efforts to establish routes for the professional recognition for youth workers. In England the major routes to a professional youth work qualification are by taking a higher education intermediate level qualification, a university degree or a postgraduate qualification. The National Youth Agency (NYJ) is the agency responsible for accrediting higher education programmes taking into account such elements as involvement of local employers in programme governance, fieldwork arrangements; and incorporation of principles, ethics and values of youth work, such as democracy, voluntary participation and active learning, in the course work (Morrey and Drowley 2005).

5.4.2 Role of National Adult Education Associations

Latvia also involves various levels of government in its predominantly public authority-oriented system of recognition policy. Although the system is decentralised, its quality requirements and accreditation procedures are undertaken by a central supervisory authority, the Ministry of Education and Science. However, in an attempt to create a monitoring system, the Latvian Adult Education Association was established in 1993 to function as a coordinating body in the system of adult education and learning. Adult learning extends across other policy sectors and is organised by regional local governments, covering broad fields that include vocational and in-service training for business or sector-specific needs. This has had positive repercussions for non-formal and informal education in Latvia, particularly through the projects of the European Social Fund (Šiliņa 2008).

In Switzerland, the Swiss Federation for Adult Learning (SVEB) is the umbrella organisation of adult education and lifelong learning in Switzerland. This non-governmental organisation represents nationwide private and state institutions and associations responsible for adult education on a cantonal level as well as institutions, in-house training departments and personnel managers. It also extends its reach to individuals who are active in adult education (lifelong learning).

5.4.3 The Role of Adult Learners

Smith and Clayton (2011) provide insights into the importance of acknowledging adult learners as a stakeholder in the processes of recognition, validation and accreditation of non-formal and informal learning. Acting on the perspectives of adult learners is critically important for the validation of learning outcomes in the vocational education and training sector. Adult learners are in a powerful position to comment on the relevance and quality of content and pedagogy of programmes. Their insights and perspectives can play a critical role in determining the appropriateness of learning contents and processes. Adult learners are more likely to respond to "internal motivators" rather than "external motivators" (Laird 2007; Knowles 1990, p. 63). Thus, Smith and Clayton argue, there would seem to be an imperative for those designing, developing adult learning programmes to identify, understand and incorporate the "internal" motivators for adult learners to learn, such as self-esteem, recognition, better quality of life, increased job-satisfaction and greater self-confidence, more than external motivators include job-security, better jobs, promotion and higher salaries.

5.5 Summary

This chapter aimed to highlight the various partnerships between stakeholders which drive the coordination and implementation of RVA as these are essential to the success or failure of recognition policies and practice. While most systems aim to operate with shared responsibility, often the balance is tipped towards either the business sector or public authorities. There are pitfalls with any system that relies too heavily on one sector or another, but stakeholders are integral to the functioning of any framework of recognition of non-formal and informal education, so they must be included constructively in the process of policy-making.

Cooperation with industrial organisations and the private sector can be advantageous, partly because this enables employers harmonise labour market needs with those of the adult learners. However, there are issues associated with this, most notably that the capacities promoted by a heavily industry-influenced recognition system will often be narrowly focused around market sector skills. These skills will not always correlate with the broader set of valuable capabilities that ought to be covered by recognition (see also the example of Australia in Chap. 6). Government involvement, even in predominantly industry-based recognition systems, is therefore desirable if this is to be avoided.

Public authorities have an important role to play through a broad range of activities including: the development of goal-oriented public policies on RVA; the identification of key sectors requiring sustained efforts to build human capital; collaborative work among different ministries; managing the accreditation of official providers for assessment and certification services for productive, voluntary, education and government activities; adjusting educational curricula to the productive sector's needs, through the use of standards of competence and learning outcomes; and establishing a national system of equivalences for formal educational programmes (adult, vocational and professional levels).

Examples show that the shared responsibility or "social partnership" model based on close cooperation between the government, social partners and other societal stakeholders is becoming an inevitable feature of the development and implementation of RVA policies and practice. While the term "social partners" includes employee and employer organisations, Seddon and Billet (2004) define "social partnerships" more broadly to include partnerships enacted by the government, by the community, or negotiated through a broker system that provides advice and structured programmes for pathways to further education or employment and social inclusion. Social partnerships operate as "learning networks" because they provide opportunities for active, collaborative learning at the local level and link communities with networks of external educational and employer bodies. Only active engagement by a wide group of stakeholders can result in the development and implementation of RVA.

A unique feature of stakeholder involvement in the adult learning sector has been the engagement of adult educators. They have promoted RVA as a social movement for social justice and adult participation, including the development of access to higher education, most notably in the UK, USA and Canada. A lot of advocacy for RVA has been undertaken by organisations and networks like CAPLA in Canada, CAEL in the USA, and the Open University network for access to adults in the UK.

In developing countries, RVA is still in the process of being implemented. In most countries it exists mostly as policies on public documents. Nevertheless, these are countries with vast decentralised systems of non-formal and adult education with the aim to create lifelong learning opportunities for all. NGOs and voluntary agencies, as well as local and district governments are active in imparting non-formal education to socio-economically weaker sections, disadvantaged groups, the unskilled and unemployed, while a number of government ministries are also involved in skills development. Given the vastness of many of these countries, it will be important to highlight the role of regional local authorities in RVA implementation. Other, equally important factors in the implementation of RVA in developing countries include the establishment of resources for the training of RVA practitioners, the development of regulatory frameworks to ensure quality in non-formal and private educational sectors as well as strategies at the macro-level to provide solutions for the complex problems of groups that experience disadvantage (Singh and Duvekot 2013).

With a broad range of interests at stake, many objectives formulated in RVA policy respond to economic goals, such as driving labour market integration, improving the utilisation of competences within enterprises, and enhancing labour mobility in the informal and formal sectors. Other objectives relate more closely to education and training system reforms, the efficiency of learning systems, and the transparency of qualifications and certifications. In all countries, however, promoting and facilitating the integration and empowerment of marginalised social groups and individuals (uneducated and unemployed) and strengthening the motivation for lifelong learning are highly important policy objectives.

While lifelong learning presupposes a diversity of recognition forms and options according to the interests at stake, linking the efforts of all stakeholders and national authorities is essential for delivering access to education and recognition of all competences. All actors must be responsible for rendering competences visible and documenting them and enabling the process towards a qualification, diploma or certificate in cooperation with national authorities, and without neglecting coherence, transparency and quality. Recognition policies therefore need to reflect directly the level of cooperation between education, employment, economic and civil society actors.

Chapter 6
Features of Best Practice from Country Examples

Although no single model of recognition is universally transferrable, successful aspects of different systems can be usefully transmitted between countries. This chapter illustrates where this can occur, describing experiences ranging from countries with established practices of recognition to those which are still in the process of establishing systems of recognition.

This section spans the fields of standards and methods of assessment, the delivery of recognition practices, and quality assurance. The first field of enquiry highlights a variety of standards and methods used in different sectors (education and training sectors, employment and enterprise sectors, non-governmental organisations and community-based learning voluntary sectors, etc.) within the countries examined in this study. Consideration is also given to how assessment methods meet the given standards and the type of learning outcomes and competences used by countries as reference points for the recognition of non-formal and informal learning. The second field of inquiry concerns the delivery of recognition, particularly the role of education and training providers in recognition, as well as the professional development of trainers, assessors, advisors and counsellors. Finally, consideration is also given to the theme of quality assurance – an issue which cuts across all of the previous topics. Here, we examine the arrangements put in place by countries to support the recognition of non-formal and informal learning by way of developing policy guidelines, quality criteria, coordinating delivery, and strengthening the credibility of the recognition process. Quality is greatly influenced by how terms are defined and who sets the criteria by which each term is understood. Often those who create the policies also set the definitions and create the assessment standards (Werquin 2012). Moreover, there is a difference between standards set by stakeholders in the education sector and those in industry, and often, adult learners are not taken into account in decisions about assessment standards (Smith and Clayton 2011). There are also questions of who is given the authority to determine quality. This section deals with some of these issues.

© UNESCO Institute for Lifelong Learning 2015

M. Singh, *Global Perspectives on Recognising Non-formal and Informal Learning*,
Technical and Vocational Education and Training: Issues, Concerns and Prospects 21,
DOI 10.1007/978-3-319-15278-3_6

6.1 Developed Countries

6.1.1 New Zealand

Recognition of Prior Learning (RPL) originates in the 1980s and is very much dominated by the NQF discourse. In New Zealand, RPL is also known as Accreditation of Prior Learning (APL and credit transfer).

Scope of RVA

In New Zealand, RPL takes into account formal, non-formal and informal learning. In the case of informal learning, recognition of existing competences may lead to an increased willingness among employees to take part in workplace training or learning. Depending on the workplace or education environment, the RPL procedure may be determined by the entry requirements of the provider or, in the case of the validation of employment skills, by employers. In all cases, a clear rationale for RPL is necessary. For example, when the qualification requirements for early childhood education teachers changed, teachers without tertiary qualifications were able to be assessed for competences gained in their role as a teacher. Assessment is generally conducted at the admissions stage. Constraints arise from the cost of RPL activities, which are met by the individual and the respective (tertiary) education organisation, and which vary according to the level of assessment required.

Standards and Methods of Assessment

In New Zealand, learning outcome statements reflecting the standards of qualifications dominate the discourse on the recognition of learning outcomes from non-formal and informal learning. Learning outcomes approaches provide the basis for the final assessment, regardless of whether the learning outcomes result from formal, non-formal or informal learning.

An outcomes-based framework allows for flexibility in learning pathways, and supports the portability of qualifications across education and employment jurisdictions. Each outcome statement must include information on the expected learning outcomes of a qualification, or identify other potential qualifications following completion of a given qualification. Where qualifications are standalone, and do not prepare graduates for further study, the outcome statement must clarify this. Finally, outcome statements must specify areas in which a graduate may be qualified to work, or the contributions possible to their community (Keller 2013). In New Zealand no differentiation is made between RPL and assessment against the designated learning outcomes or standards which make up qualifications.

There are a number of approaches to assessing workplace learning and/or competences. These range from ongoing assessment towards qualification for entry level learners, to a process of Recognition of Current Competence (RCC), usually across a range of qualifications accounting for experience and performance history in the workplace. Experience may be supported by formal off-job training. The latter is focused on actual performance/competence in a role or function in relation to specified standards or learning outcomes (Bowen-Clewley et al. 2012; Competency International 2011).

Some learners are assessed on the basis of attested prior performance, for example using evidence from previous jobs. Others are assessed on the basis of a portfolio of evidence or by challenge assessment without completing a programme of learning.

Validation in both the labour market and the education system occurs through expert facilitators following a process of profiling, facilitation and assessment. Recognition is carried out by: interviewing potential candidates to find out the qualifications, or parts of qualifications, that best reflect personal comprehension; taking a holistic approach to a candidate's understandings, ensuring they are explored and expressed; valuing the insights that each learner brings; and providing expert facilitation to extract the candidate's learning, and to enable them to understand the level of presentation they need to achieve. During the profiling procedure, each candidate is interviewed about their experiences, understandings and goals. This is to ensure that the candidate is suitable for the RPL process and to help the candidate select the qualification or part of a qualification that best reflects their learning from experience. Facilitation refers to the support provided to candidates in preparation for their assessment.

Delivery of RVA

Expert facilitators enable each candidate to express their understandings appropriately and to understand the requirements of the qualification. The facilitators take a holistic approach to ensure that all of a candidate's understandings are valued, explored and expressed. Facilitation can be at a distance or face-to-face, on an individual basis or including group work. Expert facilitators are used to measure and validate informal learning against outcomes of qualifications listed on the NZQF and learning outcomes of standards on the *Directory of Assessment Standards.*

The form of assessment will vary depending upon the qualification sought. If the qualification is at level 5 of the NZQF, the assessment will be conducted by a panel of two or three expert assessors. In the case of level 6 or 7 (degree level) qualifications, a larger panel comprised of both academic staff and outside experts will be convened.

Quality Assurance

Quality assurance occurs within the assessment phase leading to a recognised qualification. Qualification developers must meet NZQA's listing requirements, which comprise six components: qualification definition; qualification type and level; outcome statement; credit value; subject area classification; and qualification status.

The Credit Recognition and Transfer Policy (New Zealand Qualifications Authority 2002), which is used by tertiary education organisations, recommends that education providers have their own administrative and practical arrangements in place for RPL/APL. This policy relates to individual learners, employing organisations, industry and professional bodies, and educational organisations, including a number of institutes of technology and polytechnics in New Zealand which have been designated Centres for Assessment of Prior Learning. This policy states as a key outcome that "credit will be granted for recorded success, whether or not it forms part or all of a complete qualification".

The following overarching and operational principles apply across the education sectors in consideration of RPL and credit transfer:

• The qualification, course, and programme development and design should promote and facilitate credit recognition and transfer.
• The key focus of credit transfer decisions should be on the benefit for learners and supporting effective learning pathways.
• Transparency in credit recognition and transfer decision-making across the education system is a critical factor for supporting and encouraging the on-going involvement of learners in education and training.
• The credit transfer and recognition should be able to operate across different cultures and national borders, and robust policies and procedures must be implemented to support this.
• The credit award as a result of either RPL or recognition of current competency is of equal standing to credit awarded through other forms of assessment and should be transferrable once awarded.

Both the industry and education sectors follow the same governing policy for recognition (Keller 2013).

The NZQF and the NZQA have not been without criticism in New Zealand. While its introduction into the TVET sector has been mostly accepted, RPL has faced resistance from schools and especially within the higher education sectors (Govers 2010).

6.1.2 Australia

The focus on recognition in the Australian context is on the VET sector rather than on the higher education sector. In Australia, VET is the overarching term for technical and further education colleges, private colleges and community-based provision.

Standards and Methods of Assessment

As in New Zealand, qualifications can be awarded directly through assessments against the unit standard, and can take place in the workplace, provided they are conducted by qualified assessors and are supported by relevant evidence.

While RPL continues to be a part of assessment against all accredited qualifications, it now also includes assessment that is oriented towards credit processes along with credit transfer and programme articulation arrangements (Cameron 2011).

RPL in Australia normally comprises five identifiable elements:

- the provision of information and support to individuals who may seek to have an RPL assessment, and the planning and development of RPL processes and practices, including determining assessment strategies and evidence requirements;
- interpreting and understanding units of competence and determining quality assurance mechanisms and feedback arrangements;
- identifying and assessing background, experiences, learning, skills and competences, and the quality and reliability of the evidence provided;
- review and appeal mechanisms; and
- certification of recognised competences (Australia. DEEWR 2008).

E-portfolios to support RPL have been found to be useful in diverse contexts, such as recognising the business and administration skills of rural women and supporting assessment in fabrication and welding, with a strong focus on photo and image evidence. Boyle (2008) carried out research into the use of e-portfolios for skills recognition with indigenous arts workers using *Skillsbook* to upload MP3 files, videos, photos and a range of text documents. Eagles et al. (2005) suggest that indigenous learners transfer knowledge more easily through oral processes such as storytelling, speech, song and dance. In higher education, e-portfolios are used to capture and present professional standards, graduate attributes and students' reflective skills. Perry (2009) and Boyle (2008) have highlighted the increase in the use of e-portfolios for gaining recognition or credit towards a formal VET qualification.

These authors also note that these forms of RPL are more effective after enrolment than the "traditional methodology of RPL assessment conducted up-front and prior to training" (Bowman et al. 2003, p. 47). Cameron (2011) makes a distinction between "up-front" enrolment-recorded RPL and RPL that occurs through forms of early progression, accelerated learning, or challenge testing after enrolment (Bowman et al. 2003; Bateman 2006; Hargreaves 2006).

Delivery of RVA

As in New Zealand, qualifications can be awarded directly through assessments against the unit standard, and can take place in the workplace, provided they are conducted by qualified assessors and are supported by evidence for assessment purposes. There are however concerns about the credibility of some industry-based assessors' capacity to make valid judgements about the attainment of learning outcomes. Self-reflection, including reflections in group settings is seen by adult learners to be a powerful process for identifying and validating learning outcomes (Smith and Clayton 2011, pp. 457–458).

Work-based action research in Australia (Mitchell and Gronold 2009) reports on a project designed to help assessors see their own strengths as advanced practitioners (particularly in their case studies) rather than focus on personal deficits.

Quality Assurance

Australia has a strong focus on the reliability and transparency of its processes. It is able to ensure this by establishing a national framework for the recognition of competences, delegating the oversight mechanisms to the states and territories and giving the responsibility for accreditation and certification to registered agencies. This diverse system highlights the strengths of a well-established government role in managing and overseeing the stakeholders' participation in recognition.

In Australia, the Australian Qualifications Framework has adopted the National Policy and Guidelines on Credit Arrangements adopted by the government in 2009 (Australian Qualifications Framework Council (AQFC) 2013). In Australia, RPL policy development has been a dynamic process. There is a tendency towards summative assessment and credit processes within VET and higher education sectors (Cameron 2011). However, developmental approaches continue to exist in small pockets of activity, particularly in relation to indigenous Australians.

Taking into account the insights and perspectives of adults is a critically important process for the quality of the validation of learning outcomes in the vocational education sector. Smith and Clayton (2011) note that adults are concerned that current processes for validating learning outcomes address quantity rather than quality of the evidence collected. The extensive use of written tests and examinations disadvantages learners with inadequate literacy skills and second language speakers, who are excluded by the structure of assessment processes. Moreover, adult learners are concerned about the inconsistent assessment standards and processes across providers. Ultimately, competency-based standards are not regarded as better than the grade system because the former does not promote a motivation for achieving excellence.

6.1.3 Republic of Korea

The Academic Credit Bank System (ACBS) was established in 1998. The Korean approach to RVA is heavily oriented towards academic qualifications, and is embedded in education and training. It represents a 'provider model' of RVA and relies on the accumulation of credits through a variety of educational provider types, both public and private. ACBS comprises formal, non-formal and informal elements.

Standards and Methods of Assessment

The ACBS documents and recognises outcomes from various non-formal learning activities by granting credits and conferring degrees when certain numbers of credits are accumulated. At the moment, six sources of credits are recognised by the ACBS:

- Credits from traditional higher education institutions.
- Credits from non-formal education and training institutions accredited by the ACBS division of the National Institute of Lifelong Education (NILE).
- Credits recognised for "Accredited important intangible cultural properties" curriculum. ACBS accredits master craftsmen and their apprentices engaged in artistic activities regarded as traditional and cultural heritage.
- Credits from part-time courses in traditional higher education institutions.
- Credits recognised for vocational qualifications by the ACBS (above the level of industrial technician)
- Credits transferred from the Bachelor's Degree Examination for Self-Education (BDES) under the Law of Bachelor's Degree. It is possible to obtain a bachelor's degree without attending a regular college or university by passing the examination operated by NILE. There are four exams for obtaining a bachelor's degree, all held once a year.

The ACBS is a summative process that includes *counselling, documentary evidence and degree conferment* (NILE 2013). Learners obtain assistance from advisors in each educational institution, or through the ACBS counselling teams, who help in planning the course, assigning the appropriate subject, or choosing the most appropriate forms of assessment. Individuals who have accumulated diverse learning experiences in informal or non-formal learning settings have to submit documentary evidence to obtain credits. The type of document varies according to the type of institution conferring the degree (Baik 2013). The degree conferred through the ACBS is equivalent to a bachelor's or associate degree under the Higher Education Act, and is conferred by the Ministry of Education, Science and Technology, or the president of the university or college. There is no legal discrimination between university graduates and ACBS degree holders. There are however some concerns expressed about the quality of education in the ACBS and differences in social prestige.

In addition to the ACBS, the Republic of Korea has an e-portfolio and curriculum vitae called the Lifelong Learning Account System (LLAS), containing an individual's lifelong learning activities. Individuals' diverse learning experiences are accumulated and managed within an online learning account. Unlike the ACBS, the learning results include not only those attained at the higher education levels, but also various other kinds of learning experiences that can be used as educational credits towards degrees or skills qualifications. The LLAS is like a savings account for lifelong education. Individuals can set up their own account, deposit different lifelong learning experiences, and plan ahead about how to "invest" their learning experiences in moving up the career ladder. The LLAS incorporates information from both the academic qualifications system and the vocational qualifications system. *Learning records* can be used to review learning activities, check fields previously studied, and plan further. Learning records can be used to obtain a primary school certificate, exemption from secondary school courses, and for public and private employment purposes.

Quality Assurance

To maintain and control the quality of the ACBS, the Korean government's approach relies upon the quality of accreditation of various types of non-formal education institutions (Republic of Korea. Ministry of Education, Science and Technology 2008). Accreditation determines whether the quality of their programmes and courses is equivalent to those of universities or colleges. Accreditation criteria include the requirement that instructors hold at least the same qualifications as a full-time professor at a junior college; classroom environments and equipment must be adequate for teaching and learning; and programmes must comply with the standardised curriculum and syllabus for each subject.

The Korean government, together with the National Institute for Lifelong Education (NILE) and the Ministry of Education, Science and Technology, evaluates curricula provided by all non-formal education institutions twice annually, as well as the credits earned, learning experiences and activities of individuals.

The accreditation of non-credit courses within so-called Lifelong Learning Centres is undertaken by NILE. Lifelong Learning Centres have a wider scope than the degree-centred ACBS. They are considered to be better equipped to take account of informal learning and establish a lifelong learning career management system assessing the results of non-formal and informal learning from accredited institutions (Republic of Korea. NILE/Ministry of Education, Science and Technology 2011). There is a well-defined procedure of assessment-accreditation (Baik 2013).

6.1.4   Japan

Japan's system of recognition comprises three parts, which relate to higher education, social education and work-related learning opportunities.

Standards and Methods of Assessment

The national high school equivalency examination is a certification system under the School Education Act of 2007 to enable people who have learnt mostly in informal or non-formal settings and who have not graduated from high school to access a higher education institution such as a university, specialised training college, or vocational school. This programme is directed at persons aged 16 years and older, including young unemployed school leavers, older workers, and women who have left their jobs to concentrate on child-rearing or due to illness.

In addition to the above recognition system allowing access to higher education, Japan utilises and recognises learning achievements of adults in the context of volunteer work. The Social Education Act of 1949 (amended in 2006) clearly sets out that government should utilise adults' learning achievements for adult volunteer activities. More broadly, as the 2006 amendment states, "society shall be made to allow all citizens to continue to learn throughout their lives and to apply all the outcomes of lifelong learning appropriately to refine themselves and lead a fulfilling life" (Japan. Ministry of Education, Culture, Sports, Science and Technology (MEXT) 2008, p. 3). In some cases, a certificate is issued by a third party agency to acknowledge knowledge, skills and competences gained through volunteer service. Practical learning activities that encompass volunteer work play a major role in promoting community development in Japan.

In the context of non-formal learning and vocational training in the workplace, Japan has introduced proficiency tests for the certification of vocational skills. These tests and standards serve as a mechanism to measure vocational knowledge and skills gained by workers.

Professional organisations and companies are expected to take advantage of the certification system in the coming years to assess the level of vocational capabilities and award qualifications. Many adult education activities are also increasingly valued by private-sector companies (Japan. Ministry of Education, Culture, Sports, Science and Technology (MEXT) 2008).

A portfolio system called the Job Card System was established in April 2007 to enable people with limited opportunities for vocational skills development, such as women or single mothers finished raising their children, to enhance their capabilities and find stable jobs. Clients are initially made aware of employment opportunities and are then guided in identifying appropriate areas of activity through career counselling. This is followed by practical job training that combines workplace practice and classroom lectures. The evaluation of this training and work experience is noted on their cards for use in their search for employment.

6.1.5   United States of America

Referred to in the USA as Prior Learning Assessment (PLA), RVA is located almost exclusively within the higher education sector, and is used not for access, but to assign academic credit towards a degree for learners who have been admitted through other means. Over the last 40 years, PLA has been applied for adult learners, and PLA opportunities for students have increased (Bamford-Rees 2008). Leading organisations include the American Council on Education (ACE) and community college boards (the latter are non-profit associations of colleges). Key partners in this area include the Council for Adult and Experiential Learning (CAEL), employers, labour organisations and regional accreditation commissions. US institutions primarily target adult learners returning to school and employed, unemployed and under-employed workers.

Standards and Methods of Assessment

In the USA, there are formalised and less formalised methods of assessing non-formal and informal learning.

Formal, standardised means of evaluating non-formal and informal learning include tests that are designed to measure the general academic skills and knowledge normally acquired through a 4-year programme of high school. Nearly 15 % of all high school diplomas issued each year in the USA are acquired through this testing process. These tests were designed in 1945, when ACE, through its Office on Educational Credit and Credentials, developed the high school equivalency General Education Development (GED) Programme, and, through its Commission on Accreditation of Service Experiences, began evaluating military experience for college learning (American Council on Education (ACE) 1981). For decades, colleges and universities have trusted ACE to provide reliable course equivalency information to facilitate credit award decisions. Participating organisations include corporations, professional and volunteer associations, schools, training suppliers, labour unions and government agencies, assessing courses from Arabic to Waste Management.

ACE also operates a Credit by Examination Programme that compares and evaluates the results of examinations used for granting professional licences and certificates to assess whether the results reflect the same level of achievement as traditional college classwork. Credit recommendations are published in a Guide to Educational Credit by Examination. The guide is distributed to college and university officials on a regular basis and can be used to grant academic credit. The American Council on Education's College Credit Recommendation Service (CREDIT) connects workplace learning with colleges and universities by helping adults gain access to academic credit for formal courses and examinations taken outside traditional degree programmes.

The College Entrance Examinations Board (founded in 1900) began using exams to assess university-level learning as far back as the 1930s, and created the College Level Examinations Programme (CLEP) in 1967. CLEP is a collection of five examinations in English Composition, Humanities, Mathematics, Natural Sciences, and Social Sciences and History. CLEP is used to validate non-formal learning by determining its equivalence to what is usually taught during the first year or two of college. About 30 additional subject examinations correspond to specific college courses taught across the country. Many colleges and universities accept CLEP credits.

Other standardised examinations that assess dozens of subjects and are acknowledged by colleges and universities include the Thomas Edison College Examination Program, the Defence Activity for Non-Traditional Education Support, the New York University Language Examinations and the Advanced Placement Program exams administered by the College Entrance Examinations Board.

Less formalised PLA methods include individualised student portfolios and programme evaluations of non-credit instruction. The expectations for RPL applications, especially written portfolios, are substantial (Michelson 2012). In most

RPL institutions, students must frame their learning within the content or learning outcomes of a particular module or course. Some flexibility is an inherent characteristic of a module, and some institutions grant students credit for interdisciplinary clusters of knowledge rather than specific content of a module (ibid., 14). Because of the academic demand of the process, one approach is for portfolio-development to be taught by lecturers in academic development, thus building competences of academic writing into RPL. The pedagogical frame of RPL typically combines methods of credit transfer and accumulation with a broadly developmental and liberal-humanist focus in which students are encouraged to gain not only credit toward a degree, but greater intellectual self-confidence, heightened self-knowledge, insight into academic norms and communication skills. Many community colleges, for example, offer non-credit training programmes with content that may be comparable to some college-level courses. Some states are working to identify the credit equivalences of these programmes so that the students earn some college credit (Van Noy et al. 2008).

Delivery of PLA

There are a number of higher education institutions that have been serving the adult learner population for many years, and they have developed their own brand of PLA methodologies. These new "adult learner friendly" colleges (including the Community College of Vermont and the Thomas A. Edison State College of New Jersey) adopted this "cause", and became leaders in establishing PLA policies and practices. According to Travers (2011), their PLA programmes embraced the philosophy that an adult could acquire college-level learning outside the formal classroom setting; an individual could have college-level learning that was not part of the curriculum; and an individual could have a capacity that formal testing cannot assess. These institutions gave birth to the work on how outcomes from non-formal and informal learning could be assessed at an individual level. Funding for PLA services is generally the responsibility of individual educational institutions. Assessment fees are normally charged to the individuals undertaking assessment.

Quality Assurance

Quality assurance in higher education remains a top priority as resources continue to diminish and demands for excellence increase. In the USA, accreditation is granted to higher education institutions through non-profit agencies that are structured and operated independently from federal or state governing bodies. Regional accrediting bodies such as Middle States Association of Schools and Colleges provide specific overarching frameworks and catalogues of critical questions that enable institutions to assess their programmes. For example, the New England Association of Schools and Colleges (2005) states that each of its standards articulates a dimension of institutional quality, and that by examining the efforts of an institution to address these dimensions "the Commission assesses and makes a determination about the effectiveness of the institution as a whole" (p. 1) (Travers and Evans 2011).

Regional accreditation bodies also set PLA guidelines for institutions; depending on the particular PLA principle to which an institution subscribes, the guidelines allow for varying degrees of institutional flexibility. For example, the New England Association of Schools and Colleges (2005) restricts individualised PLA to the undergraduate level, but allows flexibility in programme structure. The philosophy, policy and practice for accepting Prior Learning Assessment credits, established by individual institutions, must reflect local faculty agreements (Travers 2011, p. 251). However, as Travers and Evans (2011) argue, prior learning assessment programmes have unique qualities compared to other academic programmes, and therefore require their own set of protocols for programme evaluation. And yet, by using similar types of evaluative structures, the effectiveness of the programmes using PLA and those not using PLA can be compared to each other.

The Council for Adult and Experiential Learning (CAEL) has, for over 30 years, promoted a set of ten voluntary quality standards to ensure that PLA programmes are consistent with academic integrity. The Ten Standards for Assessing Learning are as follows:

• Credit should be awarded only for learning, and not for experience.
• Assessment should be based on agreed and publicised criteria for the level of acceptable learning and made public.
• Assessment should be treated as an integral part of learning, not separate from it, and should be based on a comprehension of learning processes.
• The determination of credit awards and competence levels must be made by appropriate subject matter and academic or credentialing experts.
• Credit or other credentialing should be appropriate to the context in which it is awarded and accepted.
• If awards are for credit, transcript entries should clearly describe the type of learning being recognised, and should be monitored to avoid redundant credit for the same learning.
• Policies, procedures and criteria applied to assessment, including provision for appeal, should be fully disclosed and prominently available to all parties involved in the assessment process.
• Fees charged for assessment should be based on the services performed in the process, and not determined by the amount of credit awarded.
• All personnel involved in the assessment of learning should pursue and receive adequate training and continuing professional development for their functions.
• Assessment programs should be regularly monitored, reviewed, evaluated and revised as needed to reflect changes in the needs being served, and the purposes being met (Fiddler et al. 2006).

The question of quality assurance in terms of competence-based education and assessment as an alternative to course-based assessment has been the subject of recent research in the USA (Wilbur et al. 2012). Their findings, which have implications for the quality of delivery of PLA by assessors, suggest that the descriptive criteria in competence-based education and assessment serve as a guide for students and for assessors; while there is a need for clarity and specificity, there must also be flexibility within the standards and criteria that allows assessors to represent the diversity in learning through experiences, and not merely through prescriptive assessments; the assessment of portfolios was enhanced in those cases where assessors were able to discern the development of students' ideas and reflections on their learning processes; and, finally, that the expertise of evaluators is an important factor in judging whether the outcomes of PLA processes merit the allocation of credits (Wilbur et al. 2012).

Research on authentic assessment has also been highlighted as an integral part of learning, and therefore the characteristics of PLA must honour diverse forms of learning. The authentic assessment approach was developed some 20 years ago by De Paul University School for New Learning (SNL) in Illinois, USA (School for New Learning (SLN) 1994). SNL constructed four qualities that embrace the diversity embedded in students' experiential learning and self-directed inquiry. These qualities are: clarity, flexibility, empathy and integrity. The SNL approach integrates these qualities at the formative, summative as well as programme levels.

In formative assessment, clarity means providing clear and accessible feedback that is descriptive and helpful in defining students' accomplishments and communicating expectations. Flexibility encourages juxtaposition of multiple points of view, while empathy entails honouring adults' perspectives within a trusting relationship. Integrity in formative assessment is when feedback presents subsequent learning activities to guide learners in an honest, accurate and constructive manner to demonstrate the necessary criteria.

In summative assessment, clarity is about articulating criteria for the demonstration of competence and how learning will be evaluated. Flexibility entails honouring diverse interpretation of content, critical analysis, and reflection. Empathy is when assessment validates the authentic voices in the context of their learning. Integrity means that qualified assessors must directly assess the learning evidence as defined in the criteria. At the programme level, clarity in accountability benchmarks enables shared analysis of on-going improvement efforts; flexibility engages those closest to the targeted assessment to define and reframe multiple paths of inquiry. For programme assessment, multiple perspectives are integrated, in collecting information and interpreting meaning. Integrating the expectations and standards of the college and the university must be completed and assessment processes and results monitored accordingly.

Using the above qualities developed by SLN, Wilbur et al. (2012) have argued with regard to competence-based assessments that in order to honour diverse learning processes, the criteria for PLA must be flexible for learners to engage in authentic learning rather than following prescribed pathways. The researchers formulated five standards:

- Credit or its equivalent should be awarded only for *learning*, and not for *experience*.
- Assessment should be based on standards and criteria for the level of acceptable learning that are both agreed upon and made public.

- Assessment should be treated as an integral part of learning, not apart from it, and should be based on an understanding of learning processes.
- The determination of credit awards and competence levels must be made by appropriate subject matter and academic or credentialing experts.
- Credit or other credentialing should be appropriate to the context in which it is awarded and accepted.

With respect to programme evaluation, Hoffman et al. (2009) have drawn on CAEL's Ten Standards to identify five critical factors: (1) Institutional mission and commitment; (2) Institutional support (financial, administrative, and faculty); (3) PLA programme parameters, (4) PLA evaluator development; and (5) PLA programme feedback and evaluation, Travers and Evans 2011; Travers and Evans (2011) propose a ten-by-five matrix that provides a structure from which a PLA programme can be evaluated.

These efforts to drive the transition from course-based to competence-based programmes highlight the priority afforded to the subject of quality assurance and the objective of honouring diverse learning experiences.

6.1.6 Canada

Prior Learning Assessment and Recognition (PLAR), as it is called in Canada, is a tool that assists several target groups, including:

- older workers – with or without formal credentials – wishing to identify their prior learning and have it assessed for employability or certification reasons;
- immigrants who require recognition of competences acquired outside Canada;
- members of marginalised groups who have not had their learning valued for a number of reasons;
- human resource managers and counselling practitioners tasked with supporting adults who have work and life experience but little confidence in their skills and abilities (Council of Ministers of Education (CMEC) and the Canadian Commission for UNESCO 2008, p. 50).

PLAR is used by the different sub-sectors of education and training to varying extents. Most public colleges recognise prior learning in at least some of their programmes. Some universities also recognise it – often in programmes offered through continuing education. British Columbia, Quebec and Ontario offer PLAR to adults at the secondary level, with a particular focus on individuals who have not completed secondary education. For example, in Ontario, the Ministry of Education provides funding to school boards to offer PLAR to adult learners who are working towards a secondary school certificate or diploma (CMEC and the Canadian Commission for UNESCO 2008, p. 50).

PLAR is present in most of Canada's public colleges. A distinction is made between assessment for academic credit (located primarily at college level) and assessment of knowledge, skills and competences for personal development, training needs assessment and employment. In both cases, it involves comparing the adult's learning achievements to standards or requirements set by credentialing bodies (CMEC and the Canadian Commission for UNESCO 2008).

While progression through access to academic qualifications still remains the key aspect of PLAR (Van Kleef 2011), opening up access and progress in skilled and professional occupations in the labour market is now reported as the key employment issue in Canada (CMEC 2007; OECD 2008, p. 14). An example is the Foreign Credential Recognition of adult learners, which is a process of verifying the equivalency of educational and professional experience obtained in another country. The Canadian government, through the Department of Human Resources and Social Development, plays a facilitative and funding role. But the recognition of credentials for regulated occupations (i.e. with respect to the fulfilment of licensing requirements) is mainly a provincial and territorial responsibility that has been legislatively delegated to regulatory bodies (CMEC 2007; OECD 2008, p. 14).

Standards and Methods of Assessment

Canada's first efforts to establish national RPL standards occurred when the Government of Canada funded projects lead to the development of 14 PLAR Standards through the Canadian Labour Force Development Board (1990–1999). The Canadian Association of for Prior Learning Assessment (CAPLA) expanded on this work in 1999 with the development of practitioner benchmarks and later, on assessor, advice and facilitator competencies. Currently CAPLA has begun work in collaboration with a wide range of stakeholders to develop quality assurance guidelines for the field of practice. A Pan-Canadian Framework for the Assessment and Recognition of Foreign Qualifications was developed in 2009 by Canada's forum of Labour Market Ministers and the Foreign Qualifications Recognition Working Group continues to guide and support the implementation of the Framework (Kennedy 2014).

The country note for Canada on the recognition of non-formal and informal learning (RNFIL) activity (OECD 2008) lists the three key PLAR mechanisms:

- The *challenge mechanism* is one in which the student may be permitted to challenge the school, college or university concerning the requirement to achieve specific units of credit through a taught course and examination.
- *Equivalence* enables students to demonstrate that previously acquired qualifications should count for exemption from parts of a qualification. This mechanism relates to arrangements for the transfer of credit from one situation to another. Agreements allowing credit transfer between colleges within a province are normal across Canada, and occasionally between colleges and universities. This practice is widespread between provinces/territories. Credit transfer arrangements almost never exempt the candidate from the final examination. Thus, for example, a midwife or mechanic may be able to demonstrate that they have all

the knowledge, skills and attitudes for qualified entry, but they still have to take a written exam for entry. Indeed, much PLAR activity is in preparation for a final examination (OECD 2008, p. 11).

- *The portfolio* is a commonly accepted tool for PLAR. One noteworthy instance of the use of the portfolio is at the Prior Learning Centre in Halifax, Nova Scotia, for personal development and career planning. The centre supports the applicant, who submits evidence to assemble the portfolio. The Centre also advises on opportunities to fill gaps through further training. This can help learners come to grips with written examinations for professional entry. The portfolio process has been a valuable support for those facing barriers of poverty, low formal schooling, social isolation, and lack of workplace experience (CMEC and the Canadian Commission for UNESCO 2008; see also Prior Learning Assessment (PLA) Centre 2008). Workers in community-based organisations have a history of experimentation with the use of portfolio-based assessment.

Delivery of PLAR

Use of PLAR in university-based Adult Education programmes. In Canada, Prior Learning Assessment and Recognition is considered a central element of an "adult-focused post-secondary institutions" (Council on Adult and Experiential Learning (CAEL) 2000). "Adult Education" refers to formal programmes of study to prepare individuals to become educators of adults, and is distinguished from "adult education" (lower case), the broad activity of providing education for adults (c.f. Spencer 2008). According to a survey of PLAR, Wihak and Wong (2011) report, 8 of the 11 responding universities reported making use of PLAR in their Adult Education programmes for admissions or for advanced standing (i.e. acknowledging learning from experience in the form of academic credits). The survey considered the following aspects:

- *Information.* All eight universities using PLAR indicated that they make considerable effort to inform students about its availability.
- *Support provided to applicants in having their learning assessed.* There is considerable variability in the amount and nature of support offered in terms of portfolio development courses, individual guidance, written information versus personal guidance.
- *Methods used to assess learning.* The predominant method used to assess learning is the paper-based portfolio, supplemented by interviews and/or demonstrations. The e-portfolio, Wihak argues, creates potential barriers for those adult learners who are not computer literate or do not have convenient access to computers (Wong 2004). In addition, there are issues relating to privacy, the time required to master software, and the compatibility of computer hardware and software.
- *Course-based or programme based PLAR.* In some cases, PLAR processes require that applicants have taken specific non-credit programme(s). In other

institutions, applicants holding a trade, business, or journeyperson certificate are granted a certain number of credits.

- *Faculty compensation.* While at some universities, assessment of PLAR is considered part of academic duties with no additional compensation, in others a fee is paid for the time involved in the assessment, or an honorarium based on the number of course credits the applicant is petitioning. These are part of the institution's collective agreement with the faculty members.

The Certificate in Adult and Continuing Education (CACE) a non-credit programme, uses a DACUM-like self-assessment instrument reflecting thirteen competences with 229 associated performance elements. Wihak and Wong (2011) call for different theoretical lenses that focus both on the prior learning of adults who apply to Adult Education programmes, as well as the learning required in Adult Education programmes.

Research perspectives on PLAR in university-based Adult Education programmes depend to a large extent on the theoretical position adopted with respect to prior learning. Sullivan and Thompson (2005) argue that adults' knowledge and skills can be identified and stated in terms of behavioural outcomes. Fenwick (2006), describing a much less formal process used in PLAR at the University of Alberta, argues that knowledge in Adult Education should not be codified in the reform of desired competences, as this reinforces the mainstream voice. Instead, Fenwick advocates a stance derived from complexity theory, according to which PLAR should focus on the processes of knowledge creation, rather than on knowledge as a product. Such an approach would shift the emphasis to portfolios, interviews and extended conversations. Joining Fenwick (2006) and Harris (2006), Wihak and Wong (2011) recommend that research must regard both the content and the processes of learning within and outside the higher education context. They argue that Adult Education scholars must have a theoretically articulated stance with regard to PLAR within their own discipline. Only then can university-based Adult Education programmes play a greater leadership role in encouraging increased use and acceptance of PLAR within the broader academic community.

Quality Assurance

The criteria for PLAR in academic and workplace settings were developed by the Canadian Institute for Recognising Learning in 2006. The Institute works with educators, workplaces, governments and occupational groups to develop standards and processes for quality assurance, and facilitates the integration of immigrants. The quality principles it advocates are accessibility, accountability, criterion-referencing, efficiency, equity, fairness, legality, equality, the right of appeal, transparency, validity and reliability (Morrissey et al. 2008).

As in the USA, attempts are being made to implement quality criteria which support the use of competences as units of measurement for assessment in PLAR. This development reflects pressure to implement and improve current assessment measures following the adoption of legislation to ensure that immigrant professionals are treated equitably in licensing processes (Van Kleef 2012). Van Kleef explores

Baartman et al.'s (2007) criteria for quality in assessing competences as a framework for quality. According to Baartman et al. (2007, p. 261), competency-based assessment programmes should display the following characteristics: Acceptability of all stakeholders of the assessment criteria, including benchmarks for relevant and sufficient evidence, and meaningful post-assessment feedback; Authenticity with regard to the degree of resemblance to a competency-based assessment for the future workplace; Cognitive Complexity, i.e. the extent to which thinking skills are integrated into competency standards; Comparability, i.e. assessment should be conducted in a consistent and responsible way; Cost Efficiency, i.e. the time and resources needed to develop and carry out competency-based assessments must be comparable to the benefits; Educational Consequences, determining whether the assessment program yields positive effects on learning and instruction; Fairness, i.e. the fair chance that candidates can demonstrate their competences; Candidates and staff should have insights into the benefits of multiple methods of assessment and tools; Fitness for purpose means selecting tools that can best demonstrate the relevant learning; Fitness for Self-Assessment means competency-based assessment programmes should simulate self-regulated learning; Meaningfulness is the value for stakeholders involved; Reproducibility of decisions refers to the need for assessment decisions to be accurate over situations and assessors; Transparency ensures that the assessment programme should be understandable to all stakeholders (p. 261).

PLAR nurses and staff of the School of Nursing at York University in Toronto support the use of holistic statements of competences as units of measurement for assessment, and also support the use of multiple assessment tools that combine both traditional, standardised testing and competency-based assessment methods which meet the principle of "fitness for purpose". However, Van Kleef argues that questions remain concerning the applicability of quality measures in educational assessment to quality measures in the assessment of prior learning for professional registration, given their very different conditions, purposes and participants (Van Kleef 2012).

There are no immediate plans to systematise PLAR in Canada, although RVA practice will be formed and enriched by the quality assurance project "Ensuring Quality Assessment through Training and Collaboration" currently underway through CAPLA and its partners (Kennedy 2014)

6.1.7 South Africa

RPL has existed in South Africa for over 15 years now. Technical arrangements for the recognition of Prior Learning (RPL) are highlighted in the OECD (2007) country report. In South Africa, the term RPL is used for the recognition of non-formal and informal learning. It is defined as a comparison of prior learning and experience (howsoever obtained) against the learning outcomes required for a specified qualification. Learning is measured in terms of learning outcomes for a specific qualification, and may lead to achievement of credits towards the intended qualification.

RPL can be either for *credit*, usually associated with general and further education and training; for *access*, usually associated with higher education (Samuels 2013); and for *advancement* of current requiring new certification.

RPL is implemented in a variety of contexts, ranging from Further Education and Training (FET), General Education and Training (GET) and higher education, to Adult Basic Education and Training (ABET) and workplace-based training. There are three main target groups for RPL:

- the access group, including under-qualified adult learners wishing to up-skill and improve their qualifications, and candidates lacking minimum requirements for entry into a formal learning programme;
- the redress group, including workers who may be semi-skilled and even unemployed, who may have worked for many years, but were prevented from gaining qualifications due to restrictive policies in the past;
- and candidates who left formal education prematurely and who have, over a number of years, built up learning through short programmes.

Different approaches to RPL have also emerged since Harris (1999) highlighted these through her research in South Africa. The range of approaches includes: credit-exchange (the ability of the individual to perform certain job tasks to a predetermined standard), developmental (the emphasis is on what the learner has learnt – rather than matching competences to pre-agreed standards, the curriculum and institutional prescriptions are used to determine 'acceptable' prior learning), radical (the focus is on the collective rather than the individual – only the experience of the emancipated group counts as knowledge), and the Trojan horse (an enquiry into the social construction of knowledge and curricula through which both experiential knowledge and discipline-based knowledge approach (and complement) each other). Therefore, while RPL in South Africa on the one hand is highly standardised and centralised through close association with the NQF and the SAQA, on the other hand it recognises the different strategies in implementing RVA for different target groups – "access", "redress" and "credit/qualification attainers".

The current revised policy seeks to position RPL in relation to the following key priority areas: (1) access to quality learning pathways for all South Africans, including unemployed persons; (2) redress of past unfair discrimination in education, training and employment opportunities; (3) fair recognition of workforce knowledge and skills in South Africa.

Standards and Methods of Assessment

The South African Qualifications (SAQA) Act was passed in 1995, and provides the context for South African education and training, including RPL, in the post-Apartheid era. The new NQF Act was passed in 2008 and came into effect on 1 June 2009. The new South African NQF comprises three sub-frameworks and ten levels. Three types of qualifications are recognised: certificates, diplomas and degrees. The key issue is that qualifications and standards must be registered in the national qualifications framework, which, with the latest reforms, also includes units and modules. If the outcomes of informal and non-formal learning are registered in this way, they are recognised.

The process of RVA is described as identifying what the candidate knows and can do, matching the candidate's skills and knowledge to specific standards, assessing the candidate against those standards, and crediting the candidate.

The overall approach outlined by the SAQA in its Guidelines is not only for industry-based models, as it is considered to be a generic process for both workplace and institutionally-based accreditation of prior learning (APL) (Samuels 2013).

The form, quality and sources of evidence leading to the attainment of credits depend on the particular qualification; care should be taken neither to require too much evidence nor to expect the candidate to cover the syllabus in its entirety. In implementing RVA, candidate support should not be underestimated, and should as far as possible include the possibility for candidates to choose the assessment methodologies with which they are most comfortable. The "nested" approach towards standards generation and qualifications specification is a useful way to understand what should be assessed in an RPL process.

There are relatively common stages for RVA. The inclusion of preparation, assessment and, when applicable, an appeals process is indicated in the SAQA Guidelines. The recognition practices are largely summative, linked to the NQF-registered qualifications and standards. They also allow for access to institutions (incl. bridging, undergraduate and graduate programmes) as well as upgrading workplace performance; for example in the real estate, construction and insurance industries. The role of social partners (employers and trade unions) in the learning process and in the process of RVA is emphasised.

Delivery of RPL

Criteria for implementation of RPL have been developed for SAQA, the Quality Councils, for providers, for recognised professional bodies and for RPL practition-ers (SAQA 2012a). Practitioners should be registered as an assessor, workplace assessor and/or moderator with the relevant body; should undertake specific RPL-related continuing professional development activities; and adhere to a code of conduct (SAQA 2012a). Assessors are required to identify equivalencies. Prior learning is often unstructured, tacit and intuitive, requiring the assessor to identify equivalencies to the required evidence in order to prove applied competence through an integrated assessment of the learning field.

Quality Assurance

The SAQA (2012b) has issued guidelines for the implementation of RPL, which highlight RPL as a holistic approach to the process and execution of assessment that is both incremental and developmental. The quality of assessment within the NQF relates to reliability, validity, authenticity, sufficiency and currency. There is no fundamental difference between the assessment of previously acquired skills and knowledge, and the assessment of those acquired through a current learning programme; the only difference lies in the route to the assessment.

Quality assurance of RPL was further reflected upon in the Resolution and Working Document on RPL (SAQA 2012a) that resulted from the National RPL Conference: *Bridging and expanding existing islands of excellent practice*, hosted by SAQA in February 2011. The document notes that:

- RPL needs to take into account an improved understanding of RPL practices across education, training, development and work; assessments and moderation need application against agreed standards, qualifications, part-qualifications outcome statements and other descriptions of learning;
- an effort should be made to allow standard practice to grow within sub-sectors, rather than imposing top-down standardisation;
- the concept of RPL needs to be taken beyond traditional reliability and validity, to include quality indicators such as acceptability to stakeholders, fitness for purpose, transparency, and fair consequences. Moreover, several other potential indicators require exploration in judging the quality of RPL assessments;
- The measurement of equivalence is very complicated. Qualifications at the identical NQF level have similar cognitive demand, but are not necessarily equivalent. At the same time, curriculum comparisons are a robust means to establish comparability of cognitive demand.
- Modules on RPL advising, administering, pedagogy (mediation), assessment and moderation, for example, need to be developed for the development and professionalisation of these specialised services.
- Finally, mutual understandings of quality assurance need to be developed.

A revised policy on RPL (SAQA 2012b) highlights the following principles of quality assurance: (1) The focus is on what has been learnt and not on the status of the learning site; (2) Credit is awarded for knowledge and skills through experience and not for experience alone; (3) Learning is made explicit through assessment and/or other methods that engage the intrinsic development of knowledge, skills and competences acquired; (4) Candidate guidance and support, the preparation of evidence and the development of an appropriate combination of teaching-learning, mentoring and assessment approaches are core to RPL practice. Notwithstanding all the features listed here, "RPL is generally considered to be a developmental process, and not an end it itself." (SAQA 2012b, p. 10)

6.1.8   *Austria*

In Austria, two types of RVA mechanisms currently exist in the educational sector (Austria. Federal Ministry of Education, the Arts and Culture 2011):

1. those that focus on access to external examinations and are set in the formal system, and/or aim at formal education and training qualifications; and

2. those that are mostly set in the further education and training sector, and take the form of competence audits, portfolios and similar tools, which have personal use for individuals.

Standards and Methods of Assessment

In the first case, examples include:

1. the acquisition of the lower secondary school leaving certificate by adults;
2. the awarding of the professional title of *Ingenieur* (engineer) as a result of exceptional admission to the apprenticeship examination;
3. providing access to university entrance qualification examinations for skilled workers, and graduates of 3- to 4-year full-time courses at VET schools (*berufsbildende Schulen*);
4. providing access to an upper secondary school leaving examination, which is externally organised, and provides direct access to higher education;
5. providing access to continuing VET courses at universities as well as courses at universities of applied sciences for persons who have not completed the upper secondary examination;
6. providing access to evening schools (VET colleges and secondary academic schools) for adults by allowing participants to provide evidence of acquired knowledge in a context of an modular examination.

In the case of RVA mechanisms set in the formal system and/or aiming at formal education and training qualifications (external examinations), the assessment methods for recognition correspond to those used in the formal system. Written tests and oral exams are the most commonly used methods for external examinations, and competences are usually assessed according to standards set in the formal system. In the case of the apprenticeship leaving exam – as well as in the case of exceptional admissions – both theory (usually written) and practice are emphasised, and candidates are expected to furnish evidence of their practical know-how and job-related skills.

In the second case, Austria has developed methods of assessment that are supplementary to traditional assessment. There are, for example, no mandated approaches to the implementation of RVA in the further education sector or the non-formal education sector. A variety of portfolio approaches is applied in the initiatives developed at adult learning institutions. In some cases, the portfolio is combined with an assessment centre. Examples of this practice include the competence portfolio for volunteers used by all Austrian adult education associations, the competence profile "KOMPAZ" designed by the Adult Education Centre Linz, the Competence Balance used by the Tyrol Centre of the Future, or the family competences portfolio (Brandstetter and Luomi-Messerer 2010; Prokopp 2011). The Academy of Continuing Education (Wba) uses a combination of portfolio approach and 3-day assessment, the so-called "certification workshop", where candidates demonstrate their professional, personal and social skills and competences (Brandstetter and Luomi-Messerer 2010; Prokopp and Luomi-Messerer 2010).

While RVA mechanisms are set in the formal system, some preparation courses take place in the non-formal system and are statistically recorded for the further education and training sector (Markowitsch et al. 2008). Many of the recognition mechanisms set in the formal system or aimed at the formal education and training sector are linked to preparation courses to support candidates, but these courses are generally not compulsory. The availability of support measures, such as information and awareness-raising, guidance, counselling and financial support varies depending on the recognition mechanism or initiative.

Thus, while RVA assessment is not separated from traditional assessment, mechanisms have been put in place in Austria that are supplementary to traditional assessment, such as guidance and counselling and financial support. Austria has also explored opportunities for RVA in adult learning institutions that are outside the regulatory function of the education system and labour market.

Quality Assurance

Despite the differences in the nature of RVA in the two sectors and the likely tension between the regulatory aspect of quality assurance measures on the one hand and the broadening of access to adults in adult learning institutions on the other, Austria (Austria. Federal Ministry of Education, Arts and Culture 2011; see also, Republik Österreich 2011) has recommended that RVA processes be supported by the widespread implementation of the following principles and practices:

- the provision of guidance and counselling;
- financial support for institutions and/or individuals;
- regional and temporal accessibility of mechanisms;
- the adoption of a modular approach;
- the recognition of partial certifications.

The quality principles set out in the European Guidelines for Validating Non-formal and Informal Learning are considered by the Federal Ministry of Education, the Arts and Culture to be suitable for planning and implementing RVA processes in the country.

6.1.9 Germany

In Germany, as in Austria, non-formal and informal learning are an integral and institutionalised part of the education and training system. In addition to procedures aimed at formal recognition and the labour market, steps are also being undertaken to promote lifelong learning, with the long-term aim of providing more effective ways of achieving recognition of competences acquired through non-formal and informal routes in different educational domains.

Standards and Methods of Assessment

RVA for facilitated admission to courses or examinations. Germany has a variety of procedures to recognise non-formal and informal learning in different learning environments:

In the Vocational Education and Training sector clear conditions are provided to candidates seeking admission to examinations as external students (*Externenprüfung*) upon completion of a dual system of vocational apprenticeship. Candidates with previous employment experience may take the examination (without having attended formal classes). The following conditions apply:

- Admission must be preceded by a period of employment at least one and a half times the length of the prescribed training period for that particular occupation. This minimum period may be waived if the candidate can demonstrate that they have acquired the vocational expertise that justifies admission to the examination;
- Periods of employment also include training periods in other relevant apprenticeship trades;
- Foreign qualifications and periods of employment abroad are taken into account;
- Qualification in a recognised apprenticeship trade can also be obtained by persons who have not gone through dual training (usually a requirement), but can instead provide evidence of relevant employment or training;
- Admission to the external student examination is granted by competent bodies solely on the basis of documentary evidence.

In the higher education sector, RVA is facilitated by developing equivalences and credit point systems. Usually recognition mechanisms in higher education recognise the competences and study programmes that people have acquired in vocational training, continuing vocational education and training and in the workplace (Germany. Federal Ministry of Education and Science (BMBF) 2008, p. 48).

Although traditional assessment methods such as tests and examinations are used to assess outcomes from non-formal and informal learning against standards in vocational education and training, examinations are designed in such a way as to take into account active learning processes (Frank 2011), so that competences from non-formal and informal learning can be assessed in an authentic and holistic manner. In fact, the concerned parties regularly undertake structural and content-related changes with regard to training regulations with the aim of making assessments more authentic particularly at the level of initial and continuing education and training.

Like Austria, Germany has developed methods of assessment that are supplementary to traditional assessment methods. Instruments such as the ProfilPASS (Germany. Federal Ministry of Education and Science (BMBF) 2008) have been developed to record the training, learning and work biographies of individuals. The central task for users is to complete their own biography, and it is recommended that they receive qualified guidance for this. The ProfilPASS system comprises the ProfilPASS tool and a guidance concept.

Advisors are trained at so-called "dialogue-centres" in the methodology of documenting competences in a 2-day preparatory seminar. The training of advisors is coordinated at the national level by the ProfilPASS Service Centre of the German Institute of Adult Education and the Leibniz Centre for Lifelong Learning (DIE) (Germany. Federal Ministry of Education and Science (BMBF) 2008, p. 44).

The ProfilPASS places emphasis on self-exploration and self-reflection. It is to a lesser extent an instrument providing an exact measurement of competences. The notion "competences" comprises both cognitive and motivational dimensions. A basic requirement of motivation is empowering individuals by helping them to improve their self-esteem and self-confidence, rather than undertaking an exact measurement of abilities (Preißer 2005). The various steps in the ProfilPASS are:

1. Biographical interviews to stimulate users to narrate activities and episodes of successful performance.
2. Small group discussions to highlight personal competences.
3. Self-assessment through performance of their identified competences.
4. Developing a vision for the future by combining users' own preferences and choices with the competences they themselves identify.

Expanding the Use and Availability of RVA

Many researchers (Münchhausen 2011) have pointed out the huge potential as well as the challenges in validating competences of low-skilled employees (part-time or casual workers), whose number in the German labour market is increasing. Many authors also note that unlike in other European countries, RVA in Germany does not cover the needs of low-skilled workers (Beinke and Splittstößer 2011). There are barriers to the formal recognition of competences acquired by part-time and casual workers in Germany. Low-skilled workers are frequently unable to participate in external examinations, which focus on theory, and where assessment standards and methods are still highly structured (ibid.).

These authors argue that RVA mechanisms are more effective after enrolment in retraining or rehabilitation programmes rather than prior to training, which is often the case in the traditional methodology for RVA. Many researchers also note the importance of taking into account the subjective and contextual nature of the competences of low-skilled workers (Koch and Strasser 2008, p. 45f.), and argue that validation processes should be individualised and flexible.

In light of this, research studies are being undertaken (Münchhausen 2011) that highlight the huge potential of developing diagnostic instruments to strengthen the informal learning of low-skilled employees in the context of organisational learning. These diagnostic instruments could measure progress and "competence gain" by comparing the competence profiles of atypical employees at the beginning and conclusion of their work on the basis of a range of competence dimensions.

Münchhausen's study has shown that non-traditional diagnostic instruments give a better picture of competence gain among part-time and casual workers than traditional assessment instruments such as external examinations and tests; the latter still tend to predominate the German initial and continuing vocational education and training system. By using diagnostic instruments, it was found that low-skilled employees do not necessarily perceive their work negatively, but that they do so only in relation to the end of contract, age, duration and social status. In fact, contrary to common perceptions, low-skilled worker learn new tasks, and try to overcome challenges; they have the same access to information and further learning opportunities as the others in the organisation; they are cognisant of criteria, such as complexity, decision-making, and holism; they view age as a critical employment factor, resulting in a loss of personal confidence and an increasingly defensive attitude over time, and feel pressured to seek other employment as their contract reaches its conclusion; they are more likely to be influenced by their personal, social and methodological competences, than by their professional competences. An important conclusion that emerges from the study on competence validation of atypical workers is that casual and part-time workers frequently possess "hidden" stores of knowledge. In the process of informal organisational learning they develop new knowledge which contributes to increased self-confidence. An important goal of RVA should be to strengthen informal learning through the recognition of competences in the workplace.

In view of the ever-increasing number persons in low-skilled jobs, contractual and part-time work, various measures have already been taken in Germany to validate informally acquired competences. It is felt, however, that further discussions are needed in relation to the development and implementation of: recognition infrastructure; guidance and counselling; assessment procedures; assessment standards; transparent and quality assured systems that support and complement the existing education system (Seidel 2011).

Quality Assurance

Germany (Germany. Federal Ministry of Education and Science (BMBF) 2008) highlights a series of legal, social and individual conditions that must be met to realise the vision of an open learning system.

- A social as well as a legal foundation for RVA must exist.
- Existing recognition procedures must be improved and new procedures with facilitated admission to courses or examinations developed.
- The system of documentation, recording and recognition with different, intermeshing procedures must be transparent.
- A culture of trust in respect of self-evaluation procedures must be maintained.
- The motivation and the ability to both reflect and perform self-evaluation and, most of all, a willingness and ability to continue learning must be a precondition for recognising all forms of learning.

6.1.10 Denmark

Standards and Methods of Assessment

While summative recognition links validation of non-formal and informal learning to standards in the education system, formative recognition links validation to human resource management through mapping, notional levelling, personal or career development planning.

Approaches to validation differ depending upon whether it is conducted to facilitate further learning, for career advancement purposes or to document voluntary and leisure activities.

In the *educational sector*, the recognition of informal and non-formal learning is conducted in relation to the standards utilised in the formal education and training system. Competence assessment in Denmark is always tied to educational objectives and the admission requirements of specific education programmes. Validation is located exclusively within the education system in Denmark.

In the area of *voluntary and leisure activities*, *My Competence Folder* was developed in co-operation with social partners, stakeholders from voluntary organisations and various agencies of civil society. Compiled on a voluntary basis, the folder gathers together information/documentary evidence on completed formal education, uncompleted education or training programmes, as well as competences acquired in working life, through voluntary activities, or through non-formal and informal learning. The folder consists of a CV-style framework or portfolio. There are other frameworks and methods for documenting "real competences", as they are called in Denmark.

In the work domain, the systematic identification, documentation and assessment of employees' competences already figures in enterprise-level competence development systems. Enterprises may choose their own points of reference for the RVA of employees; alternatively, state-approved education or training programme standards can serve as reference points (Denmark. Ministry of Education (UVM) 2008).

In spring 2011, a committee was established in order to develop an action plan and a model of RVA. The model describes a process of VPL divided into four stages. (1) The educational institution identifies one or more study objectives or admission requirements against which a candidate is to be evaluated; (2) the educational institution is responsible for the specific counselling and guidance relating to the process of prior learning assessment; (3) the educational institution conducts the assessment process; and (4) the educational institution carries out guidance and counselling to determine how the individual candidate can use his or her prior learning assessment, including a plan for a subsequent educational programme.

The model illustrates how the education pathway of the candidate can be combined with a job and employment pathway. In addition, the model clarifies different roles and responsibilities of stakeholders through the stages of the overall process. In order to ensure transparency in the overall process, all stages must include clear guidelines and assessment criteria.

It is the educational institution, which is responsible for conducting prior learning assessment on the basis of educational standards, admission requirements and competence objectives against which the candidate wishes to be evaluated. In the processes of documentation and assessment in educational institutions, the documentation work is referenced against the specific educational objectives and requirements. Both the applicant and the educational institution contribute to the documentation process.

According to Danish law, assessment must be conducted solely by the educational institution offering the study programmes to which a specific assessment is related. Other stakeholders can be in charge of information, identification, guidance and counselling, in a broader perspective, in the phase leading up to the assessment process ("the pre-phase"). These stakeholders include i.a. trade unions, employers' associations, job centres, unemployment insurance funds, civic education institutions, study committees and "eVejledning" (online guidance service), who can all take care of this part of the process and often in collaboration with the educational institution.. In "pre-phase" companies can, among other things, define new tasks and future business plans through the matching of competence profiles. For individuals, both employees and jobseekers, this part of the process may include documentation of what they have previously learnt. For companies and individuals, the pre-phase helps to clarify and identify objectives and the direction for career development, and it helps create a potential plan for the types of formal education which would be relevant in future.

Delivery of RVA

RVA practitioners are key to the RVA process in Denmark. Practitioners include individuals delivering information, advice and guidance; those who carry out assessments; the managers of educational institutions, and a range of other stakeholders with important but less direct roles in the validation process.

The largest group of practitioners are counsellors/guiders and assessors. According to Danish legislation, the qualification requirements for assessors are the same as for those, who teach in the formal educational system. Educational institutions are responsible for ensuring that assessors are appropriately qualified and must ensure that assessors are able to attend necessary courses and training to conduct VPL assessments.

A number of different initiatives have been undertaken to drive the professionalisation of practitioners in the field of RVA. In the vocational education and training sector, the Ministry of Education has implemented competence development initiatives for practitioners. In the voluntary sector, the Danish Adult Education Association (DAEA) the umbrella organisation for non-formal adult learning offers a training programme for teachers and guidance counsellors, who are being trained as "prior learning guides". The learning outcomes of the DAEA course are formulated as enabling participants:

- To relate guidance and counselling to the process of identification and documentation of prior learning based on the latest research;
- To use tools for identification and documentation of prior learning including the tools developed by the Ministry of Education especially for non-formal adult education, voluntary associations and voluntary work;
- To teach and support others to work as a 'prior learning guide' (*sparringspartner*).

In the formal education and training sector, the National Knowledge Centre for Validation of Prior Learning (NVR) has organised several seminars, courses and conferences in the past 5 years. In 2011, the Knowledge Centre was asked to develop a module for the formal diploma programme, which is now offered at university colleges. The module, entitled "Realkompetence" (RVA), is positioned at level 6 within the Danish NQF and corresponds to ten credit points within the European Credit Transfer System (ECTS). The module targets employees in educational institutions who work with VPL (e.g., counsellors, teachers, coordinators and managers); counsellors at job centres; youth counsellors; counsellors in trade unions; and counsellors in non-formal adult education. Admission requirements include a short-cycle higher or medium-cycle higher education and a minimum of 2 years of relevant vocational experience. Applicants with other and equivalent background may gain admittance through VPL.

Integrating experience from practice and theoretical knowledge, the course enables students to gain the competences to undertake and develop relevant tasks for all phases of the VPL process, including tasks across educations and sectors.

Although many of the practitioners in the field of RVA also fulfil other tasks, it is obvious that the performance of RVA practitioners is essential to ensuring quality and building trust in the outcomes of the validation process. At the same time, there is a growing demand for training by counsellors/guiders and assessors in Denmark.

Quality Assurance

Danish VPL legislation grants individuals (from 18 or 25 years depending on the educational field) the right to have prior learning experiences validated in relation to specific goals in adult education and continuing training. The legislation focuses on the needs of the individual and aims to make the process as accessible and flexible as possible. A key aim is to motivate those with little or no education to participate in lifelong learning by facilitating the recognition of prior learning. Principles for assessments and quality assurance in the VPL legislation are:

- VPL is an individual right.
- The responsibility to contribute to the documentation of prior learning rests with the individual.
- While a user fee may be charged, low-skilled workers enjoy free access to this service.

- Competence assessment should relate to the objectives and admission requirements of the education programme.
- Competences should be recognised no matter where and how they are acquired, but without compromising the quality or standard of the education.
- The methods used must ensure that assessments are reliable.
- Assessment results are to be documented by the issuing of certificates.
- Individuals are able to appeal prior learning decisions to an appeal board, the Qualifications Board.

The Ministry of Education and the Ministry for Science, Innovation and Higher Education both provide funding to VPL measures. The range of measures conducted at no cost to participants includes: the assessment of reading, writing, spelling, arithmetic and mathematics skills in Preparatory Adult Education or in courses staged within the vocational training system; competence assessments within adult vocational training (GVU and AMU); competence assessments for entry to general adult education programmes; and general adult education competence assessments in connection with competence certificates. Within higher education, institutions are able to levy fees for VPL and these vary from one institution to the next.

The implementation of quality VPL is a major concern for all stakeholders. In autumn 2010, the National Knowledge Centre for Validation of Prior Learning (NVR), in association with the Centre for Development of Human Resources and Quality Management (SCKK), conducted a project on the professionalisation of staff working in VPL, especially in educational institutions. This project was one of the most important initiatives to improve quality in Danish VPL to date (Denmark. SCKK 2010).

The handbook on RPL (Denmark. Ministry of Education (UVM)) stresses the need to apply valid and reliable methods in the assessment and validation of prior learning in order to safeguard legitimacy. Institutions must develop transparent guidelines for practitioners. A recent study (Andersen and Laugesen 2012) highlighted the findings of a web-based survey on quality assurance in education institutions. The survey addressed the following dimensions of quality: (1) The availability online of information on an institutions procedures and standards for VPL; (2) The availability of documentation to ensure accountability; (3) The criteria/standards used for assessment; (4) The role of participants in evaluating the VPL process. The evaluation showed that there is still considerable potential for improvement in the area of quality assurance.

Drawing on the findings of an evaluation study on the status of validation of prior learning in adult education carried out in 2010–2011 the Danish Ministry of Education has identified four areas for improvement:

- Mapping guidance and counselling activities prior to VPL
- Broadening the scope of VPL to include business and employment
- Developing a quality code for VPL
- Increasing public access to information on VPL.

6.1.11 Norway

In Norway validation of prior learning is in most cases linked to the formal education system. It is accordingly geared to the requirements of the national curriculum, and aimed at granting access or shortening the duration of existing education programmes/courses.

The two major environments for non-formal education and training in Norway are working life and adult education (delivered through NGOs). There is a comprehensive provision of learning activities, targeted at attaining qualifications and career enhancement as well as personal development. Surveys have shown that employment is the most important arena for learning, but that a systematic approach is often lacking, especially in small enterprises.

Norway is in the process of developing a national qualifications framework for the recognition of formal, non-formal and informal learning. At present industries set their own standards in cooperation with the relevant ministries, working in close cooperation with the VET education system.

Standards and Methods of Assessment

While Norway is still in the process of developing a national qualifications framework, validation processes in the formal education and training system are facilitated by the outcome-based design of national curricula. Thinking in terms of learning outcomes (Christensen 2013).

During the development of its national validation system, Norway laid the foundation for a varied set of methods and tools for the documentation and validation of competence and skills, and these methods and tools were piloted widely.

Upper secondary school level is the area where validation of prior learning is most often put to use, with good results. Assessment at this level is tied to the requirements of the national curricula, both in theoretical and vocational subjects, and the results are documented in a so-called "Individual Competence Proof". The following methods are widely used:

- *Dialogue-based methods* include discussions between assessors and learners (one-to-one), often supported by computerised or manual tools and combined with portfolio assessment, self-assessment and testing.
- *Portfolio assessments* are based on written documentation, photographs etc., and are often used to support post-admission communication and to tailor courses to individuals' knowledge and skills.
- *Vocational testing* is carried out in vocational subjects. It combines interviews and practice, both to chart the learner's background, training, work experience, language skills and objectives, and to observe his/her skills in practice. This form of assessment addresses both the theoretical and practical aspects of a trade. Vocational testing provides adults with an opportunity to show what they can actually do in their own fields.

In the voluntary sector, the Personal Competence Document (PCD) is a tool for mapping and documenting competences based on self-evaluation. The development of this tool was the result of the national validation project. The Norwegian Association for Adult Learning (NAAL) – a national umbrella organisation for 19 study associations with around 600,000 participants per year – has the overall responsibility for maintaining the PCD, which is accessible on the NAAL website. NAAL offers presentations, information and guidance regarding the PCD to organisations and institutions.

In the employment sector, a system for documentation was agreed between social partners in the context of the Basic Agreement for 2006–2009 which states that "The enterprise is requested to have a system for documentation of the individual employees' experience, courses and practice related to the conditions of work." The new basic agreement for 2010–2013 continues this focus, stating that "It is important that the enterprise has a system for documenting the individual's experience, courses and practice related to the employment relationship." While documenting competences is considered useful, small companies, in particular, struggle to implement competence development. In Norway, 83 % of enterprises have fewer than 20 employees, and allocating time and resources for competence development as part of their human resource management system or for helping employees to acquire a qualification, is a financial and organisational challenge. One solution which seems to work well is for small enterprises to form learning clusters or networks.

Delivery and Quality Assurance

Assessors are expected to possess expertise relevant to the conduct of assessments. Validation results must be consistent irrespective of the location at which RVA is undertaken. RVA processes must be clearly described and the necessary competences defined. County authorities are responsible for ensuring the quality and training of staff, which is carried out in regional assessment centres. Annual courses and seminars are held for assessors, and mentoring services are available to inexperienced assessors. Normally, assessors have a professional background in the trade or area of education in question (for VET), or both. Trained assessors are registered on regional lists maintained by assessment centres.

Organisational and coordination mechanisms constitute an important component of the Norwegian national system for the validation of prior learning. Service centres, where adults can have their experience and prior learning validated, exist in all counties. Funding is delegated to the 19 counties, and regional centres provide information and guidance. They are also responsible for the quality of the validation process and for training assessors. Often, upper secondary schools also function as assessment centres. In order to offer the same opportunities to job-seekers who wish to have their competence validated, projects have been initiated to improve cooperation between the education system and the Labour and Welfare Administration. Employers' bodies and trade unions are important stakeholders at the national and regional level, and drivers in the realisation of policy goals and practice (e.g., by offering apprenticeships and other training schemes in enterprises locally, thus supporting adults in VET schemes).

6.1.12 Finland

Scope of RVA

Unlike the RVA systems in Denmark and Norway, which link RVA to the formal education system and curricula, in Finland, RVA is oriented to competence-based vocational qualifications, offering the adult population a flexible method of renewing and maintaining its skills with a particular focus on vocational competences.

Standards and Methods of Assessment

The idea behind competence-based vocational qualifications is that candidates must meet certain requirements, which are described in terms of learning outcomes and competences (acquired formally, non-formally or informally e.g., in the workplace), and which can acquired by combining different learning methods to fit a candidate's needs.

Competence-based qualifications are defined in terms of three levels: (1) Upper secondary vocational qualifications are entry level qualifications indicating that individuals have the competences for entry to an employment in the field; (2) Further vocational qualifications indicate the vocational skills required by skilled workers in the field; (3) Specialist vocational qualifications indicate that individuals are in command of the most demanding tasks in the field. Moreover, through the acquisition of competence-based qualifications adults are eligible to apply for admission to study programmes at polytechnics or universities.

The Finnish RVA system is characterized by an elaborate support system of individualised preparatory training for those seeking to attain a qualification. More specifically, support for candidates consists of the preparation of "individual plans". These include details of the competence test that candidates are required to take as part of a qualification or its modules; where and how the test will be taken; whether the candidate's vocational skills need to be supplemented before the qualification can be obtained; and the means of supplementing existing skills (on-the-job training or participation in a programme of preparatory training).

Individualised learning has not only resulted in a steady increase in the numbers of adults seeking recognition, it has promoted greater cooperation among employers, workers and the education sector. The tests are open to everyone, regardless of age, work experience or educational background. Although preparatory training may not always be necessary particularly for those who already have broad and all-round professional competences, practice has shown that competence tests are in most cases completed in connection with the support of preparatory training.

Delivery of RVA

Assessment of the competence-based tests is carried out by experts in the field of training as well as representatives from the work domain. The learning outcomes are recognised and validated in the context of competence-based tests, in which candidates must demonstrate the expected learning outcomes and competences by participating in authentic work assignments. In addition, candidates are expected to take part in a process of self-assessment.

In the Finnish system, the awarding body is separate from the training and test provider. The qualification certificates are awarded when all the required modules of a qualification have been completed. The Qualifications Committee is the awarding body, and certificates are official documents. In addition, the Finnish National Board of Education has recommended that an international supplement be issued to the candidates together with their competence certification.

An important feature of the Finnish RVA system, particularly in the adult VET system, is the introduction of training towards specialist qualifications for adult educators. The aim is to strengthen the ability of vocational teachers' to operate within the competence-based qualifications system for adults. The training is organised by the Finnish National Board of Education and is funded by the government. However, a recent study (Jokinen 2010) has revealed a growing trend towards enrolment in "fast learning" that is programmes driven by market-needs. This trend will come at the cost of valuing expertise obtained through learning and experience prior to the training programme.

Overall, however, there is a high level of satisfaction with the Finnish system of competence-based qualifications and in particular with the flexibility that it renders in promoting a more fluid, interpersonal and semi-bureaucratic "agent identity", one which is different from the "subject-specific" nature of traditional teacher training (ibid.).

6.1.13   France

Standards and Methods of Assessment

In France, assessment puts the individual at the centre of the RVA process, and assessment plays an essential role in the processes of recognition. As Feutrie (2008) points out, VAE legislation passed in 2002 introduced a shift from a learning approach to an approach based on evaluation, and in this sense, he argues that "assessment procedures have to help candidates become conscious of unplanned learning that is hidden in activities, and understand that it has a value. The procedures also need to make learning outcomes visible, help the candidates organise learning outcomes in a way that suits the standards of the relevant qualification, and prepare the candidates to meet the jury under the best conditions" (Feutrie 2008, p. 168).

The validation of prior learning spans the entire a learning process, from the acquisition of competences to their refinement, demonstrating an increasing capacity to solve problems. The objective of this process is not to identify knowledge or skills, but to verify whether candidates can demonstrate that their schemes of thinking, the models they use, their methodologies, are relevant. The objective is not only to award qualifications, but to steer candidates' personal and professional progress, and to provide them with the tools to do so (Feutrie 2008).

Alongside the VAE system, France has a system of recognition with a substantial focus on formative assessment. This system was established under the *Bilan de Compétences* Law of 1991 and is a formative procedure that takes stock of occupational and personal experience. The *Bilan de Compétences* has the following objectives:

- to take stock of occupational and personal experience;
- to identify acquired knowledge, competences, attitudes related to work, training and social life;
- to make explicit the potential of the individual, to collect and arrange elements to define a personal or occupational "project";
- to help manage personal resources, in order to organise occupational priorities;
- to assist in career choices and career changes.

There are two stages to the *Bilan de Compétences*: The first is that of self-assessment (*auto-évaluation*), which is assisted by regional service centres. These assessments are used to build up an occupational or training plan. The candidate is requested to map their needs and expectations; and information, methods and techniques are then provided to the candidate. In the second stage, assistance is provided to candidates to analyse their motivations and occupational interests, to identify competences and occupational aptitudes and, eventually, to assess their general knowledge. This information enables candidates to define their opportunities for mobility. Candidates then receive advice from a reviewer on the steps necessary to reach their objectives.

Methods of assessment are declarative as well as simulated. The main method is the declarative one, usually in a written application describing the activities that candidates have undertaken related to the desired diploma or degree. A clear analysis and description of the acquired experience that these activities have enabled them to build up is required. Candidates attach all the documents that can demonstrate and prove this acquired experience: work certificates, examples of professional achievements, assorted attestations, and so on. A less common method is to present a real or simulated situation in which candidates demonstrate their acquired experience by performing profession cases, candidates appear before a board of examiners for an interview.

Validation of acquired experience is broken down into five phases. The first comprises consultation, information, and guidance. An applicant enters the second phase if their application conforms to the legal and administrative rules. Thirdly, the application is prepared, usually with the assistance of an advisor. In the fourth phase the VAE board evaluates the application. Finally, there is monitoring following the board's evaluation, particularly if the board instructed the candidate to further develop his or her project and to complete the certification process. Benchmarks for assessment are criteria based on the guidelines of the profession and the required qualifications (Paulet 2013).

Holistic assessments are used, requiring candidates to describe their prior work experience and to present an analysis explaining how they acquired the skills and knowledge, what they did to do so, where, in what context, by solving what problems, and what results they obtained. By asking candidates to adopt a more objective view, the board can better understand whether the acquired experience is closely dependent on the context in which it was obtained or whether it is transferable to other situations.

Post-assessment is an important feature of VAE in France. Following the board's decision to award a qualification, reject an application, or grant it only partially, candidates are given instructions indicating how to build on their experience to attain full certification: additional training modules to be successfully completed; further professional experience to be acquired; a report or dissertation to be written, and so on. The formulae vary and must be applied on a case-by-case basis.

Delivery of RVA

Professionals are identified to help candidates. Most universities have established validation centres that call on professionals to help candidates analyse their experience, present them in a legible manner and link the outcomes of their experiential learning with the requirements of the qualifications. This is a further example of how the French system successfully promotes guidance for individuals throughout their educational pathway.

Members of the board are trained to maintain rigour when assessing the acquired experience in terms of the skills, know-how and knowledge which candidates have obtained through non-formal learning and wish to demonstrate other than by academic examination.

Validation is not simply about reporting on the results of an assessment in the summative sense. The updated system obliges boards of examiners to adopt new attitudes. Two main approaches are pursued. One is for the board of examiners to weigh an individual's experience against the standards and references of the qualification; whereas the other is based on a developmental principle, which takes into account the individual's experience as a whole.

6.1.14 Portugal

The New Opportunities Initiative (NOI) for recognising the non-formal and informal learning of adults with low qualifications, together with a set of measures for implementing the National Qualifications System, was placed at the highest governmental level, and institutionalised within the mainstream of the education and training system. The recognition of prior learning was a major factor in this process of institutionalization (Gomes 2013).

Standards and Methods of Assessment

The experience of Adult Education and Training Courses (AET Courses) in Portugal had long shown that some trainees, while lacking proper certification, possessed the competences necessary to validate all of the Competence Units within a specific Key Competences Reference Framework. In other words, these trainees did not in fact need to attend or complete a course within the traditional curricular structure of the AET programme. This opened the way to the creation, in 2000, of the National System of Competences Recognition, Validation and Certification (RVCC System) for the recognition of validation of non-formal and informal learning.

The first six RVCC centres were organised by various different kinds of institutional bodies: a business association, a vocational training centre directly managed by the public employment services (Institute of Employment and Vocational Training), a state school, a vocational education school, a local development association and a protocol-based management vocational training centre. These were the first specialised units in the implementation of RVCC processes, enabling academic equivalence to be granted for Year 4, 6 or 9 of schooling.

As with the AET courses, the institutional existence of the National Agency for Adult Education and Training (a public organisation reporting to the Ministry of Labour and Social Security and to the Ministry of Education[1]) was decisive for the launch of the two modalities (the RVCC System and the AET courses) that played a core role in shaping the current adult education and training system in Portugal.

In the period between 2006 and 2011, a national network of RVCC centres emerged, incorporating over 450 New Opportunities Centres, while maintaining the institutional variety of organisational bodies with a nuclear structure that trains their technical teams in the implementation of RVCC processes.

The national network of New Opportunities Centres comprises various stages of intervention, including initial diagnosis and forwarding (Almeida et al. 2008),

---

[1]ANEFA ceased to exist in 2003, giving rise to a division of responsibilities between the then Ministry of Labour and Social Security and the Ministry of Education, wherein the management attributions of these modalities were divided, respectively between the Institute of Employment and Professional Training (IEFP) and the Directorate General for Vocational Training (DGFV). This situation remained in force until 2007, when the current National Agency for Qualification, I.P., was set up, once again a public institute reporting to the Ministry of Labour and Social Security and the Ministry of Education, which were attributed with the responsibility for implementing the New Opportunities Initiative and management and coordination of the National Qualifications System. Today, the current institutional body in charge of managing the education and training policies is the National Agency for Qualification and Vocational Education, I.P. and significant changes have occurred in the RVCC system and in the national network of centres dedicated to this kind of processes.

guidance and orientation. New technical elements were incorporated within the teams, in particular for the candidates' guidance and counselling stages. New concepts and procedures such as partial certification, vocational certification or dual certification were also developed.

Adult education and training courses opened the path towards dual certification for adults. Together with the recognition of non-formal and informal learning, adults were guided through training pathways and education pathways. In the latter case adults could have their uncompleted secondary school education validated (Year 12 of schooling). Several pedagogical principles were applied in the context of the dual certification system, including:

• Application of a reference framework for key competences
• Modular organisation of adult education and training curricula
• Local construction of curricula
• Procedural, qualitative and guiding assessment
• Personal and social mediation

The curricular organisation and pedagogical strategies used were particularly well adapted to people with low school qualifications, who faced the challenge of acquiring competences for a specific professional area (or key competences for study) while also gaining a higher secondary school certificate.

The key innovation introduced in these adult education and training courses was the introduction of customised training pathways comprising only those modules where learners displayed deficits (Gomes and Rodrigues 2007; Rodrigues 2009). Today modular training units are used by adult working populations to overcome specific competence deficits. Modular training enables certification and is a significant qualifications pathway within the framework of the National Qualifications System, together with the recognition of competences acquired in non-formal and informal contexts.

The New Opportunities Initiative was the most ambitious public intervention in adult education and training in Portugal's recent history (Guimarães 2009; see also Guimarães 2012).

Quality Assurance

The Quality Charter of the New Opportunities Centres (Gomes and Simões 2007) and the self-evaluation model based on the common assessment framework (CAF) made up the instruments of quality assurance. New financing models were established and new technical and methodological guidelines were developed and disseminated. Finally, an administrative management and information system for adult qualification procedures was designed and developed. This is now used by all RVCC Centres and training bodies, thus making it possible to obtain rigorous statistical information (SIGO), and enabling detailed monitoring of the New Opportunities Initiative and the respective issue of course certificates and diplomas for academic pathways.

More than 1.5 million adults have enrolled at a New Opportunities Centre and more than half a million people have been certified in this period.

6.1.15 Scotland

In the late 1980s, the Scottish Qualifications Authority (SQA), in collaboration with numerous higher-education institutions, developed the Accreditation of Prior Experiential Learning (APEL) mechanism. Based on the portfolio approach, APEL has remained a marginal institutional activity within further and higher education of some newer or "post-1992" universities and a few professional areas such as nursing, health and social care (Whittaker 2011). One of the main reasons for this marginalisation is the demanding nature of compiling portfolios, especially for adult returners who have been out of the educational system for some time (Whittaker 2011). As a result of this, the application of APEL has largely been limited to an "assessment on demand" tool for dispensing credit.

Standards and Methods of Assessment

In a project dealing with RPL in career guidance in formal schools undertaken by Skills Development Scotland, the following features were highlighted:

- Learning and skills gained through informal learning are mapped against the appropriate level of the Scottish Credit and Qualifications Framework (SCQF).
- Careers advisors are identified to select pupils in formal schools and undertake RVA profiling against the SCQF.
- RPL profiling was undertaken as an individual or group process to ascertain whether the peer-support dimension of a group model enhanced the experience for the participants. Evaluation aimed to investigate the applicability of the model to other contexts and a wide range of client groups, including the long-term unemployed and individuals facing redundancy.

In the context of a project dealing with RPL for workers in the health and care sectors it was found that

SCQF RPL resource pack and profiling tools supported both the formative and summative processes of recognition. The formative process involved learners building their confidence, developing their capacity to think and write reflectively. The summative process of recognition involved a staged approach to evidence-gathering enabled assessment towards and SVQ in health and social care.

- Three types of organisational learning culture were identified: expansive, restrictive and passive-restrictive. These were found to be linked to the sector. The care sector, for example, is more likely to hold an expansive attitude to learning and training than production sectors. The generic aspects of the model and material have broad applicability within the social services sectors for workers at all levels.

- There was a strong emphasis on carrying forward the pedagogical approach developed in the context of the community setting to the workplace.
- Demystifying SVQ assessment systems and language were important to help learners progress more quickly through the qualification.
- Mentors held focus group discussions with learners. The self-confidence generated through the identification of strengths and skills, and understanding their relevance to current work roles, led to greater confidence within the workplace itself.
- Mentors play an important role in the quality of the learner experience. Mentors need to be given sufficient time, training and continuing support to carry out this role effectively (Whittaker 2008). Mentors need to be given opportunities to use their role as a means of achieving their own professional development goals.

The following recommendations were made (Whittaker 2011) in the context of a higher education project to integrate quality assurance and flexible entry (Whittaker et al. 2006) at all Scottish higher education institutions:

- Recognition of informal and non-formal learning should be integrated within mainstream curriculum design and delivery. Learning outcomes need to be defined in a way that supports a variety of means of achieving them and flexibility in mode of assessment, without detracting from the quality of the provision (Whittaker et al. 2006).
- Parity of esteem between different modes of learning should be undertaken already at the curriculum design stage of programmes. It would help individuals to translate their knowledge into forms that are deemed appropriate for assessment and credit rating which requires them to move away from informal learning to something that is more easily understood by the "academy" (Whittaker 2011, p. 189).
- Learners seeking credit within programmes through informal learning should not be subjected to more demanding levels of assessment than those seeking credit through the formal route. Alternative assessment frameworks need to be considered (Whittaker 2012).

Quality Principles

Developing the SCQF RPL Guidelines (SCQF 2005) with nationally agreed principles for the recognition and credit-rating of non-formal and informal learning has been an important stimulus for RPL in Scotland. Earlier RPL took place within the context of institutional projects.

As part of the development of the national SCQF RPL Guidelines, a review (commissioned by the Quality Assurance Agency (QAA) for Scotland, the Scottish Qualifications Authority (SQA), the Universities of Scotland and the Scottish Executive) (Whittaker 2005) revealed that:

1. Linking RPL to the Scottish Credit and Qualifications Framework (SCQF) could facilitate the identification of further learning pathways as part of an educational and career guidance process;
2. Awarding of specific credit within the context of formal programmes is an important function of RPL, equally important, however, is the formative role of RVA in terms of personal growth and development;
3. Making explicit key outcomes of formative recognition was important;
4. The need to change from the term "accreditation" to "recognition" of prior informal learning, would enable a broader conceptualisation of the use and outcomes of the process;
5. Formative recognition can be undertaken in the community or workplace (Whittaker 2011, p. 179);
6. There was also a need to move to more streamlined methods embedded within curriculum design and delivery;
7. The process of evidence-gathering should be appropriate to the type of recognition undertaken and to its purpose.
8. Since the launch of the guidelines in 2005, RPL activity in Scotland has focused on research and development at sector level (Whittaker 2011).

6.1.16 England

Across the whole of the UK, the Accreditation of Prior Learning (APL) has distinct characteristics. Although it was established in the early 1990s, it was not then connected to any government policy. In this sense it was a "bottom-up" approach. The system for recognising APL tends to have a higher education focus and is established as a method of recognising non-formal learning for people who have relevant knowledge and experience but have no qualification through the formal education system.

Pokorny (2011) highlights the changes in APEL priorities and practices from a broader access agenda to one that is suited to a global economic agenda focused predominantly on the accreditation of learning for work-based contexts (UK. QAA 2004, p. 1). She points out that prior to 1992 APEL was located in the polytechnic sector under the Council for National Academic Awards (CNAA), which was responsible for awarding over half of undergraduate degrees in the UK, and was used for admission purposes. However, this form of learning was considered to pose a threat to academic standards and knowledge development by and through the academy.

Currently, institutions of higher and further education in England are encouraged to demonstrate a greater willingness to engage with and respond to the specific skill demands and needs of employers – this means providing more flexible, accessible and tailored courses designed with employers to equip students for the workplace. This is reflected in the launch of the foundation degree qualification in 2000, one of the government's responses to this agenda within which, Pokorny laments, RVA is treated as mere "alternative entry" to the start of a course, which is a rather restricted definition of APEL's focus on the foundation degree benchmark status (Pokorny 2011).

Standards and Methods of Assessment

Awarding credits to employment-based training programmes rather than individual assessments is becoming the common practice. These degree programmes usually have more generic learning outcomes than traditional degrees, plus a high level of negotiation around the practice-based content of the programme, which can make them more amenable to APEL (cf. Pokorny 2011).

APEL is thus becoming subsumed under work-based learning (WBL) or the accreditation of employment-based learning and training. Haldane and Wallace (2009) describe how technology can assist with APEL guidance in quality WBL programmes (which successfully recruit around 1,000 students per year). APEL is also financially more attractive because guidance and assessment can be delivered within the curriculum. This is because the Higher Education Funding Council for England (HEFCE) does not fund pre-enrolment APEL processes (Gallacher and Feutrie 2003).

WBL has certain features that can support APEL, but a WBL degree does not of itself resolve "concerns about what and how high level knowledge gained outside of universities is recognised and legitimised" (Pokorny 2011).

The National Vocational Qualifications (NVQ) framework was informed by employers and embraced APEL as a means by which experienced workers could demonstrate their competence against established standards of performance, reducing or obviating the need for training. Despite criticisms levelled at this approach due to its labour market orientation, the NVQ framework, says Pokorny, did much to promote APEL at pre-degree level in vocational education. It also opened up potential APEL-based pathways to higher education through higher level NVQs.

Quality Assurance

The guidelines for quality assurance, issued by the oversight body of the APL system, the Quality Assurance Agency (QAA) for Higher Education, state a range of important principles that pertain to APL (United Kingdom of Great Britain. QAA 2004). Among their stipulations, they insist that "decisions regarding the accreditation of prior learning are a matter of academic judgement... [and that] the decision-making process and outcomes should be transparent and demonstrably rigorous and fair" (CEDEFOP 2007, p. 7). Furthermore, "where limits exist on the proportion of learning that can be recognised through the accreditation process, these limits should be explicit" (CEDEFOP 2007, p. 7). In this way, the UK system for APL seeks to ensure high standards while still reaching all those who are in need of recognition for their non-formally attained skills and knowledge.

6.2 Developing Countries

6.2.1 Philippines

Non-formal and informal learning is an important means of acquiring skills for many adults in the Philippines. The Philippines has developed the alternative learning system, which awards the same qualifications as in the formal system. Alternative learning programmes exist within all subsectors of the education and training system, spanning basic education, Technical and Vocational Education and Training (TVET) and higher education.

Standards and Methods of Assessment

At the basic level, RVA is typically offered within the community-based Alternative Learning System (ALS). The ALS exists parallel to the formal school system and addresses the learning needs of those who wish to acquire basic literacy skills as well as functional literacy skills recognised as equivalent to both primary and secondary levels. It is important to note that RVA at the basic level is usually undertaken after enrolment in a non-formal or informal programme rather than prior to enrolment in a programme.

The ALS consists of two components: the non-formal Accreditation and Equivalency Programme and the Informal Education Programme (InfEd)

The Accreditation and Equivalency Programme is implemented through different modalities such as radio broadcasts, digitalised learning, TV episodes, face-to-face learning using print modules, and self-directed learning. Those who pass the Philippine Education Placement Test for Basic Education Level are recognised as primary or high school graduates. The results of the test are also accepted by technical/vocational and higher education institutions as well as for employment purposes, particularly in jobs that require an elementary or high school diploma.

The Informal Education Programme recognises competences gained by individuals following completion of short-term, interest-based courses in community learning centres. The competences promoted within community learning centres include social, economic, cultural, aesthetic, physical, spiritual, political literacies, which are considered necessary for the well-being of the community. The competences acquired through InfEd are evaluated by resource persons in community learning centres. The competences attained through all forms of learning are then documented in a passport. These passports can be used for equivalency purposes in obtaining employment, for further learning in the context of basic education, or for purposes of social recognition in the community.

At the level of TVET, workplace competences are assessed, validated and certified against competence standards developed by the Technical Education and Skills Development Authority (TESDA). The National Certification (NC) or the Certificate of Competency (CoC) are issued to those who meet the competency standards and pass the Competency Assessment and Certification for Technical and Vocational Education (TVET). This recognition of workplace competences against TVET standards and levels is considered by the government to promote the productivity, global competitiveness and quality of Filipino middle-level workers.

In higher education, the accreditation of prior learning toward a college diploma (undergraduate level) takes place in the context of the Expanded Tertiary Education Equivalency and Accreditation Programme for Baccalaureate and Master Levels (ETEEAP). This programme falls under the jurisdiction of the Commission on Higher Education (CHED). Individuals who have acquired work experience and expertise through non-formal and informal training are awarded appropriate academic degrees by CHED-accredited higher education institutions.

There are also schools and open learning systems which recognise the non-formal and informal learning and experience of learners for admission to non-accredited courses. The non-traditional open distance learning system of the Polytechnic University of the Philippines' (PUP), for example, assesses 72 units of college education, together with RVA of non-formal and informal learning, in relation to college courses at the PUP and the Far Eastern University.

Delivery of RVA

To promote non-formal and informal education programmes in communities, ALS implementers in co-ordination with local government officials draw up a profile of the community and its programme objectives. This information is disseminated through town meetings. On the basis of these overall programme objectives, community learning centres and non-formal educational programmes arc able to develop specific learning objectives.

The non-formal education and InfEd Programme clients are mostly early school leavers from elementary and secondary schools. They come from depressed and marginalised communities in rural and urban or remote hard-to-reach geographical areas. Some represent groups who have served in penal and rehabilitation institutions. Many also belong to indigenous communities. This population represents about 45 % or 40 million of the total Philippines population. Whilst some ALS clients are of school going age (6–15 years old), the majority are beyond the school going age (over 15 years old). Despite the socio-cultural and economic circumstances of these groups, there is a strong motivation to participate in these programmes and they view ALS as "second chance" education.

Support to learners in the ALS programmes is provided through the use of CD-ROM modules, workbooks, livelihood projects and microfinance, leadership training; and a referral system for graduates/completers. NGOs and community-based organisations play a significant part in implementing community education programmes and in developing assessment tools for non-accredited programmes round topics such as leadership, community organisation, environmental competences and enterprise development. NGOs use an array of assessment methods such as small group discussions, peer assessment, life-story workshops and narratives, and assessment around entrepreneurship knowledge and skills.

In the TVET sector, TESDA has developed a dual system of training (at school and in the workplace) for the continuing education and training teachers of TVET. It is based on curriculum developed from competency standards and is modular in structure Quality assurance

For the TVET sector, the quality assurance of the recognition of non-formal and informal learning is based on Training Regulations promulgated by TESDA. These regulations lay down the minimum training requirements to be complied with by all TVET providers (schools, training centres, enterprises). Programme delivery is competence-based, allowing learners free entry and exit. For each Training Regulation there is a corresponding assessment tool that is used for national assessment, which also covers RVA. These assessment tools consist of varied methods of assessment such as demonstrations, oral questioning, portfolio assessments, third party reports, interviews, and written tests. In this way, TESDA opens assessment, validation and certification to all interested applicants regardless of their educational background.

In the case of its Alternative Learning Programme, the government plans to promote quality assurance by incorporating the ALS program into the Philippines Qualifications Framework (PQF). In preparation for this, the government envisions the establishment of a national test covering both formal and non-formal basic education within the Alternative Learning System (ALS), which will be administered for both school students and community-based learners. Additionally, formal basic education has already introduced functional literacy as its goal, which is also the goal of non-formal basic education within the ALS. By creating such synergies between formal and non-formal learning the Department of Education hopes to accommodate the recognition of non-formal and informal learning in its PQF.

6.2.2 Thailand

Recognition of non-formal and informal learning at the basic level falls within the remit of the Office of the Non-Formal and Informal Education (ONIE), a service of the Ministry of Education. This office is responsible for setting the criteria for RVA (Thailand. Ministry of Education, Office of the Non-Formal and Informal Education (ONIE) 2008).

Standards and Methods of Assessment

The reference points for RVA of non-formal and informal learning are the national curricula at the primary and secondary levels. In order to promote comparability between non-formal and informal learning, the Office of Non-formal and Informal Education (ONIE) has developed the Non-Formal Education (NFE) Equivalency Programme. The Ministry of Education has developed and issued a national curriculum, which has been adjusted to serve as a guideline for the development of curricula based on local needs and contexts for use in non-formal education programmes.

The accreditation of educational achievements in the Thai basic education context has concentrated on four significant components. The first is basic knowledge, which is understood as the Thai language, mathematics, English and science. The second is vocational development, which consists of knowledge and abilities in the area of vocational and occupational skills. These abilities include problem solving, occupational administration, computer competences, working attitudes and professional ethics. The third component is quality of life improvement, which is an evaluation of an individual's perception of the value of family life and the skills that contribute to a happy life. It also focuses on the promotion of healthy living, both physically and mentally, and attitudes to religious principles and ethics in everyday life. The final component is social and community development, which concerns an individual's ability to apply their own potential for leading a good life in a community. This involves a strong family focus, but also participating in and supporting the activities that benefit the community and society as a whole.

In accordance with the NFE Basic Curriculum B.E. 2551 (2008) standards, the Office of the Non-Formal Education Commission has developed a range of non-formal and informal education programmes, including:

• Basic education equivalency programme
• Education for occupational development
• Education for life skills development
• Education for community and social development

Credits accumulated by learners are transferable within the same type or between different types of education, regardless of whether the credits are acquired through formal, non-formal or informal education, vocational training or work experience.

Support provided to learners from disadvantaged backgrounds through the development of active learning methodologies, such as dual education and/or training, cooperative learning, constructivist learning, project-based learning in various settings, be they on-the-job settings training programmes, internships or placement programmes in collaboration with industry, employers, trade unions, civil society agencies and community-based organisations.

Quality Assurance

Accredited non-formal educational establishments are expected to formulate regulations and guidelines to be followed by all personnel concerning the criteria of assessment. Some of the quality criteria are: (1) Learning assessment must include knowledge, skills and broader competences such as moral, civic, values, and personal attributes of honesty and integrity. (2) Assessment must take into account competences related to quality of life activities contributing to personal, career and social development in the context of family, the community and society.

In addition, quality assurance alludes to the quality of non-formal education provision, and the arrangements that non-formal educational establishments make in regard to the National NFE Quality Assessment Test at the end of each semester.

Credit transfers of educational results, knowledge and experiences are undertaken by non-formal education establishments, based on the guidelines and criteria formulated by ONIE. ONIE is currently trying to develop techniques to recognise informal learning through workplace learning.

One of the aims of the Thai National Qualifications Framework is to serve as a reference to the learner/worker in the workplace or other learning settings. Given that pathways for further learning are defined in an NQF, this should provide learning opportunities to those who would like to update and upgrade their competences in the workplace and gain qualifications through the of validation of experiences or recognition of prior learning. In this way, the NQF would provide the enabling environment and tool for valuing the competences an individual possesses. At the same time, individuals obtaining certificates through this programme will have the same rights and qualification as those who obtain certificates in the formal schooling system. Establishing the standard for these methods and NFE learners is therefore still a work in progress and a challenge for ONIE.

6.2.3 Bangladesh

Recognition of Prior Learning in Bangladesh is a sub-component of a larger project aimed at increasing the access of underprivileged groups to TVET, which was initiated in the context of Bangladesh's National Skills Development Policy in collaboration with the Dhaka office of the International Labour Organisation (ILO) (Arthur 2009). The project's aim is to develop RPL for Bangladesh that would cater for skills gained both formally and informally.

Given the fact that Bangladesh has a large informal sector, the Ministry of Labour and the Ministry of Overseas Workers in coordination with the ILO's office in Dhaka is conducting a project to develop and implement the recognition of prior learning for this sector. It is hoped that RPL will result in the recognition of competences gained but not previously recognised in the informal sector of the Bangladesh economy. RPL is expected to provide some informal sector workers with opportunities to move to employment in the formal sector. This particularly important benefit of RPL will affect some 80 % of the working population of Bangladesh (Arthur 2009).

The Government considers RPL also advantageous as a means to address the challenge of early school leavers. Many citizens leave school before completing the eighth grade of the general education system and, because of this, are unable to enrol in formal skills training programmes. However, the government has removed this requirement, so that early school leavers are now able to access formal skills courses programmes with the aid of RPL. Access through RPL enables individuals to gain entry or admission to a particular course or qualification without necessarily meeting some of the standard prerequisites such as completion of Year 8. RPL would enable early school leavers and workers in the informal economy to demonstrate that they have the necessary knowledge, skills and competences to undertake a training course or meet the prerequisites at a specific level of the NTVEQF.

Standards and Methods of Assessment

In Bangladesh, RVA is linked to the National Technical and Vocational Quali-fications Framework (NTVQF). The NTVQF provides a uniform framework for establishing course assessment requirements and course entry points. It is expected to provide the basis for an effective RVA process. However, the overall success of linking RPL to NTVQF will hinge on the incorporation of industry advisory groups alongside government agencies and NGOs in the development of RPL infrastructure and assessor training etc.

It has been proposed that RVA methodology and tools not be based exclusively on centrally set examinations. However, centrally set challenge tests will be used for moderation purposes. This will, the project implementers believe, maintain the integrity of the system in its infancy.

The introduction of a portfolio system (Competency Log Book) to document evidence of competences gained within the informal economy has also been proposed (Arthur 2009).

Delivery of RVA

Like Burkina Faso and Benin, Bangladesh has a well-developed traditional appren-ticeship system. This invites the involvement of master craftspersons and resource persons from NGOs as RPL assessors in technical training centres and technical skills centres. Assessors will be trained to use reasonable adjustment processes for informal sector workers during the assessment process.

At present training institutions (both public and private) have few incentives to respond to market needs, especially in the informal economy. One of the critical issues in the development of an RVA system in Bangladesh will therefore be to allow public and publicly financed institutions greater autonomy in selecting training and assessment programmes, hiring assessors, and generating revenues by selling these services. The potential advantages of allowing the private sector a key role in the management of TVET institutions will be the greater market responsiveness to the needs of the informal sector (Arthur 2009). However, the government will need to provide incentives to NGOs to provide RPL services to the informal sector initially (ibid.).

Several levels of training for assessors have been proposed, targeting NGOs, technical and training centres, technical skills centres and master craftspersons (in both rural and urban settings). These training opportunities will be oriented towards individuals already qualified in workplace assessment as well as those requiring foundational training in this area.

Assessors will be trained to collect evidence, design assessment instruments, plan and organise assessment, assess competences, carry out reasonable adjustments, validate assessment instruments, and carry out appeal processes. It is hoped that the latter training interventions will promote transparency and enhance the integrity of the RPL system by laying the basis for a culture in which assessment decisions can be questioned and appealed.

Social inclusiveness is an important consideration in the RPL system. Since 80 % of employment is generated in the informal economy, support mechanisms need to be put in place that will enable the disadvantaged to access RPL. It is foreseen that NGOs and other public/private partnerships will expand the provision of RVA to socially marginalised groups in the informal sector. Costs, location and literacy issues will also need to be addressed and an acceptance of reasonable adjustment criteria will be required (Arthur 2009).

RPL is expected to be piloted as an integral component of the new NTVQF. The initial target of RPL will be the National Pre-Vocational Certificate 1 and Certificate 2 (NPVC 1 and NPVC 2). It will include training for assessors/trainers and be limited to four industry groups already identified. RPL could also target an industry group suggested by industry skills committees (Arthur 2009).

Quality Assurance

In Bangladesh, RPL will build on already existing models of collaboration between public and private institutions. It is envisaged that collaboration will produce a series of checks and balances, ensuring that quality assurance is built into the RPL system. There is expected to be a single TVET body, which will be responsible for co-ordinating the overall training system, providing oversight, financing of training, curriculum development, supervising skills tests, RPL, certification and accreditation (Arthur 2009).

6.2.4 Mexico

Like the Philippines, Mexico displays a sub-sectoral approach to RVA, with different approaches in primary and secondary education, higher education and the employment sector.

Standards and Methods of Assessment

In *primary and secondary education*, successful assessment can result in the award of credits or certification through the recognition of skills relevant to the Educational Model for Life and Work (Modelo Educación para la Vida y el Trabajo, MEVyT). Within this programme modules are organised around everyday life skills and oriented towards the development of competences.

The assessment processes facilitate learning and accreditation for people from diverse geographical and socio-cultural environments. The assessment of learning outcomes is viewed as a formative and ongoing process, allowing young people and adults to identify the progress and limitations of their learning.

Rigour and fairness are maintained through the use of assessors who are neither involved in the educational process or learning facilitators. Instead the final assessment, accreditation and certification are undertaken by a third party assessor authorised by the Secretariat of Public Education.

Recognition of non-formal and informal learning in basic education begins with a series of diagnostic tests. A diagnostic test allows individuals to discover how their knowledge, skills and wider competences align to basic education and schooling certification. These tests result either in the issuing of a primary or secondary certificate, or the applicant's referral to the appropriate level of participation in basic education.

Mexico also uses traditional examinations for assessment in the basic education sector, as certification at these levels is a requirement for admission to programmes leading to baccalaureate and higher education qualifications. While this may appear to create inflexibilities, the broader standards described in the MEVyT programme help to ameliorate this by enabling broader learning to be directly assessed.

At the baccalaureate and higher education levels, assessment is organised around a set of national criteria and standards, and is directed at citizens aged 25 years and older who have acquired knowledge corresponding to this level through self-guided learning and work experience.

Competences are assessed through a process divided into three parts. First, knowledge of Spanish, mathematics, natural sciences, social sciences and the contemporary world, as well as reasoning and verbal skills, are assessed through a general knowledge examination. Following this, candidates complete a written examination covering the subjects of science, technology and the arts, including themes related to social, historical, and current affairs. Finally, students are required to take an oral examination chaired by two examiners. Candidates are evaluated against a baccalaureate graduate standard on verbal expression and their cultural and educational background.

In the case of citizens aged 30 years and older wishing to pursue a bachelor degree, assessments are held at the Centre for the Assessment of Higher Education. Both standardised tests and practical assessments are used. General examinations, interviews, presentation of a thesis and a final oral exam are used to determine candidates' performance against the criteria. An additional practical assessment is required in some areas such as health and engineering. Bachelor degrees in early childhood education follow a slightly different process. Students in this area take a general exam and those who do not pass must complete a second practical assessment, which includes the presentation of a lesson plan and a video of the candidate teaching a sequence of activities related to their lesson plan.

The awarding body is the Ministry of Education, which is responsible for issuing bachelor degrees and professional licences. Professional bodies are involved in the whole accreditation process from examination design through to the actual oral examination of candidates.

RVA for workforce development and employability is closely associated with the National System of Competency Standards (NSCS), which has been developed by the National Council for Standardisation and Certification of Labour Competences (CONOCER) and under which RVA is organised, regulated and implemented (García-Bullé 2013).

The Mexican Qualifications Framework has been established by the General Directorate of Accreditation, Incorporation and Revalidation, within the Ministry for Public Education. CONOCER is participating in linking the NSCS and the Mexican Qualifications Framework. These linkages are expected to contribute to labour mobility within the country or a region. CONOCER promotes development of certifiable standards for the use of RVA of competences by employers and workers, accredits the assessment and certifications unit standards, and issues the official "labour competence certificates".

Although assessments are oriented to the competitiveness of a particular economic sector and relevance in the labour market, they are nevertheless oriented to a holistic notion of competences. The various types of competences include, functional and labour competences (e.g. knowledge and abilities required to execute a particular function in any service or manufacturing activity); social competences, meaning the capability to build relationships of trust with others through productive collaboration both in work teams and social networks; attitudes, referring to entrepreneurship, such as the capability to achieve goals, self-esteem, resilience, personal will and strength to fight for one's beliefs; intellectual competences, meaning the capabilities to generate new ideas and innovation; and ethical competences, namely the core values that help to identify what is right and what is wrong, what is good or bad for the social group to which people belong.

Different methods and instruments are combined. The mechanism for the evaluation and certification of competences is based on portfolio evidence, observations of real life performances, interviews, or proof of knowledge. When required, an evaluation of attitudes, behaviour and personal values is carried out through "360° evaluations" including workshops, case resolution and presentations, as well as simulated scenarios and assessment centre models.

Assessment is accessible to all. CONOCER does not deny access to any candidate, firm, trade union or institution that approaches an evaluation centre to go through the assessment and further certification processes; all candidates who decide to participate in the process are accepted for the evaluation and certification process.

Information to key players is an important element of the RVA system. Following initial contact, candidates, firms, trade unions and institutions wishing to engage with the RVA system receive a statement detailing their rights and obligations and the cost of the process.

RVA is voluntary. Applicants undertake a voluntary diagnostic test in order to receive a preliminary assessment of their level of competences. Various options for addressing skills gaps are available. Based on the preliminary assessment of their level of competences, applicants decide whether they want to go directly to the evaluation process, or improve their competence through a particular training programme or additional work experience.

6.2.5 Mauritius

The RVA system in Mauritius has a clear rationale and is designed to bring people back into education and training. *Employers* recognise and use RVA because it provides them with qualified and motivated personnel. Pathways for further learning have been clearly defined within the Mauritian Qualifications Framework (MQF), attracting significant interest from *trade unions*. The success of the recognition system in Mauritius would not have been possible without the vital role played by the *government* in supporting the initiative (Allgoo 2013).

Standards and Methods of Assessment

Mauritius has deployed a learning outcomes-based qualification framework for the establishment of RVA. In the process of recognition, care is taken that a candidate's claim to validation is made against the MQF and that the qualification issued is the same as would be obtained through the formal system (Allgoo 2013). In addition, in line with its objectives, the Mauritius Qualifications Authority (MQA) has developed more than 110 outcome-based qualifications within the MQF. These comprise a number of unit standards that enable RVA, clearly defining pathways on the MQF and encouraging lifelong learning.

A candidate who acquires a certificate through RVA has the possibility to progress further on the NQF. In so doing, they not only re-enter the education and training system but also climb the social ladder.

The RPL model as set up by the MQA comprises three phases: Pre-screening; Facilitation; and Assessment. Once a candidate makes an application for RPL to the MQA, the application is pre-screened. Following a successful outcome in the pre-screening exercise, an RPL facilitator, registered with the MQA, is assigned to the RPL candidate. The facilitator guides the RPL candidate through the process of building a portfolio over a period of 3 months. The portfolio is a collection of evidence, comprising personal details, employment history, evidence of skills and knowledge, non-formal courses, life-experience learning, community and voluntary activities, and relevant experience in the selected trade.

The evidence to be submitted may comprise any or all of the following: statements of results of formal education; sample of work produced; performance appraisal reports; references from current or previous employers; job descriptions; details of formal training, seminars, conferences and workshops attended which are relevant to the RPL application; certificates of participation/achievements/awards; letters of recommendation; video tapes, tape recordings and/or photographs of work activities; specific details of work and/or participation in projects; and written testimonials from managers or colleagues.

Once the portfolio has been completed, the RPL candidate then submits it to the MQA, and it is forwarded to the awarding body for assessment. The assessment is carried out through an interview and at the end of the process, the RPL candidate either obtains a full qualification, no qualification or a partial qualification, known as a "Record of Learning".

Delivery of RVA

With regard to process development and implementation: (1) the roles of facilitators, advisors and assessors are clearly defined and contextualised. (2) *Facilitators* are registered and appointed by the MQA to communicate to the learner the different options that can be offered after conducting a pre-assessment. (3) Rigour is maintained through the use of trained RVA *assessors* who review the portfolio of the applicant; compare the evidence provided with the performance criteria; and make judgements as to whether the applicant wholly or partially meets the requirements. (4) Assessors check whether the evidence submitted conforms to the following recognition principles: validity (is the evidence relevant?); sufficiency (is there enough evidence?); authenticity (is the evidence a true reflection of the candidate?); currency (is the evidence provided reliable within the context?). (5) A clear and easy-to-follow, process of assessment is developed and used: identifying what the learner knows and can do; matching the skills, knowledge and experience of the learner against standards; assessing the learner; acknowledging the competences of the learner; crediting the learner for skills, knowledge and experience already acquired; and issuing a record of learning/qualification.

Quality Assurance

Under the Mauritian Qualifications Authority (MQA) Act 2001, training providers have to seek accreditation for their programmes prior to delivery. Accreditation of programmes enables the MQA to set benchmarks for quality management arrangements in education and training for the TVET sector. MQA envisions the creation of so-called Learners' Accounts within a National Qualifications Framework Information System (NQFIS) – a data base comprising records of achievement for each Mauritian learner from the primary to tertiary level, as well as the technical and vocational sectors. Additionally, the NQFIS will provide useful and relevant information on the labour force. As such, this information system will provide employers and educational providers the possibility to match the skills available on the labour market with those placed on the MQF. The MQF will also act as a reference for the individual once his/her achieved learning has been recorded in the database.

6.2.6 Namibia

In 2009, the Namibia Qualifications Authority (NQA) and the National Training Agency (NTA) were assigned the responsibility of overseeing the development of a national policy on the recognition of prior learning. An RPL steering committee with representatives from the different sectors was constituted to work on the draft policy. Following a consultative process, principled approval was granted by the Minister of Education. Full implementation will commence once the policy has been ratified.

The policy enables candidates to earn credit for unit standards or full qualifications which are in line with the NQF. Within this context RPL refers to a broad spectrum of processes all aimed at achieving a particular outcome, including the recognition of prior certification, recognition of non-certificated formal learning, recognition of non-certified non-formal learning, articulation, credit transfer and mutual recognition (Namibia. Ministry of Education 2009).

Standards and Methods of Assessment

At the secondary school level, Namibia has successfully developed equivalency systems. This allows learners to flexibly transfer between conventional schools and Open and Distance Learning (ODL) providers.

According to legislation enacted in 1997, the Namibian College of Open Learning (NAMCOL) is required to provide study opportunities to adults and out-of-school youth to upgrade their professional and vocational skills and their level of general education (Namibia. Government of the Republic of Namibia 1996). Similarly, institutions of higher learning are required to facilitate access for some students through open and distance learning programmes. The Centre for External Studies at the University of Namibia and the Centre for Open and Lifelong Learning at the Polytechnic of Namibia also offer tertiary education programmes through the distance-learning mode of study.

Applicants for RPL enter into an assessment agreement with the college before undergoing a series of assessments to demonstrate their competence. The assessment process involves pre- and post-interviews, portfolio development and proficiency tests. Following the assessment process, candidates are given written feedback on the outcome of the assessment.

Quality Assurance

The Namibian College of Open Learning (NAMCOL) has developed an institutional policy on RPL to broaden access to its post-secondary programme. The policy defines RPL as "the process of identifying, matching, assessing and crediting the knowledge, skills and experience that candidates have gained through formal, informal or non-formal learning" (NAMCOL 2008). At present, the policy is being applied to enable candidates to gain access into the college's post-secondary programmes at certificate and diploma levels.

The National RPL policy places emphasis on the following elements to ensure the quality of the RPL process: (1) Parity of esteem; (2) Awards obtained through RPL will not indicate whether or not they were obtained via the RPL route and will be treated as any other qualification award; (3) Articulation between sectors and pathways is ensured in terms of the NQF; (4) Quality is not to be compromised. The policy guidelines explicitly speak of high quality of the occupational and unit standards as well as that of assessment. The intention of these guidelines is to ensure that RPL candidates enjoy equal opportunities for social and economic advancement. (5) A system of RPL that is planned, structured and well-resourced will have clear procedures, competence standards and related assessment tools, qualified assessors and portfolios; it will ensure sustainable funding and buy-in by all stakeholders; and will possess a simple, easily understood system.

The RPL policy is currently at the initial implementation stage. The stakeholders involved are employers, training providers, and government and different quality assurance bodies. The NQA provides technical support through capacity building.

6.2.7 Benin

Benin does not have an established system of recognition and validation of learning outcomes and competences. Instead, recognition of non-formal and informal learning takes place on a case-by-case and ad hoc basis, and there are no official recognition procedures or frameworks. Nevertheless, Benin has been able to develop criteria and standards of recognition in those areas where an informal system of recognition has begun to operate.

Standards and Methods of Assessment

In Benin, the focus of recognition is on the assessment of competences towards a vocational qualification in the context of the country's technical and vocational education and training certification system. The two certificates that are being promoted in close connection with recognition processes are the Vocational Skill Certificates (*Certificat de Qualification Professionnelle*, CQP) and the Occupational Skills Certificate (*Certificat de Qualification de Métier*, CQM).

Delivery of RVA

While Benin does not have a national qualifications framework, various government ministries and professional organisations are working in close partnership to transform traditional apprenticeships into a regulated dual training system. Recognition of non-formal and informal learning needs to be seen in the context of the reforms in the Beninese traditional apprenticeship system and its evolution into a dual system of training (workplace-based and school-based) (Walther and Filipiak 2007).

The dual system of training is designed to help young, uneducated individuals to acquire vocational qualifications, which are registered in the *Directory of Training and Professional Qualifications*. Central to the running of a dual training system is the employment of traditional master craftsmen, who train their apprentices to the CQP level. These master craftsmen-trainers are invited to update their skills beforehand by attaining an advanced vocational qualification, building on the competences they already possess. This in turn is improving the quality of training imparted to apprentices. The extent to which RVA is being used before and after acquiring the CQP and CQM qualifications could provide an interesting area of future research.

Quality Assurance

The dual system of training which has been developed in Benin in close relationship with the traditional apprenticeship system includes the acquisition of literacy and cognitive skills of craftspeople, employees and micro-entrepreneurs as well as young people (Walther and Filipiak 2007).

6.2.8   Burkina Faso

In Burkina Faso the informal economy accounts for up to 90 % of total employment. Only about 5 % of the workforce receives formal initial training and the rate of formal continuing training is very low. Formal Technical and Vocational Education and Training (TVET) plays only a minor role (Savadogo and Walther 2013). The majority of workers acquire skills through informal or non-formal training that includes on-the-job training, self-training and traditional apprenticeships.

Given the high importance of the informal sector in the economy and its relevance for productivity, donor agencies such as the French Development Agency (ADF) in collaboration with local professional associations and national authorities are exploring new opportunities to recognise and certify competences acquired through traditional apprenticeships.

RVA in Burkina Faso needs to be placed in the context of the country's skills development policy agenda, which foresees a shift from a diploma-oriented system of education and training to a skills development system targeting early school leavers and workers in the informal economy. The shift is to be seen in relation to the move away from a formal school-based TVET system to one which integrates the diversity of the formal, non-formal and informal pathways. Finally, and most importantly, the skills development framework signals a shift away from a knowledge-based national certification framework to a framework recognising and validating all types of skills and work experiences (Savadogo and Walther 2013).

The new paradigm of skills development will include the establishment of an outcomes-based National Qualifications Framework (NQF) with several pathways, including school-based training, apprenticeship training, workplace training, and one of the pathways will be the recognition of formal and non-formal learning and skills.

Chapter 7
Sharing Learning: Cross-Country Observations

Based on the foregoing analysis, this concluding chapter reflects on the emerging cross-country/regional patterns, convergences and divergences, and comments on challenges and critical factors that impact on and are conducive to the implementation of RVA. The aim is to push the RVA agenda forward towards a set of global/international benchmarks and strategic areas that will facilitate the exchange of ideas across countries and at the same time enable countries to develop their own understandings and judgements of what might be required in their own country contexts.

To facilitate this learning process, it is useful to focus on differences and common features in a dynamic way by focusing on the following themes:

1. The strategic value of RVA
2. The multidimensional and multi-targeted approaches to RVA
3. Features of best practice and quality RVA processes
4. Challenges and future country directions in RVA

These themes provide useful points of reference for sharing learning on RVA policy and practice across countries, and between developed and developing countries.

7.1 The Strategic Value of RVA

There is little doubt that a cohesive and coherent approach to RVA is essential. Starting with the strategic areas that have emerged out of this analysis (Chaps. 3, 4 and 5), this section will look at some of the differences and commonalities within themes on RVA's strategic value.

© UNESCO Institute for Lifelong Learning 2015   159
M. Singh, *Global Perspectives on Recognising Non-formal and Informal Learning*,
Technical and Vocational Education and Training: Issues, Concerns and Prospects 21,
DOI 10.1007/978-3-319-15278-3_7

One *first lesson* that can be drawn from the country examples is that targeted *policies, legislation and sector-wide education reforms* play an important role in promoting the cause of RVA. Legislative reform raises the profile of non-formal and informal learning, attracts attention from private stakeholders, and facilitates linkages between qualification sub-frameworks more generally. These improve take-up of RVA and can add to the legitimacy of new RVA systems. Countries show a wide variety of approaches to the policy and legislative context in which the recognition of learning from non-formal and informal settings occurs. A distinction can be made between those countries which have inclusive policies and a legal framework for RVA, and those which have set policies and legislation in some subsectors of the education and training system. The former are more likely to be among the countries moving in the direction of developing RVA systems or quasi-systems that include financial provision, quality assurance, and a high level of acceptance in society. Several countries have subsumed RVA under laws regulating NQFs and their regulatory bodies. The case of the USA, however, demonstrates that RVA activity levels can be high in the absence of specific government policies, legislation or national qualifications frameworks. In the USA, there is a tradition of locating recognition policies and processes at the level of an institution or organisation.

The second lesson is that *recognition policy must be calibrated with broader policy objectives.* These objectives can be educational, economic, social and cultural aims which governments seek to promote. Whatever the case, providing guidance for a country's recognition policy through concrete policy objectives is important for the overall success of the initiatives. A significant point concerns the value of expanding the objectives of the recognition process to include the reduction of inequality, poverty and social exclusion in both the education system and broader society. Regardless of whether this is achieved directly or indirectly, opening up further learning opportunities via RVA is a constructive step to diminishing engrained and persistent inequality and promoting sustainable development. There are opportunities for RVA even where there appears to be a general shift of RVA priorities and practices from a broader access agenda to one that is suited to a global economic agenda. RVA could provide a means for higher education institutions to attract experienced students, many of whom may be unemployed because of the global economic downturn. While "external" goals such as employment and qualifications are served by RVA in many contexts, RVA needs to speak to the "internal" dimensions – the aspiration of individuals to be recognised for what they already know, to be given access to new learning opportunities and to contribute to society through creative and meaningful work. RVA is essential for recognising the skills that already exist in the workplace and informal economies, creating learning pathways where gaps exist.

The third lesson is that the involvement of all stakeholders is essential to the success or failure of recognition policies. While most systems aim to operate with shared responsibility, often the balance is tipped towards either industry- or public authority-learning arrangements. Very often the role of agencies of civil society and the adult learning sectors are neglected. The benefits of RVA are associated with the involvement and interests of various stakeholders. Recognition policies should therefore reflect the level of cooperation between education, economic and civil society actors. *Creating a coordinated structure linking the efforts of all stakeholders and national authorities* is essential for access to education and recognition of competences for all domains. All actors should be responsible for rendering competences visible, while enabling the processes towards a qualification, diploma or certificate in cooperation with national authorities ensuring coherence, transparency and quality.

The *fourth lesson* is that the anchoring of RVA into explicit and holistic strategies of lifelong learning and the broad vision of an open learning society are important factors conducive to the implementation of RVA. However, once lifelong learning has been identified as an important overarching strategy, there are a number of interpretations of lifelong learning that play a crucial role in determining the scope of the resulting RVA policy. The EU places an emphasis on the dual goal of lifelong learning: employability and citizenship. As Rogers (2014) and Knoll (2006) argue however, across Europe more generally, vocationally-oriented continuing education and training (after initial education) has been a new site for promoting lifelong learning until now. There is also a call for more informed lifelong learning policies and practices enabling the recognition and accessibility of informal knowledge in the workplace as many aspects of informal job-related learning are increasingly found to be essential to becoming and remaining knowledgeable workers (Livingstone and Guile 2012).

In developing countries, by contrast, lifelong learning plays a role in basic education and training. Lifelong learning in these countries is connected to non-formal rather than formal education. Here, learning is not only life-long, it is life-wide. Learning is promoted through engaging with the cultural practices of the learner's communities. Lifelong learning tends to be directed at the need for further learning opportunities for people who may never return to the education system, as well as for those skilled and semi-skilled workers in the agricultural and small-scale industrial sectors. It is also there to assist workers and minority groups working for low wages in small enterprises. Clearly in these contexts RVA has a great potential yet to be tapped. For example, RVA could pay great attention to cultural practices, to adults' informal knowledge, and knowledge traditions outside the formal system. RVA could be understood as a pedagogical device rather than a mere technical exercise. Skills development programmes could be reformulated as skills recognition programmes focussed on what people know and have, not what they lack. In this way RVA could identify skills bases for alternative forms of economic and ecological development. At the same time this could contribute to the development of individual and collective self-esteem. Equally important will be to give greater attention to curriculum developments that bring alternative knowledge systems into non-formal educational institutions.

7.1.1 Multidimensional and Multi-targeted Approaches to RVA

Based on the review of RVA in different country contexts we found that RVA is focused on three different aims, namely:

- RVA as a means to achieve an official qualification.
- RVA as an entry door to formal tertiary education institution.
- RVA as a means to make competences and learning visible.

This multidimensional perspective is important. RVA should be seen as an attempt to integrate different modes (reflective, formative and summative recognition) and different settings (work, family, community, voluntary, social work, sports) into lifelong learning. While in some cases RVA is a real opportunity to avoid a complete cycle of training, it is more often than not a part of a learning, professional or personal path.

RVA as a Means to Achieve an Official Qualification

Learning outcomes, with their emphasis on achievements rather than pathways are clearly important in opening up qualifications to non-formal and informal learning, and in providing comparability between non-formal and formal programmes. RVA can be seen as an alternative route to achieve a qualification. However, countries differ with regard to whether they reference RVA against existing formal education and training standards and institutions, or on national qualifications frameworks based on learning outcomes/competences. Within this fundamental division, there are differences in the way countries understand and define learning outcomes and competences according to their contexts and social and economic needs. In addition, there are stark divisions between developed countries and developing countries in the development of NQFs. The different approaches to linking RVA to national reference points – which are not mutually exclusive – can be grouped as follows.

The first group of countries, where RVA is an accepted route to qualifications, consists of Australia, New Zealand, France, Portugal, Finland, Scotland, South Africa, Mauritius and Namibia. NQFs establish common references and quality systems, and allow for the formal equivalence of qualifications recognised through RVA and formal course assessments. Quality assessment is a key feature of qualifications frameworks within this group. NQF developments such as the SCQF provide opportunities to challenge assessment approaches that dominate the formal system. Higher level definitions of "competence" through programme level outcomes or level descriptors contextualised in different occupational or professional areas can accommodate unstructured learning experience and can extract the transferable knowledge, skills and understanding which are comparable to that gained through formal learning (Whittaker 2012). Furthermore, outcome statements in qualifications frameworks have been shown to include information on graduate profiles, employment pathways and education pathways (New Zealand).

In Australia, given the comprehensive and overarching character of the Australian Qualifications Framework (AQF), linkages between secondary education, TVET and higher education sub-frameworks can be established through the recognition of prior learning.

A *second group* of countries are those that place an emphasis on national vocational qualifications frameworks with hardly any reference to the general formal education system. Bangladesh, Namibia and Burkina Faso have either developed or are in the process of developing such frameworks. In the view of these countries, skills development and a focus on labour market requirements are beneficial to both overall economic and social development as well as individuals seeking employment. Shifting to competence-based approaches in National Vocational Qualifications Frameworks (NVQFs) has made the recognition of relevant skills and knowledge more achievable. The adoption of a pragmatic stance with respect to skills development, and the role of NQFs in vocational education and training, offers greater potential for the recognition of existing skills, particularly those found in the large informal economies of these countries. Furthermore, the skills orientation of NQFs and competence-based training are less contentious compared with the typically content-driven, discipline-based approaches of general education and university education programmes (Allais 2010). A similar development is to be seen in England's National Vocational Qualifications (NVQ) framework, which despite being criticised for its focus on behavioural output measures of specific task and skills did much to promote APEL at pre-degree level in vocational education as well as opening up potential APEL-related pathways to higher education through higher level NVQs (Pokorny 2011). In the longer term, developing countries should consider recognising non-formal and informal learning not only in their TVET sectors, but also beyond skills development, in their higher education systems (Arthur 2009).

The third group includes countries with approaches that recognise learning outcomes which relate to skills and occupational standards in specific economic sectors. The approach adopted in Mexico is to make visible, validate and certify the vast reservoir of experiential learning from working life, within sectoral (occupational standards) recognition systems. Although Mauritius and South Africa have overarching frameworks, they have also both developed RVA processes in certain occupations. Recognition of non-formal and informal learning within occupational standards is recognised as potentially being of great use given the weaknesses in the formal education and training sector, and the extent of informal employment and training.

Many developing countries have initiated ambitious programmes for the development of occupational standards in order to describe the employment requirements for existing and future workers. However, these developments are infrequently integrated with vocational qualifications systems, leaving the occupational standards unused, and complicating the translation process into different types of qualifications, and curricula. A clear identification of different qualification types and how they can build on occupational standards can resolve these situations (Keevy 2012). Basing qualifications on occupational standards and labour market demand, as well as linking them to higher-level qualifications and allowing for progression, raises the "market-value" of these qualifications. Case studies from countries have shown that occupational standards have been welcomed as potential instruments to support demand-led qualifications systems and they can also offer the basis to certify existing staff in enterprises and organisations.

The fourth group consists of European countries, which are in the process of referencing their NQFs to the European Qualifications Framework (EQF). The EQF is viewed as an opportunity to integrate non-formal and informal learning. Norway is discussing with stakeholders whether non-formal and informal learning should be, and through which means it could be, accommodated into an NQF in its own right (parallel approach) without having to be recognised via the formal education system (convergent approach). Austria is also making great efforts to relate learning outcomes from non-formal and informal learning that do not yet have an equivalent in the formal system. In Germany, all EQF reference levels should be achievable via various educational pathways, including non-formal and informal pathways. However, despite the willingness to introduce the NQFs, and until such time as non-formal and informal pathways to qualifications are identified, it appears that RVA will continue to be referenced against the formal educational system, rather than its direct placement in the NQF.

While the development of various NQFs in Europe has stimulated developments in educational standards and descriptions of competences and learning, countries have identified the need for further work in partnership with all stakeholders. In many countries, further efforts are required to clarify issues relating to the learning outcomes approach in terms of concepts, assessment methodologies and tools, and the balance between outcome orientation and input factors (CEDEFOP 2012).

Only further research can tell if NQFs are leading to RVA, or whether RVA is causing NQFs to be established. In any case, there are "parallel" or "divergent" tendencies in several developing countries for NQFs to serve the labour market with skilled labour, to provide a means to recognise learning that takes place outside the formal education sector, and to help those who have dropped out of the academic system to receive training oriented more strongly towards vocational practice. The recognition of non-formal and informal learning thus becomes a key issue in NQF developments. Within knowledge-based economies, parallel and divergent tendencies are apparent whereby labour markets associated with specific occupations (such as IT software engineering) drive internationally recognised individual competences to take over formal education and training programmes (Brockmann 2011). Internationally recognised individual competences of this kind require vocationally-oriented frameworks for their recognition.

It is worth pointing out that NQFs do not themselves promote RVA (Dyson and Keating 2005). Instead, this occurs through the actions of stakeholders at the workplace, individual and provider levels. For linkages between recognition practices and NQFs to be successful, they need to take into account the real world of learning and working at several levels by: (1) developing individual competence portfolios for different informal and non-formal activities; (2) linking individual learning needs and competence requirements in the workplace, the local community and region to tailor-made education and training (non-formal) offers; and (3) incorporating work-related and adult learning activities either as integral parts of accredited programmes or as part of non-accredited programmes. In the context of knowledge-based societies, Livingstone and Guile (2012) have shown, such informal and non-formal activities can develop knowledge, skills and competence in highly effective ways, and need to become an explicit feature of supporting further education, transition to work, and the social integration of individuals in society – the important pillars of education for sustainable development.

This close collaboration between workplace, community, individual and provider levels is essential for preventing the narrowing of the richness of individual experience and the inclusive, open-ended and lifelong character of learning processes. RVA needs to go beyond the mere formalisation of experience in terms of knowledge, skills and competences. Some countries, particularly the German-speaking countries, despite their distinctive focus on vocational education and training, are careful to ensure that outcome orientations in qualifications are not reduced to narrow task-related skills and knowledge, and instead include broad descriptors of knowledge, skills and competences (moral, civic and social), learning objectives, standards and quality of input (Bohlinger 2007–2008) with the aim of promoting an all-rounded individual.

Despite the growing trend towards the establishment of NQFs, the linkage of RVA to NQFs represents an ongoing challenge and many quality assurance requirements will need to be met before non-formal and informal learning can enter into the framework. Developing countries often lack the capacities and the resources to develop credible systems of assessment and certification. This is in stark contrast to developed countries, where the introduction of NQFs are policy initiatives that are seen as "supportive of educational reforms that have far reaching implications for the management and delivery of education and training, design of programmes and assessment and certification processes" (Comyn 2009). Furthermore, developing a comprehensive framework is a huge undertaking in which countries of the South are rarely able to invest, and it is remarkable that despite financial constraints many less resource-rich countries of the South have been able to come up with innovative approaches to work towards this goal in more manageable and incremental ways. In fact, many countries are now shifting from "integrated" frameworks to "sectoral" or "bridging" frameworks, whereby in the latter case, NQFs are seen as systems of coordination, collaboration and communication, wherein different sectors are able to follow sector-specific approaches but continue to be guided within a nationally coherent system. A case in point is South Africa which has laid the ground-work for this shift, moving away from the earlier post-apartheid euphoria that existed in the mid-1990s that placed far-reaching transformational expectation on the South African NQF. In the sub-sectoral approach, the TVET sector operates alongside (parallel approach) existing educational standards in the higher education sector, with labour competency frameworks for specific industrial sectors.

RVA as an Entry Door to Formal Tertiary Education Paths

In Norway approximately 5 % of all new students in higher education are adults admitted on the basis of recognised formal, non-formal and informal learning. In 2007, 67 % of adults applying for enrolment on the basis of prior learning were admitted. This proportion varies significantly between different fields of study. However, only a very small number of students apply for exemption. This indicates that many institutions were uncertain as to how the RVA procedure should be applied. Consequently, sufficient information was not provided to the target groups. The guidelines developed by Vox for RVA exemptions are an important step forward in aiding participation in higher education (Alfsen 2014).

Many universities in Europe are widening participation of non-traditional students by making pedagogical methods used for RVA an integral part of activities of guidance and counselling (CEDEFOP 2009). These services should help to increase access to higher education and help students to choose courses or pathways that are suited to their aptitudes and interests; to pay attention to learning possibilities that can favour subsequent employability; and help students to transition to the job market. While many universities in Europe already have placement services, these are usually separate from counselling services, aimed at helping adults to find a job rather than developing their professional and personal pathways (Piazza 2013). Improving career guidance services in tertiary education essentially means creating possibilities for the interaction between placement and guidance services, transforming traditional roles of teachers into one in favour of guidance, counselling, encouraging; and the provision in the university curriculum of career management courses, opportunities for work experiences, and profiling and portfolio systems. According to Bassot (2006), career guidance has a role to play in ensuring that lifelong learning is embedded into the lives of young people and adults, encouraging them to learn and to achieve their potential.

In many countries there is increasingly a trend to put a greater focus on TVET and work experience in order to help learners to progress to higher education. In the Republic of Korea vocational qualification and other learning through workplace experiences can be recognised towards higher education credits.

RVA for Making Competences and Learning Visible

The review of RVA has shown that RVA is first and foremost about making competences and learning visible. RVA makes it possible for a person to make an inventory of his/her competences, allowing those competences to receive a value and be recognised. The RVA is practiced by many people and groups as a means to become aware of their own skills to design and implement personal development plans, but also to enrich the educational paths with additional modules and enter further formal training, and as a way of better planning for redeployment and offering one's own skills and competences in the job market.

Competences and talents can be made visible not only against pre-set standards, looking for access and exemptions, but also "geared at enabling individuals to manage their own careers, articulate their own development needs and build up their own competences. Education and vocational training should respond to this, by becoming more flexible and demand-driven. Formal systems such as qualification structures and vocational frameworks will then have less of a prescriptive function in terms of personal development, and serve more as a reference framework and repertoire within which there is individual choice. These formal systems retain a function as pegs for defining the direction and level of personal development and the relevant external communication with employers, mediators, referrers, schools, etc." (Duvekot 2014, p. 24).

Studies in the USA suggest that participation in PLA programmes has various "transformational" effects on individual students in terms of self-awareness and skill development (personal, problem-solving and study skills, self-direction and self-regulation). Studies show that PLA students exhibited slightly higher tacit knowledge and processes of reflection (Travers 2011). Germany also reports that outcomes for the users of the ProfilPASS are positive. Typically, they have a greater appreciation of their own skills and, on this basis, can plan their future in a more self-confident and targeted way, and are motivated to participate in further learning. The ProfilPASS is frequently used by people who find themselves in a phase of transition or reorientation, such as those who are returning to the workplace or who are looking to set up their own business. It is also used by migrants looking for a way of coping more effectively with the German labour market.

From Nova Scotia in Canada, the Record of Achievement (ROA) project of the RPL and Labour Mobility Unit within the Adult Education Division of the Government of Nova Scotia Canada is an example of RPL methodologies that make visible the prior learning, work experience and life experiences of youngsters who may never return to school. ROA addresses the challenges faced by the close to 100,000 working age Nova Scotians with few or no formal qualifications, but who have skills and knowledge that would make them good employees in entry levels jobs. RPL is undertaken in relation to the Nova Scotia Core Employability Skills Framework. It offers the employer a validation of the skills and learning of individuals than can be measured against occupational requirements. It offers the learner an opportunity to develop a personal plan for bridging skill gaps towards securing employment or further training (Walsh-Goya and Morrissey 2014).

7.1.2 Features of Best Practice and Quality RVA Processes

Countries from across the world utilise a range of effective measures to validate, accredit and recognise learning, and while it is difficult to come up with a single "best practice" model, a range of important features, themes and principles, and successful aspects of different recognition processes have emerged in the individual country examples presented which can be usefully shared between countries. However, these features need to be placed in the context of the degree of development of RVA in the countries. For purposes of facilitating a learning process, three groups of countries can be categorised: A group of countries with a high degree of development of RVA practices: Scotland, England, Denmark, Finland, France, Republic of Korea, Australia, New Zealand, Norway, Portugal, South Africa, Canada, and the USA. A group of countries with a medium degree of development of RVA practice. In these countries, RVA is gaining momentum with the development of national policies and learning outcome and competence-based approaches: such as Mauritius, Namibia, the Philippines, Thailand and Japan. A group of countries, including Bangladesh, Burkina Faso and Benin, where RVA is still under construction.

The following features have emerged as key considerations in the development of best practice in RVA:

- Standards and methods of assessment
- Delivering RVA and strengthening professionalism
- Quality assurance of procedures and processes
- Outcomes and impacts in RVA

Standards and Methods of Assessment

The utilisation of agreed standards or benchmarks is an important feature of RVA. One example of agreed standards is a general agreement on national curricula. Workplace-specific competence demands – i.e. the competences that are necessary to perform specific tasks, such as operating certain machines, or serving customers – are another. Regardless of context, and whether it is for licensure, employment, credit or qualification, there is a need to have clear criteria for both learners and assessors so that the object of assessment is identified to all those involved. Similarly, the purpose of an assessment must be clear. It is only fair to the individual and the organisation/institution to tie assessments to specific learning or performance-based outcomes. Appropriate evaluation tools can then be used to consider how learners could gain recognition and credit for their existing skills and knowledge. At the same time learners need to understand the rationale for their RVA.

Assessment based on learning outcomes has become an important quality issue in developing RVA systems. In Japan, the purpose of assessment is not to select the best, but rather to provide an opportunity for learners to show what they are able to do. This means that learners should be properly prepared to do the best they can. A lesson to learn is that the development of the proper assessment of learning outcomes should be considered to be an important policy issue, particularly introducing procedures for assessment and recognition of learning outcomes, independent of the place, form and time of learning.

Combining traditional methods and tests with other methods such as practical demonstrations has allowed relatively flexible procedures. Each assessment tool has its strengths and weaknesses. It is important to match the assessment tool to the purpose of the assessment and in some cases, to the nature of the learner. In some cases requiring individuals to create large portfolios, for example, will prove inappropriate. Practical demonstrations and/or oral questioning might be a preferable method of assessing such individuals. Profiling skills and knowledge for the identification of learning outcomes, as practiced in New Zealand, gives learners a realistic perspective on the requirements and an effective way to demonstrate their skills and knowledge. Instead of asking people to compile portfolios or take standardised tests (in the knowledge that they are unlikely to pass), other ways of assessing what people know and can do must be considered.

While there is a growing use of portfolio methods, applicants are also turning to simpler devices, requiring only a few pages, to demonstrate their ability to meet standards. Language can be an impediment to the successful completion of portfolios. There is also discussion in many countries on how methods of portfolio assessment might be improved in order to increase openness and transparency and to better enable individuals to describe their current knowledge, skills and motivation. Japan employs a type of portfolio that resembles a CV and is used to list non-formal and informal learning in the employment sector. One of the tools employed in Portugal is a biographical and narrative-based assessment that allows individuals to present their experiences in a less formal manner. In Australia, there is an increasing use of e-portfolios for gaining recognition or credit towards a formal VET qualification. Online self-assessments are useful for enabling individuals to gauge the likely outcome of applications to regulated professions or courses.

An important feature is the growing tendency towards continuity from *formative assessment* to *summative accreditation* as seen in the steps that are necessary to identify learning-outcome equivalencies, such as increasing our understanding of portfolio methods; quality assurance guidelines; guidance and counselling knowledge; and learning-outcome descriptions. In France, a clear and easy-to-follow process of assessment and accreditation has been developed. Norway recommends the use of clearly defined and described steps and stages that can be recognised by all stakeholders, as this is important for building confidence in the system. The process can consist of certain steps, for example: (1) information and guidance; (2) description/mapping of competences, including documentation from formal and informal learning, and from work practice; (3) assessment or validation; and (4) recognition of competences – and accreditation. Each step must then be defined and described. In addition, county authorities are required to register all adult candidates who have gone through a validation process at upper secondary level into a national, digital registration system, providing long-term records of learning and skills.

While there is a clear distinction between formative and summative assessment, countries must be aware of the linkages and be clear about how assessment in recognition is to be employed for their specific educational and broader policy goals. There is an increased understanding and use of *formative assessment* in some countries. Formative assessment is used in RVA to assess learning needs and to select learning material and effective learning methods to achieve the expected outcomes. The formative role of RVA is also important in terms of personal growth and development. Acknowledging and making explicit key outcomes of formative assessment is important to its success (Whittaker 2011).

Delivering RVA and Strengthening Professionalism

The quality of RVA, including guidance and counselling hinges significantly on the capability of RVA administrators, assessors, facilitators, counsellors and guidance practitioners to set up and maintain inclusive RVA practices. RVA assessment is based on evidence and must be equitable, culturally inclusive, fair, flexible, valid and reliable, and provide for reasonable adjustment. This requires not only competent assessors and validation procedures to ensure the authority and reliability of the results, but also requires that the performance of assessors be monitored to ensure consistency in their judgements. In Australia, there is increasing action research on developing assessors' capacities, aimed at helping assessors to see their own strengths as advanced practitioners. In Portugal, professionalisation is sought through the sharing of practices, knowledge and experiences among teachers and trainers who carry out adult learning programmes and undertake validation assessments. Many countries (e.g. Australia, South Africa and New Zealand) have in place facilities for the registration of assessors. At the School of New Learning (DePaul University Chicago), the responsibility for advising, coaching the development of evidence and assessing/evaluating falls primarily to "faculty mentors" and professional experts, who serve as community-based "experts" to student programmes, helping individuals to shape a "focus area" of study and its integration within the larger degree design and requirements. The college has adopted four qualities for feedback and assessment: clarity, integrity (with regard to criteria) flexibility and empathy (Wilbur, Marienau and Fiddler 2012).

Professionalisation is, of course, not the only issue of import in this context. A recent international review (Carrigan and Downes 2010) raises concerns that assessment may alienate and frighten potential learners from marginalised backgrounds who have had negative assessment experiences in the past. This also applies to developing countries, which face major challenges when it comes to ensuring quality in the assessment of learning outcomes. Kennedy (2014) also refers to the tendency to over-assess PLAR candidates as compared to traditional learners as one of the reasons why the high demand for RPL services by Canadian-born adult learners looking for recognition by academic institutions has not materialised.

In most cases the assessment process used for RVA provides abundant additional support for applicants. The provision of information to key players is important. In several countries, professional guides and counsellors are identified, as well as trainers, to promote RVA and support candidates. In France, RVA guidance and counselling was increased, which led to the birth of a new profession, that of the APEL advisor. Mauritius, which will use Creole to facilitate RVA processes, emphasises that information should take into account the complexities of the language that often impede fair validation. In Australia a guidance document has been developed to help guidance counsellors assess the applicant's skills.

Assessors need training on effective assessment procedures, and this is the case whether an assessor is a supervisor in a workplace or a member of college faculty.

Many countries have shown that due attention should be paid during implementation *processes* to the provision of individual support to identify and document skills. The implementation of RVA should not be a cumbersome process and sufficient time should be allowed. The process of matching skills with competences described in training documentation can be off-putting for those who have had limited interaction with formal education. In Crooks, Kane, and Cohen's (1996) model, the administration link deals with the administration of assessment tasks, as task performance can be greatly influenced by the procedures followed in presenting and administering tasks. The challenges for learners resulting from this are easily underestimated.

Impact is another link in the chain described by Crooks, Kane, and Cohen (1996) and refers not to identifiable stages of the assessment process, but "the consequential basis of validity" (Messick 1989). Threats to validity can come from assessment processes being perceived as unfair as a result of exclusion from further learning opportunities due to RVA results. Negative views about the process of RVA can affect confidence in RVA. One way of ensuring confidence and fairness in the assessment could be to standardise the RVA process, from administration to feedback about the outcome. It is important that all claimants are offered the same treatment and, for example, receive guidance on the process and instruments involved. Assessment can be made more transparent by making criteria better known to the claimants.

General requirements in connection with the planning and development of RVA processes have also been highlighted. In Mauritius, RVA is yet to be extended to all sectors. The need to train RPL facilitators and assessors in all sectors prior to extending the same has however been highlighted. The identification of facilitators and assessors presents a challenge in itself and these positions are frequently filled on a part-time basis in all sectors (Allgoo 2013). The Philippines has reported that educators, instructional managers and facilitators lack the capacity to assess outcomes from non-formal learning, despite their ability to develop learning strategies using different methodologies and technologies.

Quality Assurance of Policies, Procedures and Processes

Quality assurance of policies, procedures and processes is vital for gaining trust among users. Generally, countries promote the view that core principles within which RVA provision will operate should provide a more transparent and equitable process, and facilitate mutual trust and confidence among receiving institutions. The use of SCQF RPL Guidelines by institutions in Scotland is proving to be a source of guidance, and is making possible the attainment of greater consistency and transparency. The quality principles set out in the European Guidelines for Validating Non-formal and Informal Learning are considered to be suitable for most European countries.

In the USA, a research study (Ganzglass et al. 2011) has recommended the creation of a national competence-based framework for US post-secondary education that will include certificate-level workforce education and training. The purpose is to ensure that credits acquired by currently non-credit-bearing workforce education and training, achieved in part or full through RVA, are of the same quality and have the same standing as qualifications achieved as a consequence of formal education and training.

There is already a trend in the US for some institutions to design degree programmes around student learning outcomes, or competences, rather than college credits. Evaluative frameworks are being developed in increasing numbers for competency-based prior learning assessment programmes in order to equate their effectiveness to other programme evaluation processes within institutions of higher education. Thus, instead of reinventing the wheel, CAEL standards for competency-based PLA are being interrelated with quality criteria used in the evaluation of college academic programmes with the aim of developing overarching evaluative frameworks that embed the effectiveness of PLA programmes as well.

In Canada also measures for the assessment of educational quality (e.g., CAEL standards for PLA) are applied to the assessment of prior learning in competency-based education and assessment, for example in the area of professional registration. However, there has been some scepticism expressed regarding their applicability, given their very different conditions, purposes and participants (Van Kleef 2011).

Outcomes and Impacts

An important element of quality is the issue of quality of outcomes and impacts in RVA. These will be discussed in terms of evidence on uptake; the number of certificates; use of portfolio and other tools and so on. As can be seen below, there appears to be a focus on the formal learning system and formal qualifications.

Evidence on uptake. Only a few countries such as Denmark, Norway, France, Germany, Austria and the USA have estimates on the impact on learners and their subsequent capacities to gain employment and continue into formal learning. A recent CAEL study (Klein-Collins 2010) reported that PLA students have better rates of degree completion than non-PLA students, regardless of the size, level or type of institutions. It found that more than half (56 %) of adult PLA students earned a post-secondary degree within several years, while only 21 % of non-PLA students did so (Klein-Collins 2010). A study by CAEL in 2006 (Klein-Collins 2007) into the scale and scope of implementation showed that more than half of all states had at least one agency supporting or encouraging the adoption and use of PLA methods in higher education.

Making use of RVA outcomes. Data on the use of RVA outcomes range from the number of people who appear for an examination, to the number of people who have obtained certification through RVA, and the number of credits and qualifications awarded. Data from Germany demonstrate that external students' examinations resulted in improved status for individuals and the potential recruitment of executives for companies (Germany. Federal Ministry of Education and Science 2008, p. 21). In 2008, this applied to 7.2 % of the candidates appearing for the final vocational apprenticeship examination. The number of persons who appeared for the above examination increased from 20,700 in 2000 to more than 28,000 in 2009, demonstrating that Germany makes use of RVA outcomes on a large scale.

The number of persons who apply for RVA as well as those who go through the process has been quite high in France. Since the introduction of the system in 2002, 136,000 people have obtained certification through RVA (Paulet 2013). Different ministries (Higher Education and Research; Agriculture; Social Action and Health; Employment; Youth and Sport; Defence; Culture; and Maritime Affairs) are involved in admitting candidates' applications and granting certification.

Figures for the Republic of Korea show that uptake was high in 2009. The total number of credits issued through the ACBS rose to more than 200,000 (Baik 2013). About 500 education and training institutions participated in the ACBS at that time.

In South Africa, between 1995 and 2004 the total number of qualifications awarded increased at an average annual growth rate of 4.3 %, with the highest growth in 4-year first degrees, honours degrees and master's degrees. Education & Training Quality Assurance Bodies (ETQAs) have been able to make significant progress over the last number of years and have already uploaded 2.7 million learners' records between 2006 and 2010.

Austria has also reported on take-up and has provided exemplary data for a number of initiatives and mechanisms (Brandstetter and Luomi-Messerer 2010). More than 800 candidates per year acquire the lower secondary school (*Hauptschule*) qualifications in second-chance education; approximately 5,300 persons per year take the final apprenticeship examination *Lehrabschlussprüfung* (LAP) in second-chance education; approximately 3,800 persons per year are awarded the professional title *Ingenieur*; approximately 3,000 persons have been issued competence balances at the Tyrol Centre of the Future since 2003; and about 2,000 persons have been issued the competence profile KOMPAZ at the *Volkshochschule Linz* (Adult Education Centre Linz) (Austria. Federal Ministry of Education, the Arts and Culture 2011).

In Mauritius, some 50 persons have already acquired either a full qualification or a record of learning to date. According to information gathered by the Mauritius Qualifications Authority, some of them have been promoted in their jobs while others benefited from a rise in salary. In effect, RVA has not only broadened participation in education and training, but as one RVA candidate said, "RVA has enhanced my confidence and given me a 'second chance' by recognising my experience and know-how." Additionally, a batch of 50 persons will be assessed shortly, of which 25 will be assessed against the National Certificate in Adult Literacy Level (Allgoo 2013).

Mexico has not to date carried out impact evaluations with respect to productivity or economic and social progress for workers, but CONOCER is in the process of developing the instruments and mechanisms to evaluate impact, such as building a database of firms, voluntary and educational institutions that certify workers, as well as a database of individual workers. However, the system currently has close to 70 accredited centres for assessment and certification of competences, with more than 2,000 points of contact to provide services around the country. Over the 5-year period to June 2013 CONOCER has issued more than 400,000 certificates in Mexico, i.e., 65 % more than during its first 12 years of operation since 1995. This increase, according to García-Bullé (2013), may be considered a good proxy of the value that the market perceives of recognition practices. The principle behind the growth strategy of the national network of evaluation and certification entities has been to ensure market credibility.

The transformational effects of the use *of portfolio methods and other testing tools has also been highlighted*. A 2006 CAEL survey (Klein-Collins 2007) reports that 66 % of college and university administrators accept portfolio assessments for academic credit. This is an increase from 55 % 10 years ago. Standardised tests are heavily used as indicators of prior learning. About 616,000 individuals completed the General Education Development test in 2006. Thousands of corporate courses and programmes have been assessed for credit recommendations. About 2,900 colleges grant credit or advanced standing for College Level Examinations Programme (CLEP) examinations.

E-learning modules and tools that were used to integrate RVA into guidance and counselling/placement services (Europlacement 2010; Piazza 2013) were appreciated by students and job-seekers for higher education institutions and universities in eight European countries. The tools and modules supported the self-evaluation and self-analysis processes of students and job-seekers. The e-learning path allowed students and job-seekers to reflect on their competences and experiences and to identify the weaknesses in their professional profiles. Operators of the placement services, on their part, pointed out that they became more aware of the guidance needs of students and young people.

More than 110,000 ProfilPASS packs had been issued up until July 2011, including more than 55,000 copies of a special version of the ProfilPASS for young people. The digital e-ProfilPASS now available is complemented through a comprehensive range of advisory services (Germany. Federal Ministry of Education and Science (BMBF) and the Standing Conference of the Ministers of Education and Cultural Affairs of the Länder in the Federal Republic of Germany (KMK) 2008, p. 37).

The recognition of prior learning and previous competences is a factor in the uptake of further education and training. However, research in Australia has shown that RVA appears to benefit those from socio-economic backgrounds who already have experience of and success in post-compulsory education and training. They are mid-career, established in the workforce, older, full-time, and in associate professional, professional or managerial occupations. Maher et al. (2010) found that candidates from indigenous, non-English-speaking backgrounds and women returning to the workforce are less likely to access and complete RVA than other groups. Moreover, the dominant model of RVA in Australia is the credentialing model (Butterworth 1992), and Cameron (2004) found that this approach is neither relevant nor appropriate to the needs of disadvantaged and disengaged groups of learners.

A recently published survey (Guthu and Bekkevold 2010) undertaken by Vox, the Norwegian Agency for Adult Learning, has shown that a total of 55 % of all adults completing their upper secondary education (including VET) in 2008 had undergone validation of their prior learning, and 86 % of these were granted exemption from at least one module. The survey also points out the uneven uptake. In the field of vocational training, adults are more likely to choose health and social studies, where 63 % of candidates had undergone validation, and between 89 and 92 % (depending on the level of study) gained formal recognition of learning, resulting in an exemption from parts of the training schedule.

Qualitative improvements. From Portugal, there is evidence (Gomes 2013) that the National Qualifications System and New Opportunities Initiative have enabled the emergence of a new approach to the field of adult education and training, countering the low level of involvement in lifelong learning activities (INE 2007; OECD 2011). At the level of competences, new fields of learning have been identified that increase self-awareness, strengthen soft-skills and highlight practical knowledge (in particular in the areas of information and communications technologies and different forms of literacy). There are also significant meta-learning benefits (i.e., learning how to learn). Families have gained, not only through the valorisation of adults, but also through the example parents can give to their children with respect to the importance of schooling, or through their greater capacity to keep abreast of their children's studies. These aspects have had a major impact on family reading patterns and children's success at school.

The participation by adults in the New Opportunities Initiative seems to be breaking the cycle of scholastic exclusion. Companies, which have made increasing investments in the Initiative, now have greater access to confident and qualified workers who are willing to learn. Above all, the New Opportunities Initiative is viewed by all those taking part as an instrument for restoring social justice in the field of certified qualifications, which is crucial for social participation and capacity-building. From a theoretical and methodological perspective, the Initiative is an open field of investigation where hitherto contrasting paradigmatic perspectives conceive new modes of intervention, new levels of response and new working methodologies and structuring of systems without overlooking the specific characteristics of the field of adult education and training which may and should be safeguarded (e.g., the contextualisation of learning processes, diversification of educational paths, singularisation and individualisation of working methodologies, and the effects of scale). However, a recent study has reflected critically upon the Portuguese New Opportunities Initiative (Barros 2013). It argues that certification and the promotion of individual advancement rather than collective identity are becoming more and more important goals of RVA. Concerns are expressed over the narrow focus of RVA practitioners to converge and standardise diverse and divergent knowledge forms into national standards.

Qualitative improvements can be noted in the context of the Equivalency Programmes in the Philippines. Despite low uptake, research has shown that learners take on leadership roles in the community as a result of increased confidence and access to information; they become community educators and organisers, helping other people who need education; learning livelihood skills enables them to earn an income; participants learn to participate in community affairs; parents become involved in the education of their children and learn literacy as well; learners are able to negotiate with the government regarding their rights and claims to social services; as women become more empowered – they become active in the community and have more access to information related to the health and welfare of children.

7.1.3 The Challenges and Future Directions in RVA

The country cases reveal that the focus of RVA and its various forms appear to be on formal recognition through education and qualifications systems. Workplaces, non-formal activities and community life are not yet aligned to qualifications, and RVA's potential in relation to lifelong learning and the creation of learning societies has yet to be fully exploited and utilised. It is therefore likely that patterns of RVA take-up are influenced as much by the barriers to RVA as they are by the benefits it brings. In general, it can be concluded that the factors discussed below are at one and the same time conducive to the implementation of RVA in different contexts as well as constituting challenges to the development of RVA where these have not yet been put in place.

The Unrealised Potential for RVA

The data available from the Danish Ministry of Education indicates that the potential for RVA has not yet been fully realised. Pokorny (2011, p. 11) describes the unrealised potential of APEL in English higher education despite efforts by some adult educators efforts to open up higher levels of learning. Currently, institutions of higher and further education in England are encouraged to demonstrate a greater willingness to engage and respond to the specific skills demands and needs of employers. Factors that limit take-up in the Danish context include the lack of implementation of policies and procedures by providers, and the financial crisis of 2010. Furthermore, take-up is uneven. Take-up is highest in vocational training. The Danish Ministry of Education set up a working group in 2011 with representatives from social partners, practitioners, educational providers, unions and associations with the aim of realising the full potential of RVA provision (Andersen and Aagaard 2013).

In South Africa, take-up is limited by staff and resource shortages, lack of compliance with SAQA requirements, and the fact that implementation plans and projects have been developed in only a few sectors. SAQA believes that the implementation of RPL should be expanded and driven through a national co-ordinated strategy and should receive proper funding for it to have a massive impact. The Minister of Higher Education and Training established a national RPL task team to develop such a national RPL strategy (Samuels 2013). RVA could have a major impact given the country's critical skills shortage, employability issues and historical discrimination.

Collecting Sufficient Data on RVA Impact and Outcomes

Countries acknowledge that they have not collected sufficient data about RVA outcomes to paint an accurate picture of how successfully RVA has been implemented, nor are there clearly defined benchmarks with regard to the degree to which RVA is considered desirable, and why. Given the amount of informal, undocumented RVA that potentially occurs, it is not possible to develop an accurate picture.

In the case of New Zealand and Australia, no data is available as RVA assessment is a part of the credit transfer system and is not distinguished from traditional assessment. In Canada, statistics to measure the effectiveness of PLAR as a successful intervention are difficult to find. Denmark reports that it has not systematically conducted quantitative or qualitative analyses of data relating to the outcomes and impact of RVA. The existing knowledge is based on analyses of case studies. But some small analyses indicate that RVA eases admission and/or shortens education pathways. Most of the benefits of RVA are perceived benefits. In general, policies highlight the role of RVA in creating job opportunities and improving employability and labour market mobility. However, better data on what works is needed in order to design and provide the best possible frameworks and incentives.

If an RVA policy is to be advocated, instituted, and supported, it should be possible to prove some evidence about its usefulness, and the extent to which it is achieving or is likely to achieve its objectives. The need for evidence is even more urgent in developing countries, where data is completely lacking. Developing countries need to put in place mechanisms for sourcing the available data in local contexts before, during and after the development and implementation of RVA (Keevy 2012).

Financing RVA

Costs to individuals and education systems for information and guidance, assessors, facilitators, auditors and awarding bodies represent a further systemic challenge. Canada does not have an RVA policy or a lifelong learning policy, and funding for PLAR is a matter for provincial governments. Recent research has recommended the creation of expanded financial supports through the tax system, the Employment Insurance (EI) system and other mechanisms to reduce cost barriers for adult learners and to provide stronger incentives to employers to invest in education and training for their employees. This is to be flanked by expanded public policy recognition of, and improved funding stability for, the voluntary non-profit sector as a critically important source of productive employment and learning and skills development for large numbers of Canadian adults (Canadian Council on Learning

2007). However, most funding for the adult learning sector in Canada is project-based, so that when support is withdrawn, the project cannot be sustained.

In Austria, the huge efforts and costs associated with establishing a relevant system represent a major challenge. Austria recommends ensuring financial support for institutions and/or individuals. RVA is not a cheap procedure and a considerable number of staff is necessary for the elaboration of professional references. While the recognition procedure itself need not be especially cost intensive (particularly if based on tests), the labour-intensive and time-consuming elaboration of professional standards makes up-scaling a challenging undertaking. The Republic of Korea has also reported the need for financial support and attention to this issue at a national level.

In the case of Mexico, establishing and implementing cost-sharing (state-supported and self-financing) mechanisms for the RVA of labour competences represents a major challenge. A mechanism of this kind has been put in place in France, namely the Joint Fund for Career Security (*Funds Paritaire de Sécurisation des Parcours Professionnels*, FPSPP), which is financed jointly by social partners and the state. The FPSPP is expected to provide training to a further 200,000 jobseekers and over 500,000 low-skilled employees per year. The fund emerged out of a new agreement that was negotiated with social partners in 2008 and signed in January 2009. Under this agreement unemployed workers are allowed to retain previously acquired individual training rights – the so-called "portability" feature – which they can use either while unemployed or in their next job. This legislation is very recent and its application is still embryonic, making it difficult to predict the changes that it will bring about (Paulet 2013). In France the funding of RVA is considered in relation to broader strategic issues of access, relevance and the state of the economy, rather than merely with respect to short-term operational issues.

In South Africa, the high cost of assessment and the limited number of assessment centres that focus on RVA compared with the priority given to RVA in the national policy guideline represent a significant barrier (Samuels 2013). In Mauritius, the funding of RVA has been a major issue. The pilot projects were funded by the National Empowerment Foundation, which was created to subsidise the fees of prospective, low-income RVA candidates. Namibia will soon introduce a national training levy that aims to motivate employers to fund, either directly or indirectly, the training and development of their employees. Cost is also a limiting factor in the Philippines, especially with respect to the implementation of nationwide accreditation and equivalency testing systems, individual-based portfolio assessments and other mechanisms that would allow for the better measurement and comparability of competences from formal, non-formal and informal learning.

In Denmark, recognition of non-formal and informal learning is supported by the Ministry of Education (Denmark. Institute for Evaluation (EVA) 2010). Funding is delivered through a system called the "taximeter system", which links one-off funding to institutions according to the number of RVA candidates completing competence assessments, personal study plans, training plans within specific institutions and courses of adult education and training. The amount paid to an institution varies according to the type of study programme in which a person is enrolled. Every year the taximeter rates are set in the spending bill adopted by Parliament, based on estimated costs per student completion in each of several streams. Allowance schemes for forgone earnings during participation in education and training are based on a co-financed system through public and private sources. Private sources include funding by companies through a national fund set up by the social partners and through collective agreements. Co-financing is more or less a universal rule.

In England, HEFCE declared APEL in 2007 a national priority area in the context of provision developed with employers and employer bodies (HEFCE 2007). Funding for the Workforce Development Programme included resourcing brokerage arrangements between employers, training providers and educational institutions. Pokorny (2011) sees this shift in priority in APEL in light of the dramatic changes English higher education is undergoing in funding, which from 2012 will see HEFCE funding withdrawn from postgraduate study, and all undergraduate subjects with the exception of science, technology, engineering and mathematics. Universities will be able to increase their fees and undergraduate students will be expected to pay these increased course fees through a state-funded deferred payment loan, which for the first time will be available to part-time as well as full-time students. Within this context, and by enabling experienced students to study at an accelerated rate, APEL could provide a means for universities to attract and retain experienced students, many of whom may be unemployed due to the global economic downturn.

Countries acknowledge that RVA involves costs for the individual and for the system in terms of information and guidance, assessors, facilitators, auditors and awarding bodies. They also recommend that these costs should be kept to a minimum as recognition benefits not only the individual but also society in general. Recognition needs to be seen as an investment and a right that requires accessible recognition arrangements.

Furthering Linkages Between Educational Institutions, Workplaces and Community Life

Chapter 4 analysed separately the contribution of RVA to educational, economic, social and individual development. However, we argued that these were not discrete categories. While countries tend to place an emphasis on one or another of these, its educational, economic, social and individual effects are inextricably intertwined and the real challenge in practice is for RVA to align with the needs of different sectors and stakeholders – particularly the labour market and social sectors – and to function coherently within the education and training system, and qualifications frameworks.

The distinction made between RVA in the general and vocational domains presents a particular challenge. In the Republic of Korea, academic degrees and diplomas are developed with little regard to the competence-based Korean Qualifications Framework (KQF) and the Korean Skill Standards (KSS) (Baik 2013). According to Baik, networking with relevant systems or government organisations such as the Ministry of Labour and the Ministry of Health and Welfare, as well as linking RVA to the competency-based qualifications in the KQF and the KSS, will improve the reliability of RVA measures and make them convenient for both learners and the companies and educators involved.

At the same time, the low profile of occupational standards in educational provision still needs improvement. Many occupational standards remain unused because they are not linked to educational qualifications. Their status – especially when compared with the high value attached to academic qualifications – needs to be strengthened. In some countries this strengthening of the link between academic and vocational education is seen in the establishment of middle institutional paths (further education and training, community colleges or post-secondary institutions) that promote both cognitive and applied learning, and require input requirements in the form of work experience and its recognition.

In many countries RVA is yet to be implemented as a coordinated measure across all areas of learning. Germany, for instance, reports a lack of comprehensive procedures (Germany. National Commission for UNESCO 2011). In South Africa, the three sectors of the education and training system still operate within functional silos and there is no subsector cooperation. The lack of a co-ordinated, integrated and comprehensive RVA system has led to a fragmented approach and unnecessary duplication of RVA programmes in Namibia (Murangi 2013).

Countries have also highlighted barriers to the visibility of learning across education, working life and labour market sectors as well in non-governmental agencies. This has been reported in the case of Denmark (Andersen and Aagaard 2013). Lack of inter-sectoral cooperation results in a lack of trust in the RVA system by employers, who may or may not accept qualification documents issued through validation processes in educational institutions. In some countries it is the opposite. Educational institutions and awarding bodies are sometimes sceptical of the quality of assessments undertaken in the workplace.

Forging effective partnerships between government, learning institutions, employers, individuals and non-formal training providers is the single most important factor of success of RVA in workforce development. These partnerships are vital when RVA is linked to employability and skills development, and entail a broadening of the recruitment base for both education and employment. The promotion of effective collaboration among employers, learning providers, awarding bodies and others is also the focus of Scotland's lifelong skills strategy (Scottish Government 2007a). Cooperation between industry training bodies, registered training organisations, government learning institutions is promoting RVA constructively in New Zealand (Keller 2013). Creating consensus among relevant and visible leaders, comprising employers, workers, educators and government officials, is a critical factor in the implementation of RVA for the purposes of workforce development in Mexico (García-Bullé 2013).

Furthering linkages between civil society organisations and further education and training institutions has been highlighted by Jarvis (2008). Civil society organisations could develop socio-cultural purposes, quality systems, and guidelines that explicitly incorporate values which serve the wider community and society, including sustainability, inclusiveness, biculturalism and multiculturalism for example. These goals, he argues, could be reflected in the number of initiatives to improve the quality of the providers of educational, cultural and sports services for strengthening capacities, improving the quality of individuals' lives, and improving mental and physical well-being (Jarvis 2008; Usher 2008). Proper systems of assessment and validation capable of evaluating the socio-cultural goals of non-formal learning are also needed.

The experience from Japan shows that non-profit organisations (NPO) which are conducted by volunteers and organised under non-profit legislation (formally known as the Law to Promote Specified Non-profit Activities, enacted in 2009) offer a model for recognising non-formal and informal learning through university extension programmes. The courses of one civil society group (SLG) (see Ogawa 2009) include community studies, career development, languages, children's courses, liberal arts, hobbies, sports, and special events.

Creating systematic and efficient transitions and pathways across education and training sectors and other sectors should entail exchange and cooperation among actors from educational institutions and partners from the worlds of work and social life. The widest possible involvement of such stakeholders can strengthen the systems that are eventually implemented. In this respect, it is important to establish rules and legal frameworks that take into account the interests of all the actors and that facilitate interaction and coherence of these interests.

Transcending Cultural Resistance to RVA

Evidence from countries reveals frequent resistance to the use of RVA from both higher education institutions and society in general. Many countries attribute this resistance to the fear that its introduction could result in a fall in academic standards. Research in Australia (Pitman 2009) has shown that there is a belief that the link between RVA, the learning outcomes approach and competence-based education and training promotes a reduced understanding of knowledge. There is also the perception that formal educational environments compensate for skills and attributes lacking in students with significant RVA involvement. Pitman (2009) points out that most universities in Australia offer a "blanket" RVA policy rather than anything more specific. He finds that three-quarters of this sample of universities indicate that they accept RVA, and the vast majority (90 %) provide extra resources. As Pokorny (2011) notes, in the UK, perceptions of APEL as a threat to academic standards and knowledge development by and through the academy resulted in a trend towards its application in largely WBL contexts rather than for admission to undergraduate programmes located in the polytechnic sector.

In France, the RVA movement is seeking to counter perceptions that theoretical knowledge will be compromised through RVA by ensuring its implementation across all levels of education and training. In order to make RVA an integral aspect of lifelong learning, France is undertaking broad education and training reforms. These reforms aim to enhance quality in education, particularly in the context of the increasing diversity of a burgeoning student population. To this end, France is striving to involve all stakeholders and to improve the integration of further education and training. Other elements in this reform include the improvement of pathways between initial and continuing education; the promotion of genuine links between schools, companies and services; and the creation of synergies between general education and vocational training (Paulet 2013). Through these reforms education and training will be made more relevant to the world of work and responsive to the expectations of the ever-growing number of candidates with incomplete diplomas requiring supplementary training. Increasing flexibility in these systems will require the introduction of greater numbers of educational modules that can be assessed on the basis of competence domains relevant to jobseekers and labour markets (Paulet 2013).

Highlighting the sluggish growth in the acceptance of innovative means of assessment in some organisation-driven services for adult students, workers and professions, Wong (2011) attributes this to the lack of familiarity of universities and undergraduate colleges with adult education. According to Wong (2011) RVA practice has been more warmly accepted among faculty staff who are familiar with adult education and experiential learning and who have drawn on the works of Dewey (1925), Knowles (1970, 1975), Schön (1983, 1987) and Kolb (1984), which in turn have influenced the importance of RVA in the development of independent and reflective learners.

Van Kleef (2011), using evidence from research in universities in Canada, argues for the strengthening of education and training structures (curricula, teaching practices) that subscribe to more participative and learner-centred learning, rich learning events and construction of meaning by learners. University departments that are redesigning their programmes to provide bridges between classroom-based learning and community-based or workplace-based learning are important candidates for RVA in Canada. Van Kleef advocates the recruitment of partners to develop assessment processes and curricula structures that would benefit both conventional age students and adult learners, and says that institutional accreditation processes should concentrate on effective teaching practices as an important component of quality. Wong (2011) contends that these educational experiences are similar to RVA in that they place an emphasis on personal experience, rich learning events, and the construction of meaning by learners. Learners analyse their experience by reflecting on, evaluating and reconstructing that experience. Both have in common the role that evaluation plays in situations where there is intensive immersion in the experiences and where other people are involved. Wong, citing expanding research on Community Service Learning (CSL), says that CSL can be defined as a type of experiential education in which students participate in the community and reflect on their involvement in such a way as to gain further understanding of the course content and its relationship to social needs and an enhanced sense of civic responsibility.

In developing countries resistance to RVA has been due mainly to the relative lack of academic literacy and formal theory among workplace practitioners. A combination of academic and "everyday" knowledge could help in overcoming the resistance to RVA. In Ghana the Council for Technical and Vocational Education and Training (COTVET) and the Japanese International Cooperation Agency (JICA) are currently working together on the introduction of the demand-oriented competence-based TVET curricula, which should further align the education on offer with the needs of its agro-based industrial economy (Baffour-Awuah 2013). Of central importance is the structural incorporation of creative and innovative skills acquisition elements (from work and informal learning) into the curricula on offer in education and training programmes of higher education institutions that could increase student capabilities in translating the theoretical knowledge gained in a specific programme to a wide variety of problems, situations and contexts. It is within this context that exploratory work is currently underway to establish a qualifications framework for TVET in Ghana.

Resistance to the implementation of RVA for admission purposes in higher education has implications for the domain of vocational education and its status in society. In many developing countries, vocational education and training is widely viewed as a second-tier subsystem located beneath the academic stream. As noted in our discussion around NQF developments, if solutions are to be found to the skills crises afflicting many developing countries, it is imperative that the status of vocational and occupationally-based qualifications be raised. In this respect, many countries are working to create national qualifications frameworks in order to enhance synergies between the academic, TVET and economic sectors. Keevy et al. (2012, p. 61) argue that the issue at stake is not simply one of relating qualifications to labour market demands, but rather one of developing a workforce at an advanced enough level of the education and training system, so as to benefit from the better alignment of the occupational standards and the qualifications system.

A better understanding of the concept and significance of the recognition of informal learning to the development of competences, Germany believes, is essential if RVA is to become a widespread reality in society in general, and education and training systems in particular. Germany highlights the need for social consensus on the value of this learning and a change in the culture of learning at all levels. At the same time Germany acknowledges that while informal learning has the potential to strengthen the status of vocationally relevant qualifications, evidence from Germany, (and even from Austria and Norway) has shown that outcomes from informal learning are most frequently used by individuals who already hold high academic qualifications. Strengthening informal learning of part-time and casual labour is therefore one of the foci of RVA strategies in Germany (Münchhausen 2011). Germany also recommends the development of appropriate teaching methods that would at the same time create systematic links between different forms of learning.

Teachers and educational planners need to acknowledge the existence and the power of informal learning. They should help participants to recognise the value of their existing funds of knowledge, bank of skills, frames of references and perceptions and expectations (Rogers 2014). Building new learning on the prior learning of each learner will need to be taken into account of learning outcomes-based and diversified assessment approaches in formal and non-formal learning.

Teachers should be trained to recognise their own "accepted interpretative schemes" (Rogers 2014) and need to become more aware of informal learning and what it achieves.

Other more specific limitations to RVA relate to the difficulties arising from the low up-take in vocational schools of formative assessment based on occupational profiles. The lack of occupational standards includes the lack of input requirements in the form of workplace experience in the vocational school curriculum. The lack of mechanisms for the recognition of experiential learning linked to career guidance and information on training options means that young people are unable to construct continuing training pathways (Cabrera 2010).

Communicating Opportunities Presented by RVA to Stakeholders

The generally *low level of awareness and understanding* of RVA is another challenge. Researchers claim that the concept and the opportunities it presents are still not well known among potential users and prioritised groups.

Sometimes training providers are *unable to classify knowledge* acquired through formal, non-formal and informal learning adequately. Rather, as Germany reports, they should be able to tailor courses on offer and teaching methods to reflect previous learning. Appropriate teaching methods should be developed to promote the intended informal learning so as to create at the same time a systematic link between different forms of learning (Germany. National Commission for UNESCO 2011). The need to ensure that recognised learning is fully taken into account by providers rather than repeated by developing tailor-made courses has been highlighted by Norway. Denmark emphasises the need for greater awareness of recognition schemes and their benefits among *potential users*, including citizens, businesses and their employees, education and training providers, voluntary associations and social partner organisations in the labour market (Andersen and Aagaard 2013).

Norway and Denmark advocate the development of a trusted RVA system based on the cooperation of sectors and stakeholders. Both countries seek to raise awareness of good practice among stakeholders. In Norway, although validation and recognition of non-formal and informal learning is implemented in the educational system, discussions with industry stakeholders and individuals who could profit from validation continue. Norwegian agencies showcase good practice in an effort to strike a balance between the ideals of validation and the traditional attitude that formal education is the best form of learning. Mauritius is focusing on a communication strategy to expose major stakeholders to international RVA best practice. South Africa will put in place a national co-ordinated strategy with the appropriate resources (Samuels 2013). This will be important to implement RVA on a massive scale in South Africa.

Cultural barriers at the official level have been highlighted in several developing countries. A lack of faith on the part of education officials and lack of support from management is attributed to a lack of understanding of the principles underlying recognition of non-formal and informal learning. Education officials still have a traditional outlook on education as primarily school-based learning and prioritise accordingly. A key challenge in developing countries is the need for advocacy to raise awareness and sensitise governments to the need to give due recognition to education programmes being implemented by NGOs and community organisations with a proven track record in conducting non-formal learning.

The question of how to enable education and training providers to initiate the RVA exercise and start offering opportunities to potential candidates on a continuous basis can be fraught with difficulties. Building on experiences in practice in New Zealand and Australia, Bangladesh plans to include RVA as an additional tool that can be integrated into training agendas; and to provide registered training providers with the support, assistance and training to undertake RPL at their level. In New Zealand and Australia, registered training organisations that fall under the quality assurance framework of their national qualifications frameworks are also those that undertake RVA. It is the technical and vocational providers of education and training that have more intensively been involved in RVA, perhaps because it is these institutions that have the most highly developed outcomes-based curricula, and because their courses are mostly aligned to skills development in the workplace, allowing the links between the workplace and what is taught in institutions to be acknowledged.

National agencies and specialist organisations, such as Vox in Norway, play a significant role in gathering and disseminating information on the benefits of RVA.

Making available research results to faculty staff in higher education on high-quality learning as well as co-curricular experiences can be a good way to sensitise faculty members to the significance of non-formal and informal learning. For Canada, Wong (2011) refers to one such report (NSSE 2003) that has studied graduate attributes in terms of their participation in enriching educational experiences such as co-curricular activities, internships, field experiences, co-operative experiences, clinical assignments, community service or volunteer work, foreign language courses, work or study abroad, and culminating senior experiences such as senior projects or theses.

A report on a cross-Canada study of PLAR by Aarts, Blower, Burke, Conlin, Ebner Howarth, Howell, Lamarre and Van Kleef (1999), made the following recommendations for overcoming barriers: increase efforts to communicate opportunities presented by RVA to stakeholders; increase the extent of professional development made available to RVA practitioners; to further develop RVA methodologies and further linkages between educational institutions and workplaces in order to enhance the participation of workers currently not connected to training institutions.

The development of materials to promote RVA to stakeholders and learners, including sector-specific "business cases" for RVA, has been debated and implemented in Scotland. The Universities Scotland HEI RPL Network was established in 2008 by the Quality Assurance Agency Scotland in response to national policy drivers relating to RVA, the current focus on RVA within the context of Bologna developments and the work of the "quality enhancement themes". Bringing together the main education and training providers (formal and non-formal) with employers and government, the organisation is tasked with increasing understanding, awareness, use and take-up of RVA.

Participants in the Scottish Universities RPL Network have identified key areas of activity to be explored collaboratively with Scottish, UK and international colleagues: the sharing of approaches, resources and tools in order to streamline processes and make them more accessible to learners; the sharing and highlighting of evidence of success; and the development of a theoretical framework to underpin the RVA process that can be integrated into related pedagogical developments, such as work-based learning, personal development planning and employability. All the above should inspire more confidence about RVA among university staff, thereby countering perceptions that RVA processes are not sufficiently robust as indicators of student achievement and likely future performance.

The Demand Side of RVA: Encouraging Companies and Individuals

While countries have invested in the financing of RVA and other measures designed to remove or reduce the disincentives for providers and other bodies to award RVA, less attention has been given to the demand side, for example how companies and individuals can be encouraged to access RVA opportunities as a means of advancing their learning. There is often a lack of clarity with regard to whether companies are interested in competence recognition, given their preference for employees with skills and competences acquired in non-formal and informal learning but without "formal" certificates, because of the reduced cost of employing formally unqualified or lower qualified persons. From some countries we learn about difficulties in involving employers with RVA. These difficulties centre on a range of questions: Who will conduct RVA? Where will it be conducted? Who will pay for it? What actual benefits will it hold for employers? As well as the development of infrastructure and processes, aligning RVA to career and skills development requires a huge cultural shift in employing organisations. From development work in Scotland it is clear that the whole process needs to be integrated within existing workforce development systems, rather than being developed as a separate (and potentially marginal) activity.

The various initiatives and programmes in RVA, both nationally and locally, are fuelling a debate on informal learning and appreciation of such learning and recognition, but there are still many challenges before widespread recognition can become a reality. Some countries like Germany and South Africa have recommended that public administration departments should take the lead by introducing RVA procedures that take account of informal learning and make outcomes visible. It has been found that people who are less educated and employees in low-skilled positions do not enjoy the same opportunities for on-the-job-learning as those with higher formal qualifications.

Regional and Sub-regional Cooperation

Finally, an important challenge lies in the strengthening of collaboration between all stakeholders at a local, regional and international level. Regional collaboration already being promoted in the context of the development of the European Qualifications Framework is proving to be a stimulus for European countries to reflect on how they can place non-formal and informal learning outcomes directly into their national qualifications frameworks (NQFs). In the European Commission, the Cluster on the Recognition of Learning Outcomes – the largest of the eight education and training clusters – supports countries in developing NQFs and systems for VNFIL. The cluster uses peer-learning activities to exchange good practice and channel collective efforts.

Several countries in Southeast Asia have called for more opportunities to learn from countries in the sub-region, such as Australia and New Zealand, who have extensive experience in accrediting and assessing non-formal and informal learning. This could be advocated as an agenda in the Association of South-East Asian Nations (ASEAN) and in the Southeast Asian Ministers of Education Organisation (SEAMEO) regional meetings.

As cross-border migration grows around the world, recognition across national borders becomes a pressing need. In Mexico, there are calls to support Mexican migrant workers through the recognition of their competences with a view to enhancing integration into the North American labour markets.

The recognition of learning gained outside the UK is also a theme in Scotland's higher education sector, particularly linked to internationalisation. A scoping study was undertaken by the SCQF Partnership, Glasgow Caledonian University, on behalf of Universities Scotland, Scotland's Colleges and Skills Development Scotland. The outcome was the presentation to the Scottish government of three sustainable recognition and support models for refugees and migrant workers, with potential transferability to other groups under-represented in education and employment (Guest and Vecchia 2010, in Whittaker 2011).

In Africa, the harmonisation of qualification frameworks is becoming an emerging issue in regional integration and the mutual recognition of qualifications is rapidly becoming a necessity. RVA is an important component in the Transnational Qualifications Framework (TQF) and TQF procedures and policies. In this context, Mauritius recommends that collaboration between all stakeholders be further strengthened not only locally, but also at the regional and international level. Consolidating the network to include countries which have implemented or wish to implement RVA would facilitate the collection of a considerable body of information to render the RVA system more effective.

Challenges in the Informal Economy

There are challenges specific to developing countries to which RVA policy, legislation and lifelong learning strategies need to respond. The first is skills recognition in the informal economy or informal sector. Arthur (2009) raises a number of issues regarding the planning and development of RVA for the informal economy in Bangladesh which are also relevant for other countries in a similar situation. While acknowledging that those countries which are yet to establish RVA procedures and their effective implementation face a difficult task, Arthur argues that the trend in many countries towards competence-based and learning outcomes-based systems will improve conditions for the acceptance of RVA processes. Secondly, he recommends, RVA needs to be embedded in policy, practices and funding from the outset, and priority areas need to be identified, such as the large non-formal education sector and the large number of skilled people without certification. Furthermore planning will be very important, and a relevant authority will need to take responsibility for this role (Arthur 2009). Such a process should be undertaken in collaboration with other key players such as government, industry, NGOs and social partners to ensure that a whole-of-sector approach is used. RVA information and support services should be actively promoted, easy to understand, recognise the diversity of participants and support participants with limited literacy skills. Other issues raised by Arthur (2009) are: linking RVA to NQFs; the marketing of RVA to ensure its uptake; whether any specific group (such as overseas workers) should be targeted initially to create a market process; industry needs as identified by industry skills committees; initial and on-going costs and funding; initial training of assessors and the sustainability of this process; procedures for the registration of RTOs; maintenance of a central register of qualifications; audit and moderation functions; and portfolio development.

In addition, writing in the context of RPL in South Africa, Michelson (2012) claims that RVA is essential to answer the need for a holistic analysis of workers' knowledge and skills as the basis for aligning education to social and economic development. Within this context, Michelson recommends: RVA mechanisms must be developed with clear and agreed-upon pathways from RVA to education and training and qualifications; accordingly, qualification and curriculum design must take account of the existing knowledge and skills of workers. RVA must go beyond technical approaches to skills auditing; rather it must become a mechanism to identify the best practices in mentoring, problem-solving and knowledge creation and how they can be used to inform and improve educational provision and to facilitate accreditation activities; the latter could be related to a few major industries or service sectors, such as engineering, health and construction sectors, but could also include informal horticulture and environmental protection (Michelson 2012).

Challenges in Non-formal Education

A great deal of non-formal second-chance education that takes place in the basic education and post-basic education still remains marginalised; often there are no proper frameworks to accredit non-formal education programmes; and education, vocational and occupational tracks are still separated. The study draws lessons on certain ways to recognise learning in non-formal education. Differentiating between different types of non-formal education and training could be a first step towards transforming non-formal education and training into a field of high-value educational opportunities providing real articulation and mobility. In the *first category* non-formal education is standardised through a curriculum with equivalence to formal education. Within the *second category* non-formal learning is integrated into an NQF and assessed against formal competence standards. The *third category* includes those non-formal learning programmes run by civil society organisations which are linked to community-based learning programmes, such as agricultural extension, citizenship education, health, family planning, civic education and mass media. They are frequently not seen as part of educational system, yet are an important part of personal development, livelihood and life skills and a positive alternative route to learning.

In response to the above challenges to the recognition of non-formal and informal learning, some strategic directions emerge from the country examples, particularly in relation to recognising learning outcomes in the context of community-based organisations. Firstly, countries emphasise the creation of *structures for coordinating RVA* for recognising competences and learning outcomes gained through public, private and NGO training that currently go unrecognised, including the role of local authorities in RVA implementation at provincial/territorial and local levels. Secondly, countries emphasise the establishment of *competence frameworks and alternative assessment methods* for assessing competences and learning outcomes in relation to the educational system, or sectoral and employability standards. Thirdly, they also emphasise the importance of improving the quality of non-formal learning outcomes through the establishment of *regulatory frameworks for quality* that include the development of new programmes and curricula that establish effective relationships between the workplace and educational institutions and between theoretical and applied aspects of education and training: Fourthly, the need for *professional development of community-based practitioners* has also emerged from the country examples. RVA personnel are essential to the building of bridges between non-formal, informal and formal learning. Greater recognition of RVA personnel's work as a profession, partly through the creation of quality standards and partly through further and higher education and training courses leading to recognised qualifications could enhance the quality of adult and community learning delivery as well as that of RVA. Fifthly, *accreditation mechanisms* are needed that take forward non-formal learning principles (active learning, voluntary nature of participation, socially inclusive approaches; democratic, empowering and humanistic functions.) into professional development courses for RVA personnel working in non-formal learning programmes. Finally, national authorities need to collaborate closely with NGOs to shape non-formal learning policy and practice.

7.1.4 Lessons and Issues

Critical lessons learnt with respect to the development and implementation of RVA policy and practice demonstrate the need for:

- high-level commitment by policy-makers, institutional leaders, stakeholders and practitioners at the federal, provincial/territorial and community levels;
- clear curricula and qualifications as the currency of learning;
- awareness-raising to highlight the benefits and opportunities of RVA to learners, employees, people not in education or employment, and employers;
- processes for RVA that do not hinder access for underprivileged people who lack educational opportunities;
- processes that can be trusted, are reliable and flexible, as well as rigour in terms of practitioner expertise, and funding models and pathways that ensure that participants save money;
- the provision of high-quality RVA information and support for candidates;
- the presence of strong links between the education sector and training sector, the world of work and civil society.

This study and the shift in priorities and practice in Member States have yielded valuable lessons with respect to the evolution of attitudes to learning outside formal settings; the growing willingness to think about this learning in terms of its various subsectors; and the critical nature of reference points such as qualifications, standards, curricula and frameworks against which this learning can be measured in meaningful and comparable ways. There is also a growing understanding that not all learning from non-formal and informal settings can be accredited against a set of predefined criteria, and yet such learning is clearly still important.

Most importantly, the debate over recent years confirms that RVA of non-formal and informal learning can and does play a key role in distributing the benefits of education and training – a central concern when considering disadvantaged individuals and countries. Examples from diverse contexts show that progress is being made.

Further exploration and implementation of RVA, particularly with respect to basic education and skills gained in the workplace and the informal economy would clearly have significant potential to assist with educational mobility and social and economic development. Each country summary sheds light on aspects of RVA mobility and equity that provides important learning for RVA policy, no matter what stage of education or learning reform a country has achieved. The different ways in which individuals gain a particular competence, reputation, or qualification to carry out their activities, are both varied and valid. It is critical therefore that the implementation of NQFs does not create a uniformity of approach that once again excludes the very people such systems are seeking to recognise and value.

The North-south approach has provided a unique and on-going opportunity to explore new ways of thinking about the social and economic space(s) that learning of all kinds can now inhabit. This approach has highlighted the relevance of recognition for developing countries, where access to education and training has been limited, where non-formal and informal sectors are vast, and where the enormous amount and richness of informal knowledge and wisdom are integral to the lifelong learning process practised by traditional and rural societies.

The study has emphasised that recognition is primarily about learner empowerment leading to personal development, employability and relevant qualifications in the building of a learning society. It is in this wider context that lifelong learning has its true meaning and in which recognition can open up a diversity of learning routes.

The study has stressed the importance of promoting inclusiveness in education and training. This is particularly pertinent with respect to the integration of literacy and adult basic education sectors within NQF recognition reforms. Countries are advised not to reduce non-formal and informal learning to a poor copy of formal education.

Both systemic and individual perspectives on recognition need to be united to open up the way to a more holistic and integrated approach. Systems of education need to be oriented towards the resources, capacities and motivation of individuals and groups, and not the other way round.

It has stressed the importance of global benchmarks, common issues and shared educational approaches, while at the same time taking account of the variety of contexts across countries. Keeping this debate open and continuing could have profound implications for making real equity gains for individuals and their prospects; for countries and their societal challenges; and for those interested in improved equity in education globally.

There are professionals in learning and training systems that are growing into the role of lifelong learning professionals. In these new roles, they will become the ambassadors of an open and accessible learning system that offers learning opportunities to all, and learning for any purpose in any context.

References

Aarts, S., Blower, D., Burke, R., Conlin, E., Ebner Howarth, C., Howell, B., Lamarre, G., & Van Kleef, J. (1999). *A slice of the iceberg: Cross-Canada study of prior learning assessment and recognition.* Toronto: Cross-Canada Partnership on Prior Learning Assessment and Recognition (PLAR).

Abrahamsson, K. (1989). Prior life experience and higher education. In C. J. Titmus (Ed.), *Lifelong education for adults: An international handbook* (pp. 162–167). Oxford: Pergamon Press.

Alfsen, C. (2014). Experiences with validation of prior learning in higher education in Norway. Developing guidelines for VPL towards exemptions in higher education. In R. Duvekot, B. Halba, K. Aagaard, S. Gabrscek, & J. Murray (Eds.), *The power of VPL: Validation of prior learning as a multi-targeted approach for access to learning opportunities for all.* Vught, The Netherlands: Inholland University and European Centre VPL.

Allais, S. (2010). *The implementation and impact of national qualifications frameworks: Report of a study in 16 countries.* Geneva: International Labour Organisation.

Allais, S. (2011). Using learning outcomes to make educational judgements: Some practical and conceptual issues. Bohlinger and Münchausen, op.cit., pp. 145–166.

Allgoo, K. (2013). The Mauritius model of recognition of prior learning (RPL). Singh and Duvekot, op.cit., pp. 55–63.

Almeida, M., et al. (2008). *Metodologia de acolhimento, diagnóstico e encaminhamento de adultos* (Centros Novas Oportunidades). Lisbon: National Qualifications Agency. (In Portuguese).

American Council on Education. (1981). *Guide to credit by examination.* Washington, DC: American Council on Education.

Andersen, B. M., & Aagaard, K. (2013). Denmark: The RVA-NQF linkage to lifelong learning. Singh and Duvekot, op.cit., pp. 149–156.

Andersen, M., & Laugesen, C. (2012). Recognition of prior learning within formal adult education in Denmark. *PLAIO: Prior Learning Inside Out, 1*(2). http://www.plaio.org/index.php/home/article/view/24. Accessed 23 Jan 2014.

Andersson, P., & Fejes, A. (2011). Sweden: The developing field of validation research. Harris, Breier and Wihak, op.cit., pp. 228–247.

Andersson, P., & Harris, J. (Eds.). (2006). *Re-theorising the recognition of prior learning.* Leicester: NIACE.

Andersson, P., Fejes, A., & Ahn, S.-E. (2004). Recognition of prior vocational learning in Sweden. *Studies in the Education of Adults, 36*(1), 57–71.

© UNESCO Institute for Lifelong Learning 2015
M. Singh, *Global Perspectives on Recognising Non-formal and Informal Learning,*
Technical and Vocational Education and Training: Issues, Concerns and Prospects 21,
DOI 10.1007/978-3-319-15278-3

Armsby, P. (2013). Developing professional learning and identity through the recognition of experiential learning at doctoral level. *International Journal of Lifelong Education, 32*(4), 412–429.

Arthur, J. (2009). *Recognition of prior learning. Interim report* (A Sub-component of Component 5. Increased access of underprivileged groups to TTVET). Dhaka: ILO. http://www.ilo.org/wcmsp5/groups/public/---asia/---ro-bangkok/---ilo-dhaka/documents/publication/wcms_122105.pdf. Accessed 14 Jan 2014.

Aspin, D. N., & Chapman, J. D. (2000). Lifelong learning: Concepts and conceptions. *International Journal of Lifelong Education, 19*(1), 2–19.

Atkin, C. (2000). Lifelong learning – Attitudes to practice in the rural context: A study using Bourdieu's perspective of habitus. *International Journal of Lifelong Education, 19*(3), 253–265.

Australia. Department of Education, Employment and Workplace Relations (DEEWR). (2008). *Development and state of the art of adult learning and education. National report of Australia.* (UNESCO's 6th international conference on Adult Education, CONFINTEA VI). Canberra: DEEWR. http://www.unesco.org/fileadmin/MULTIMEDIA/INSTITUTES/UIL/confintea/pdf/National_Reports/Asia%20-%20Pacific/Australia.pdf. Accessed 14 Jan 2014.

Australian Qualifications Framework Council. (2013, January). *Australian qualifications framework* (2nd ed.). Canberra: AQF Council.

Austria. Federal Ministry of Education, Arts and Culture. (2011). *Consultation questions on UNESCO guidelines for recognising all forms of learning with a focus on non-formal and informal learning.* Vienna: BMUKK, in Co-operation with 3s Unternehmensberatung Ltd.

Baartman, L., Prins, F., Kirschner, P., & Van der Vleuten, C. (2007). Determining the quality of competence assessment programs: A self-evaluation procedure. *Studies in Education Evaluation, 33*, 158–181.

Baffour-Awuah, D. (2013). Ghana: Integrating non-formal and informal learning in the new national TVET qualifications framework. Singh and Duvekot op.cit., pp. 49–54.

Baik, E. S. (2013). The Republic of Korea Academic Credit Bank and the lifelong learning system. Singh and Duvekot, op.cit., pp. 116–124.

Bamford-Rees, D. (2008). Thirty-five years of PLA: We've come a long way. In D. Hart & J. Hickerson (Eds.), *Prior learning portfolio: A representative collection* (pp. 1–10). Chicago: CAEL.

Bangladesh Ministry of Primary and Mass Education. (2008). *Development and state of the art of adult learning and education. National report of Bangladesh* (UNESCO's 6th international conference on adult education CONFINTEA VI). Dacca: MoPME.

Barros, R. (2013). The Portuguese case of RPL new practices and new adult educators: Some tensions and ambivalences in the framework of new public policies. *Education International Journal of Lifelong Education, 32*(4), 430–446.

Bassot, B. (2006). Constructing new understandings of career guidance: Joining the dots. In J. Bimrose & H. Reid (Eds.), *Constructing the future: Transforming career guidance.* Stourbridge: Institute of Career Guidance.

Bateman, A. (2006). Yes, we are there! Think piece. In S. McKenna & J. Mitchell (Eds.), *RPL – Done well in VET: Resources generated for the Reframing the Future national forums conducted in 2006.* Elizabeth: Department of Education, Science and Training – Reframing the Future. http://www.vta.vic.edu.au/docs/Skills%20Recognition/RPL+Done+Well+In+Vet-Reframing+the+Future.pdf. Accessed 16 Jan 2014.

Beck, U. (1992). *Risk society.* London: Sage.

Beinke, K., & Splittstößer, S. (2011). Validierung von Kompetenzen Geringqualifizierter: Rahmenbedingungen und zielgruppenspezifische Eignung bestehender Verfahren. Bohlinger and Münchausen, op.cit., pp. 369–388. (in German).

Bjørnåvold, J. (2000). *Making learning visible: Identification, assessment and recognition of non-formal learning in Europe.* Thessaloniki: CEDEFOP.

Blomqvist, C., & Louko, S. (2013). Finland: An outline of the national qualifications framework development and the recognition of prior learning. Singh and Duvekot, op.cit., pp. 157–162.

Bloom, M. (1984). *Taxonomy of educational objectives*. Boston: Pearson Education.

Bohlinger, S. (2007–2008). Competences as the core element of the European qualifications framework. *European Journal of Vocational Training 42/43*(2007/3, 2008/1), 96–112.

Bohlinger. (2011). Qualifications frameworks and learning outcomes: New challenges for European education and training policy and research. Bohlinger and Münchausen, op.cit., pp. 123–144.

Bohlinger, S., & Münchhausen, G. (Eds.). (2011). *Validierung von Lernergebnissen – Recognition and validation of prior learning*. Bonn: BIBB.

Bowen-Clewley, L., Farley, M., Rowe, R., & Russell, L. (2012). *So what does "being qualified" really mean? A critical perspective on a growing trend of "credentialism" and its relevance in workplaces in 21st century*. Wellington: Competency International Ltd. http://www.iaea.info/documents/paper_1162a3122.pdf. Accessed 28 May 2012.

Bowman, B., Bateman, A., Knight, B., Thomson, P., Hargreaves, J., Blom, K., & Enders, M. (2003). *Recognition of prior learning in the vocational education and training sector*. Adelaide: NCVER.

Boyle, A. (2008). *Enabling e-portfolios for skills recognition of aboriginal art workers in central Australia*. Australian Vocational Education and Training Research Association Conference, Adelaide, Australia. http://www.avetra.org.au/papers-2009/papers/55.00.pdf. Accessed 14 Jan 2014.

Brandstetter, G., & Luomi-Messerer, K. (2010). *European inventory on validation of non-formal and informal learning 2010. Country report: Austria* (European Commission, DG Education and Culture, in cooperation with CEDEFOP). London: GHK Consulting.

Brockmann, M. (2011). Higher Education qualifications: Convergence and divergence in software engineering and nursing. Brockmann, Clarke, Winch, Hanf, Méhaut and Westerhuis, op.cit., pp. 120–135.

Brockmann, M., Clarke, L., Winch, C., Hanf, G., Méhaut, P., & Westerhuis, A. (Eds.). (2011a). *Knowledge, skills and competence in the European labour market: What's in a vocational qualification?* London: Routledge.

Brockmann, M., Clarke, L., Winch, C., Hanf, G., Méhaut, P., & Westerhuis, A (Eds.). (2011b). Introduction: Cross-national equivalence or skills and qualifications across Europe. Brockmann, Clarke, Winch, Hanf, Méhaut and Westerhuis, op.cit., pp. 1–21.

Brookfield, S. D. (1986). *Understanding and facilitating adult learning: A comprehensive analysis of principles and effective practices*. Milton-Keynes: Open University Press.

Brundage, D., & Mackeracher, D. (1980). *Adult learning principles and their application to planning*. Toronto: Ministry of Education.

Butterworth, C. (1992). More than one bite at the APEL. *Journal of Further and Higher Education, 16*(3), 39–51.

Cabrera, A. M. (2010). *Qualifications frameworks: Implementation and impact. Background case study on Chile*. Geneva: Skills and Employability Department, ILO.

Cambodia. Ministry of Education, Youth and Sport (MoEYS). (2008). *New trend and present situation of adult learning and education. National report of Cambodia* (UNESCO's 6th International Conference on Adult Education, CONFINTEA VI). Hamburg: UNESCO Institute for Lifelong Learning. http://www.unesco.org/fileadmin/MULTIMEDIA/INSTITUTES/UIL/confintea/pdf/National_Reports/Asia%20-%20Pacific/Cambodia.pdf. Accessed 16 Jan 2014.

Cameron, R. (2004). *RPL and the mature-age job seekers*. Prepared for *Adult Learning Australia*. Melbourne: Adult Learning Australia.

Cameron R. (2006). RPL and the disengaged learner: The need for new starting points. Andersson and Harris, op.cit., pp. 117–140.

Cameron, R. (2009). A career and learning transitions model for those experiencing labour market disadvantage. *Australian Journal of Career Development, 18*(1), 17–25.

Cameron R. (2011). Australia: An overview of 20 years of research into the recognition of prior learning (RPL). Harris, Breier and Wihak, op.cit., pp. 14–43.

Campero Cuenca, C., Hernández Flores, G., Klesing-Rempel, U., Méndez Puga, A. N., Ruiz Munoz, M., Arévalo Guizar, G., Guzmán Máximo, G., Fernández Zayas, C., & Mendieta Ramos, M. (2008). *El desarrolo y el estado de la cuestión sobre el aprendizaje y la educación de adultos (AEA). Documento complementario de México* (UNESCO's 6th international conference on adult education, CONFINTEA VI). Hamburg: UNESCO Institute for Lifelong Learning. (In Spanish).

Canadian Council on Learning. (2007). *State of learning in Canada: No time for complacency.* Ottawa: CCL.

Canadian Council of Ministers of Education (CMEC). (2007). *OECD activity: Recognition of non-formal and informal learning (RNFIL).* Report on provincial/territorial activities and pan-Canadian overview. Ottawa: Council of Ministers of Education.

Canadian Council of Ministers of Education (CMEC) and the Canadian Commission for UNESCO. (2008). *Development and state of the art of adult learning and education. National report of Canada* (UNESCO's 6th international conference on adult education, CONFINTEA VI). Ottawa: CMEC and the Canadian National Commission for UNESCO.

Carrigan, J., & Downes, P. (with I Byrne). (2010). *Is there more than what's the score? Exploring needs and skills checking for literacy as part of a holistic initial assessment process in a lifelong learning society.* Dublin: Educational Disadvantage Centre, St. Patrick's College Drumcondra. http://main.spd.dcu.ie/main/academic/edc/documents/Soistheremorethanwhatsthescore.pdf. Accessed 14 Jan 2014.

Castells, M. (1996). *The rise of the network society* (Vol. 1). Oxford: Basil Blackwell.

Castro-Mussot, L. M., & de Anda, M. L. (2007). Mexico's national adult education programme. Singh and Castro-Mussot, op.cit., pp. 117–139.

CEDEFOP. (2007). *European inventory on validation of informal and non-formal learning.* Birmingham: ECOTEC Research and Consulting Ltd.

CEDEFOP. (2008). *How can the EQF and national qualifications frameworks facilitate the validation of non-formal and informal learning?* (Workshop 2. Implementing the European qualifications framework conference, Brussels, 3–4 June). Brussels: CEDEFOP.

CEDEFOP. (2009). *European guidelines for validating non-formal and informal learning.* Luxembourg: Office for Official Publications of the European Union.

CEDEFOP. (2012). *Development of national qualifications frameworks in Europe October 2011* (Working paper no. 12). Luxembourg: Office for Official Publications of the European Union.

Chisholm, L., & Hoskins, B. (2005). Introduction: Tracks and tools for trading up in non-formal learning. *Trading up: Potential and performance non-formal learning.* Strasbourg: Council of Europe.

Christensen, H. (2013). Norway: Linking validation of prior learning to the formal qualifications system. Singh and Duvekot, op.cit., pp. 175–183.

Coleman, J. (1988). Social capital in the creation of human capital. *American Journal of Sociology, 94*(Suppl.), S95–S120.

Coleman, J. (1994). *Foundations of social theory.* Harvard: Harvard University Press.

Colley, H., Hodkinson, P., & Malcolm, J. (2003). *Informality and formality in learning: A report for the learning and skills research centre.* Leeds: University of Leeds.

Commonwealth of Learning. (2010). *Transnational qualifications framework for the Virtual University of Small States of the Commonwealth: Procedures and guidelines – April 2010.* Vancouver: COL. http://www.col.org/PublicationDocuments/pub_VUSSC_TransnationalQualificationsFramework_April2010_web.pdf. Accessed 14 Jan 2014.

Competency International Limited. (2011). *Ensuring consistency of qualification outcomes: A discussion paper.* Wellington: Competency International Ltd. http://www.nzqa.govt.nz/assets/Studying-in-NZ/New-Zealand-Qualification-Framework/consistency-qual-outcomes.pdf. Accessed 10 July 2011.

Comyn, P. (2009, September). Vocational qualification frameworks in Asia-Pacific: A cresting wave of educational reform? *Research in Post-Compulsory Education, 14*(3), 251–268.

Council on Adult and Experiential Learning. (2000). *Serving adult learners in higher education: Principles of effectiveness- executive summary.* Chicago: CAEL.

Council of the European Union. (2004). *Draft Conclusions of the Council and of the representatives of the Governments of the Member States meeting within the Council on Common European Principles of the identification and validation of informal and non-formal learning.* Brussels: European Commission.http://www2.cedefop.europa.eu/etv/Information_resources/EuropeanInventory/publications/principles/validation2004_en.pdf. Accessed 17 Jan 2014.

Council of the European Union. (2012). *Council Recommendations of 20 December 2012 on the validation of non-formal and informal learning* (2012/C 398/01). http://eur-lex.europa.eu/LexUriServ/LexUriServ.do?uri=OJ:C:2012:398:0001:0005:EN:PDF. Accessed 24 July 2014.

Crooks, T. J., Kane, M. T., & Cohen, A. S. (1996). Threats to the valid use of assessments. *Assessment in Education: Principles, Policy and Practice, 3*(3), 265–285.

Cropley, A. J. (Ed.). (1979). *Lifelong education: Stocktaking.* Hamburg: UNESCO Institute of Education (UIE).

Day, M., & Zakos, P. (2000). *Developing benchmarks for prior learning assessment and recognition. Practitioner perspectives: Guidelines for the Canadian PLAR practitioner.* Belleville: Human Resources Canada and CAPLA.

Delors, J. (1996). *Learning: The treasure within.* Report to UNESCO of the International Commission on Education for the Twenty-first Century. Paris: UNESCO.

Denmark. Institute for Evaluation (EVA). (2010). *Anerkendelse af realkompetencer på VEU-området mv.* København: Danish Evaluation Institute. http://www.eva.dk/projekter/2010/undersoegelse-af-udmoentningen-af-lovgivningen-om-anerkendelse-af-realkompetencer-paa-veu-omraadet/rapport/anerkendelse-af-realkompetencer-paa-veu-omraadet-mv/download. Accessed 14 Jan 2014. (In Danish).

Denmark. Ministry of Education (UVM). (2007). *Denmark's strategy for lifelong learning: Education and lifelong skills upgrading for all. Report to the European Commission.* Copenhagen: Undervisningsministeriet.

Denmark. Ministry of Education (UVM). (2008). *Development and state of the art of adult learning and education. National report of Denmark* (UNESCO's 6th international conference on adult education, CONFINTEA VI). Copenhagen: Undervisningsministeriet.

Denmark. Statens Center for Kompetenceudvikling. (2010). *Statens Center for Kompetenceudvikling* (Centre for Development of Human Resources and Quality Management). København: SCKK. www.kompetenceudvikling.dk. Accessed 14 Jan 2014. (In Danish).

Depover, C. (2006). *Conception et pilotage des réformes du curriculum.* Paris: UNESCO. http://unesdoc.unesco.org/images/0015/001511/151154f.pdf. Accessed 7 Oct 2013. (In French).

Dewey, J. (1925). *Experience and nature.* New York: Open Court (1929 Rev.). London: George Allen and Unwin.

Dewey, J. (1966). *Democracy and education.* New York: Free Press (originally published 1916, New York: Macmillan).

Diarra Keita, M. (2006). *Processes, approaches and pedagogies in literacy programmes: Case study on the experience of the Institute for Popular Education* (ADEA Biennale on education, Gabon, March 27–31). Paris: International Institute for Educational Planning.

Downes, P. (2011). *A systems level focus on access to education for traditionally marginalised groups in Europe* (LLL 2010 SP5 comparative report for the EU Commission). Dublin: Educational Disadvantage Centre. St Patrick's College.

Downes, T., & Downes, P. (2007). Pedagogy of the processed. In P. Downes & A. L. Gilligan (Eds.), *Beyond educational disadvantage* (pp. 24–38). Dublin: Institute for Public Administration.

Duke, C. (2001). Lifelong learning and tertiary education: The learning university revisited. In D. Aspin, J. Chapman, M. Hatton, & Y. Sawano (Eds.), *International handbook of lifelong learning* (pp. 501–528). Dordrecht/Boston/London: Kluwer Academic Publishers.

Duvekot, R. (2010). *European inventory on validation of non-formal and informal learning 2010. Country report: Netherlands* (European Commission, DG Education and Culture, in cooperation with CEDEFOP). London: GHK Consulting.

Duvekot, R. (2014). Breaking ground for validation of prior learning in lifelong learning strategies. In R. Duvekot, B. Halba, K. Aagaard, S. Gabrscek, & J. Murray (Eds.), *The power of VPL:*

Validation of prior learning as a multi-targeted approach for access to learning opportunities for all. Vught, The Netherlands: Inholland University and European Centre VPL.

Duvekot, R., & Konrad, J. (2007, June 22–24). Towards a transnational concept of valuing lifelong learning: Some practical reflections on developing theory. In *International Conference for Research in Lifelong Learning* (CRLL). Stirling: University of Stirling.

Duvekot, R., Kaemingk, E., & Pijls, T. (2003). *The world of EVC: The application of EVC in the Netherlands in four spheres.* Utrecht: Kenniscentrum Erkenning van Competenties.

Dyson, C., & Keating, J. (2005). *Recognition of prior learning: Policy and practice for skills learned at work* (Skills working paper no. 21). Geneva: Skills and Employability Department.

Eagles, D., Woodward, P., & Pope, M. (2005). Indigenous learners in the digital age: Recognising skills and knowledge. In *Proceedings of the 8th Australian Vocational Education and Training Research Association (AVETRA) Conference: Emerging Futures – Recent, Responsive and Relevant Research.* Brisbane: AVETRA. https://avetra.org.au/documents/PA045Eagles.pdf. Accessed 16 Jan 2014.

Ecuador Ministerio de Educacion. (2008). *El Desarollo y el estado de la cuestion sobre el aprendizaje y la educacion de adultos: Ecuador national report* (UNESCO's 6th international conference on adult education, CONFINTEA V). Quito: Funcionarios Direccion Nacional de Educacion Popular Permanente (DINEPP). (In Spanish).

Eraut, M. (2004). Informal learning in the workplace. *Studies in Continuing Education, 26*(2), 247–273.

Eraut, M., Alderton, J., Cole, G., & Senker, P. (2000). Development of knowledge and skills at work. In F. Coffield (Ed.), *Differing visions of a learning society: Research findings* (Vol. 1, pp. 231–262). Bristol: Policy Press.

Eriksen, E. O. (1995). *Deliberativ politick. Demokrati I teori og praksis.* Tano: Bergen. (In Norwegian).

Ethiopia. Ministry of Education. (2006). *National Adult Education Strategy.* Addis Ababa: Ministry of Education. http://www.moe.gov.et/English/Resources/Documents/Adult%20Edu.%20Eng.pdf. Accessed 15 Jan 2014.

European Commission. (2001). *Making a European area of lifelong learning a reality.* Brussels: European Commission.

European Commission. (2004). *Education and training 2010: The success of the Lisbon strategy hinges on urgent reform.* Brussels: Council of the European Union.

European Commission. (2008). *The European qualifications framework for lifelong learning (EQF).* Luxembourg: Office for Official Publications of the European Communities.

Europlacement. (2010). *Expertising and sharing lifelong guidance for the placement (LLP-LDV/TOI/08/IT/460). Report on external evaluation.* Bologna: University of Bologna.

Faure, E., Herrera, F., Kadoura, A., Lopes, H., Petrovsky, A. V., Rahnema, M., & Ward, C. (1972). *Learning to be: The world of education today and tomorrow.* Paris: UNESCO.

Fenwick, T. (2006). Reconfiguring RPL and its assumptions: A complexified view. Andersson and Harris, op.cit., pp. 283–300.

Feutrie, M. (2008). The recognition of individual experience in a lifelong learning perspective: Validation of non-formal and informal learning in France. *Lifelong Learning in Europe (LLinE), 13*(3), 164–171.

Fiddler, M., Marienau, C., & Whitaker, U. (2006). *Assessing learning: Standards, principles and procedures* (2nd ed.). Chicago: CAEL.

Finland. Ministry of Education (Opetusministeriö). (2008). *Development and state of the art of adult learning and education: National report of Finland* (UNESCO's 6th international conference on adult education. CONFINTEA VI). Hamburg: UIL.

France. Ministry of Employment and Solidarity. (2002). *Social modernization law of 2002.* Paris: Ministry of Employment and Solidarity.

France. National Commission for UNESCO. (2005). *Recognition of experiential learning: An international analysis* (Conference proceedings, September 2005). Paris: UNESCO.

France. National Commission for UNESCO. (2007). *Recognition of experiential learning: Prospects for development in African countries* (Conference proceedings, 25–27 June). Paris: UNESCO.

Frank, I. (2011). Kompetenzorientierung in der Berufsbildung: Anforderung an Prüfungen. Bohlinger and Münchausen, op.cit., pp. 425–441.

Frommberger, D., & Krichewsky, L. (2012). Comparative analysis of vocational education and training curricula in Europe. In M. Pilz (Ed.), *Future of vocational education and training in a changing world* (pp. 235–255). Wiesbaden: VS Verlag für Sozialwissenschaften and Springer.

Gagné, R. M. (1973). *The conditions of learning*. New York: Holt, Rinehart and Winston.

Gallacher, J., & Feutrie, M. (2003). Recognising and accrediting informal and non-formal learning in higher education: An analysis of the issues emerging from a study of France and Scotland. *European Journal of Education, 38*(1), 71–83.

Ganzglass, E., Bird, K., & Prince, H. (2011). *Giving credit when credit is due: Creating a competency-based qualifications framework for post-secondary education and training.* Washington, DC: Center for Post-secondary and Economic Success (CLASP).

García-Bullé, S. (2013). Mexico. National System of Competence Standards (NSCS). Singh and Duvekot, op.cit., pp. 197–206.

Germany. Federal Ministry for Economic Co-operation and Development. (2012). *Ten objectives for more education: BMZ education strategy 2010–2013* (BMZ strategy paper 1). Bonn: BMZ.

Germany. Federal Ministry of Education and Science. (2008). *Status of recognition of non-formal and informal learning in Germany within the framework of the OECD activity 'Recognition of Informal and Non-formal Learning (RNFIL)'.* Bonn: BMBF.

Germany. Federal Ministry of Education and Science and Standing Conference of the Ministers of Education and Cultural Affairs of the Länder in the Federal Republic of Germany. (2008). *Development and the state of the art of adult learning and education: National report of Germany* (UNESCO's 6th international conference on adult education, CONFINTEA VI). Bonn: German National Commission for UNESCO, in Cooperation with BMBF and KMK. http://www.unesco.org/fileadmin/MULTIMEDIA/INSTITUTES/UIL/confintea/pdf/National_Reports/Europe%20-%20North%20America/Germany_Final__German_English_29102008.pdf. Accessed 14 Jan 2014.

Germany. Federal Ministry of Education and Science and Standing Conference of the Ministers of Education and Cultural Affairs of the Länder in the Federal Republic of Germany. (2012). *Draft bill to improve the assessment and recognition of Foreign professional qualifications.* Bonn: BMBF. http://www.bmbf.de/pubRD/anerkennungsgesetz.pdf. Accessed 17 Jan 2014. (In German).

Germany. National Commission for UNESCO. (2011). *Country report on consultation on UNESCO guidelines for the recognition, validation and accreditation (RVA) of the outcomes of non-formal and informal learning.* Bonn: BMBF and KMK and the German National Commission for UNESCO.

Gerzer-Sass, A. (2001). Familienkompetenzen als Potenzial einer innovativen Personalpolitik. In C. Leipert (Ed.), *Familie als Beruf: Arbeitsfled der Zukunft.* Opladen: Leske and Budrich.

Gerzer-Sass, A. (2005). Family skills as a potential of innovative human resources development. In L. Chisholm, B. Hoskins, & C. Glahn (Eds.), *Trading up: Potential and performance in non-formal learning.* Strasbourg: Council of Europe.

Gibbs, P., & Angelides, P. (2004). Accreditation of knowledge as being-in-the-world. *Journal of Education and Work, 17*(3), 333–346.

Giddens, A. (1991). *Modernity and self-identity: Self and society in the late modern age.* Cambridge: Polity.

Gomes, M. (2013). Portugal: Formalising non-formal and informal learning. Singh and Duvekot, op.cit., pp. 184–95.

Gomes, P., Coimbra, J. L., & Menezes, I. (2007). Individual change towards empowerment in adult education and training (ESRA 2007 European Research Conference, 20–23 September). Seville: University of Seville.

Gomes, M., & Rodrigues, S. (2007). *Cursos de educação e formação de adultos – Nível Secundário: orientações para a acção*. Lisbon: National Qualifications Agency. (In Portuguese).

Gomes, M., & Simões, F. (2007). *Carta de qualidade dos centros novas oportunidades*. Lisbon: National Qualifications Agency. (In Portuguese).

Govers, E. (2010). On the impact of government policy on programme design in New Zealand post-compulsory education. *Research in Post-compulsory Education, 15*(2), 141–158.

Guest, P., & Vecchia, M. (2010). *Scoping study on support mechanism for the recognition of the skills, learning and qualifications of migrant workers and refugees* (Final Report). Glasgow: SCQFP.

Guimarães, P. (2009). Políticas públicas de educação de adultos em Portugal: diversos sentidos para o direito à educação? *Rizoma freireano* 3. http://www.rizoma-freireano.org/index.php/politicas-publicas. Accessed 14 Jan 2014. (In Portuguese).

Guimarães, P. (2012). Critical links between recognition of prior learning, economic changes and social justice in Portugal. *Journal of Adult and Continuing Education, 18*(1), 61–76.

Guthu, L., & Bekkevold, K. (2010). *The Vox Mirror 2009: Key figures on adult participation in education and training in Norway*. Oslo: Vox.

Hager, P., & Halliday, J. (2009). *Recovering informal learning: Wisdom, judgement and community*. Dordrecht: Springer.

Haldane, A., & Wallace, J. (2009). Using technology to facilitate the accreditation of prior and experiential learning in developing personalised work-based learning programmes: A case study involved in the University of Derby, UK. *European Journal of Education, 44*(3, Part 1), 369–383.

Hall, C. (1995). University qualifications and the NZQA framework. In R. Peddie & B. Tuck (Eds.), *Setting the standards* (pp. 154–176). Palmerston North: Dunmore Press.

Hargreaves, J. (2006). *Recognition of prior learning: At a glance*. Adelaide: NCVER.

Harris, J. (1999). Ways of seeing the recognition of prior learning: What contribution can such practices make to social inclusion? *Studies in the Education of Adults, 31*(2), 124–139.

Harris, J. (2000). *Recognition of prior learning: Power, pedagogy and possibility*. Pretoria: HSRC.

Harris, J. (2006). Questions of knowledge and curriculum in the recognition of prior learning. Andersson and Harris, op.cit., pp. 51–76.

Harris, J., Breier, M., & Wihak, C. (2011). *Researching the recognition of prior learning: International perspectives*. Leicester: NIACE.

Hawley, J. (2010). *European inventory on validation of non-formal and informal learning 2010: Country report UK (England, Wales and Northern Ireland)* (European Commission, DG Education and Culture, in cooperation with CEDEFOP). London: GHK Consulting.

Higher Education Funding Council for England. (2007). Allocation of additional student numbers in 2008–09 for employer engagement. *Circular Letter Number 03/2007*. Accessed 15 Jan 2014.

Hoffman, T., Travers, N. L., Evans, M., & Treadwell, A. (2009, September). Researching critical factors impacting PLA programs: A multi-institutional study on best practices. *CAEL Forum and News*

Hoppers, W. (2005). Community schools as educational alternative in Africa: A critique. *International Review of Education, 51*(2), 115–137.

Hoppers, W. (2006). *Non-formal education and basic education reform: A conceptual review*. Paris: IIEP. http://unesdoc.unesco.org/images/0014/001444/144423e.pdf. Accessed 14 Jan 2014.

IADIS. (2012). Proceedings of the International Association for Development of the Information Society (IADIS). In *International conference on cognition and exploratory learning in digital age (CELDA)*. Madrid, Spain, 19–12 October 2012.

Iceland. Ministry of Education, Science and Culture. (2008). *The Icelandic national curriculum guide for compulsory schools. General section*. Reykjavik: Ministry of Education, Culture and Science.

ILO. (2004). *R195 Human resources development recommendation, 2004:* Recommendation concerning human resources development: Education, training and lifelong learning. Geneva: ILO.

INE. (2007). *Inquérito à educação e formação de adultos: IEFA*. Lisbon: Portuguese National Statistics Institute. (In Portuguese).

Jackson, W. (1987). *Altars of unhewn stone*. San Francisco: North Point Press.

Japan. Ministry of Education, Culture, Sports, Science and Technology. (2008). *Development and state of the art of adult learning and education. National report of Japan* (UNESCO's 6th international conference on adult education, CONFINTEA VI). Tokyo: MEXT.

Jarvis, P. (2008). The consumer society: Is there a place for traditional adult education? *Convergence, XLI*(1), 11–27.

Jokinen, E. (2010). *European inventory on validation of non-formal and informal learning 2010. From mass adult VET towards tailor-made VET – The specialist qualification in competence-based qualifications, Finland* (European Commission, DG Education and Culture, in cooperation with CEDEFOP). London: GHK Consulting.

Keevy, J. (2012). *A coordinating mechanism for the recognition of prior learning in South Africa* (Canadian Association for Prior Learning Assessment conference 21–23 October). Halifax: CAPLA.

Keevy, J., Charraud, A.-M., & Allgoo, K. (2012). *National qualifications frameworks developed in Anglo-Saxon and French traditions. Considerations for sustainable development in Africa* (ADEA Triennale on education and training in Africa, Ouagadougou, Burkina Faso, February 14–19). Tunis: Agency for the Development of Education in Africa.

Keller, A. (2013). New Zealand Qualifications Framework and support to lifelong learning. Singh and Duvekot, op.cit., pp. 131–141.

Kennedy, B. (2014). Canada: Country Profile. *UIL global observatory of recognition, validation and accreditation of non-formal and informal learning*. Hamburg: UIL.

Kirk, J. (Ed.). (2009). *Certification counts: Recognising the learning attainments of displaced and refugee students*. Paris: International Institute for Educational Planning.

Klein-Collins, R. (2007). *Prior learning assessment. Current policy and practice in the US: A preliminary report*. Chicago: Council for Adult and Experiential Learning (CAEL). http://www.pcc.edu/edserv/eac/assessment/documents/CAEL-PLA-CurrentPolicyandPracticeintheUS.pdf. Accessed 16 Jan 2014.

Klein-Collins, R. (2010). *Fueling the race to postsecondary success: A 48-institution study of prior learning assessment and adult student outcomes*. Chicago: CAEL.

Knoll, J. (2006). Informal adult education: Between formal qualifications and competences. *Adult Education and Development, 66*, 263–274.

Knowles, M. (1970). *The modern practice of adult education*. Chicago: Follett.

Knowles, M. (1975). *Self-directed learning: A guide for learners and teachers*. New York: Cambridge Adult Education.

Knowles, M. (1990). *The adult learner: A neglected species: Building blocks of human potential* (3rd ed.). Houston: Gulf Publishing Co.

Koch, M., & Strasser, P. (2008). Der Kompetenzbegriff. Kritik einer neuen Bildungsleitsemantik. In M. Koch & P. Strasser (Eds.), *In der Tat kompetent. Zum Verständnis von Kompetenz und Tätigkeit in der beruflichen Benachteiligtenförderung* (pp. 25–52). Bielefeld: Bertelsmann.

Kolb, D. (1984). *Experiential learning: Experience as the source of learning and development*. Englewood Cliff: Prentice Hall.

Kurtz, J. (2007). *Life skills-based education in secondary school foreign language classrooms: Cornerstone of a challenging vision* (International research symposium 'Looking ahead with curiosity: Visions of languages in education', 28 April–1 May). Frankfurt am Main: Goethe-Universität.

Laird, J. D. (2007). *Feeling. The perception of self*. Oxford: Oxford University Press.

Lave, J., & Wenger, E. (1991). *Situated learning: Legitimate peripheral participation*. Cambridge: Cambridge University Press.

Livingstone, D. W. (2001). *'Adults' informal learning: Definitions, findings, gaps and future research'. Centre for the Study of Education and Work* (New Approaches to Lifelong Learning (NALL) working paper 21). Toronto: Ontario Institute for the Study in Education – Advisory

Panel of Experts on Adult Learning (APEAL), Applied Research Branch, Human Resource Development, Canada.

Livingstone, D. W. (2005). Expanding conception of work and learning: Research and policy implications. In K. Leithwood, D. W. Livingstone, A. Cumming, N. Bascia, & A. Datnow (Eds.), *International handbook of educational policy* (pp. 977–996). New York: Kluwer Publishers.

Livingstone, D. W., & Guile, D. (Eds.). (2012). *The knowledge economy and lifelong learning: A critical reader*. Rotterdam: Sense Publishers.

Livingstone, D. W., & Sawchuk, P. H. (2004). *Hidden knowledge. Organized labor in the information age*. Toronto: Garamond Press.

Lloyd, S. (2012). A brief overview of the current legislation in South Africa which impacts on recognition of prior learning. *SAQA Bulletin, 12*(3), 35–52.

Lohmar, B., & Eckhardt, T. (2011). *The education system in the federal republic of Germany 2010/2011: A description of the responsibilities, structures and developments in education policy for the exchange of information in Europe*. Bonn: Secretariat of the Standing Conference of the Ministers of Education and Cultural Affairs of the Länder in the Federal Republic of Germany (KMK).

MacIntyre, A. (1981). *After virtues*. London: Duckworth.

Maes, M. (2008). *Valuing learning in the Netherlands: Landmarks on the road for accreditation of prior learning*. Hertogenbosch: CINOP Advisory.

Maher, K., Davies, L., Harris, R., & Short, T. (2010). *Scoping the potential of skills recognition in rail: Final report, March 2010*. Brisbane: CRC for Rail Innovation Education and Training Programme.

Maldives. Centre for Continuing Education. (2009). *Centre for continuing education.*www.cce.edu.mv. Accessed 14 Aug 2012.

Markowitsch, J., Benda-Kahri, S., Prokopp, M., Rammel, S., & Hefler, G. (2008). *Neuausrichtung der berufsbildenden Schulen für Berufstätige: Eine Studie im Auftrag des BMUKK* (Studies in lifelong learning, Vol. 7). Krems: Donau-Universität Krems. (In German).

Mckenzie, P. (1998). *Lifelong learning as a policy response*. Australian Council for Educational Research (ACER). Centre for the Economics of Education and Training (CEET). http://research.acer.edu.au/ceet/6

McKay, V., & Romm, N. (2006). *The NQF and its implementation in non-formal education: With special reference to South Africa, Namibia, Botswana and Kenya* (ADEA biennial). Paris: IIEP.

Messick, S. (1989). Validity. In R. L. Linn (Ed.), *Educational measurement* (3rd ed., pp. 13–103). New York: Macmillan.

Michelson, E. (1998). Remembering: The return of the body to experiential learning. *Studies in Continuing Education, 20*(2), 2017–2033.

Michelson, E. (2006). Beyond Galileo's telescope: Situated knowledge and the recognition or prior learning. Andersson and Harris, op.cit., pp. 141–162.

Michelson, E. (2012). Report and recommendation to the South African Qualifications Authority based on international models of the recognition of prior learning. *SAQA Bulletin, 12*(3), 11–33.

Miles, M. B., & Huberman, A. M. (1994). *Qualitative data analysis: A sourcebook of new methods* (2nd ed.). Thousand Oaks: Sage.

Miller, A. (2009). The world of e-portfolio. *The Knowledge Tree*, (E-Journal of Learning Innovation, Edition 18). Australian Flexible Learning Framework. Melbourne: Australian Government.

Mitchell, J., & Gronold, J. (2009). *Increasing the confidence of advanced RPL assessors*. Paper presented at the 12th Australian Vocational Education and Training Research Association Conference, Sydney. http://www.avetra.org.org.au/papers-2009/papers/35.00pdf. Accessed 16 Jan 2014.

Mitra, S., Dangwal, R., Chatterjee, S., Jha, S., Bisht, R. S., & Kapur, P. (2005). Acquisition of computer literacy on shared public computers: Children and the "Hole in the wall". *Australasian Journal of Educational Technology, 21*(3): 407–426. www.ascilite.org.au/ajet/ajet21/mitra.html. Accessed 14 Jan 2014.

Morrey, L., & Drowley, S. (2005). Quality assurance of youth work initial professional training in England. In L. Chisholm, B. Hoskins with C. Glahn (Eds.), *Trading up: Potential and performance in non-formal learning*. Strasbourg: Council of Europe.

Morrissey, M., Myers, D., Bélanger, P., Robitaille, M., Davison, P., Van Kleef, J., & Williams, R. (2008). *Achieving our potential: An action plan for prior learning and recognition (PLAR) in Canada*. Ottawa: Canadian Council on Learning.

Münchhausen, G. (2011). Chancen der Validierung informellen Lernens im Rahmen atypischer Beschäftigung. In S. Bohlinger & G. Münchausen (Eds.), *Validierung von Lernergebnissen: Recognition and validation of prior learning* (pp. 407–424). Bonn: Bundesinstitut für Berufsbildung.

Murangi, H. (2013). Namibia: Challenges of implementing the RPL policy. Singh and Duvekot, op.cit., pp. 55–63.

Naik, J. P. (1977). *Some perspectives on non-formal education. Alternatives in development education*. Bombay: Allied Publishers.

Namibia. Government of the Republic of Namibia. (1996). *Namibia qualifications authority act, Act 29 of 1996*. Windhoek: Government Printers.

Namibia. Ministry of Education. (2009). *Draft national policy on recognition of prior learning*. Windhoek: Government Printers.

Namibian College of Open Learning. (2008). *Policy on recognition of prior learning*. Windhoek: NAMCOL.

National Survey of Student Engagement (NSSE). (2003). *Converting data into action: Expanding the boundaries of institutional improvement*. Bloomington: Centre for Postsecondary Research, Indiana University.

New Zealand Government. (1989). *Education Act 1989*.http://www.legislation.govt.nz/act/public/1989/0080/latest/DLM175959.html. Accessed 16 Jan 2014.

New Zealand. Ministry of Education. (2008). *Development and state of the art of adult learning and education. National report of New Zealand* (UNESCO's 6th international conference on adult education, CONFINTEA VI). Hamburg: UIL.

New Zealand Qualifications Authority (NZQA). (2002). *Supporting learning pathways: Credit recognition and transfer policy*. Wellington: NZQA.

New Zealand Qualifications Authority (NZQA). (2011). *The New Zealand qualifications framework* (Version 2.0). Wellington: NZQA.

Norway. Confederation of Trade Unions and Confederation of Norwegian Enterprise. (2009). *Basic agreement 2010–2013 LO – NHO with supplementary agreements*. Oslo: LO and NHO.

Norway. Ministry of Education and Research. (2007). *Strategy for lifelong learning in Norway: Status, challenges and areas of priority* (Report). Oslo: RNMER.

OECD. (2007). *Qualifications systems: Bridges to lifelong learning*. Paris: OECD.

OECD. (2008). *Recognition of non-formal and informal learning: Country note for Canada. Group of national experts on the recognition of non-formal and informal learning*. Paris: OECD.

OECD. (2010). *Recognition of non-formal and informal learning: Country practices*. Paris: OECD.

OECD. (2011). *Education at a glance 2011*. Paris: OECD.

Ogawa, A. (2009, September-October). Japan's new lifelong learning policy: Exploring lessons from the European knowledge economy. *International Journal of Lifelong Education, 28*(5), 601–614.

Otero, M. S., Hawley, J., & Duchemin, C. (2010). *European inventory on validation of non-formal and informal learning. Final report: Executive summary* (European Commission, Directorate-General for Education and Culture, in co-operation with CEDEFOP). London: GHK Consultancy.

Panda, S. (2011). Continuing education and lifelong learning in the Indian sub-continent: Critical reflections. *International Journal of Continuing Education ad Lifelong Learning, 4*(1), 25–28.

Paulet, M.-O. (2013). France: The validation of acquired experience (VAE). Singh and Duvekot, op.cit., pp. 163–168.

Perry, W. (2009). *E-portfolios for RPL assessment: Key findings on current engagement in the VET sector* (Final report). Canberra: Australian Flexible Learning Framework, Department of

Education, Employment and Workplace Relations. http://learnerpathways.flexiblelearning.net.au/documents/research_reports/E-portfolios_for_RPL_Assessment_Final.pdf. Accessed 14 Sept 2014.

Philippines. National Commission for UNESCO. (2011). *Country Response on Consultation on UNESCO Guidelines for the recognition, validation and accreditation (RVA) of the outcomes of non-formal and informal learning*. Manila: BALS-DepEd./TESDA/Civil Society Network for Education Reform (E-Net Philippines).

Piazza, R. (2013). Towards the construction of a personal professional pathway: An experimental project for the recognition of non-formal and informal learning in the University of Catania. *Journal of Adult and Continuing Education, 19*(1 Spring), (pp. 101–124).

Pitman, T. (2009). Recognition of prior learning: The accelerated rate of change in Australian universities. *Higher Education Research and Development, 28*(2), 227–240.

Pokorny, H. (2011). England: Accreditation of prior experiential learning (APEL) research in higher education. Harris, Breier and Wihak, op.cit., pp. 248–283.

Preißer, R. (2005). Portfolio-building as a tool for self-reflectivity on a micro and macro level of society: The German case. In L. Chisholm, B. Hoskins with C. Glahn (Eds.), *Trading up: Potential and performance in non-formal learning*. Strasbourg: Council of Europe.

Prior Learning Assessment (PLA) Centre. (2008). *Achieving our potential: An action plan for prior learning assessment and recognition (PLAR) in Canada*. Halifax: PLA Centre.

Prokopp, M. (2010). Was bringt Kompetenzanerkennung – und wem? Ein Standpunkt. *Magazin Ewachsenenbildung. at. Das Fachmedium für Forschung, Praxis and Diskurs*. Ausgabe, 9 September 2010. http://erwachsenenbildung.at/magazin/10-09/meb10-9_06_prokopp.pdf. Accessed 16 Jan 2014.

Prokopp, M. (2011). *Anerkennung von non-formalem und informellem Lernen für Personen mit geringer formaler Qualifikation in Österreich* (Studies in lifelong learning 8). Krems: Donau-Universität-Krems (DUK).

Prokopp, M., & Luomi-Messerer, K. (2010). *European inventory on validation of non-formal and informal learning 2010: Case study of recognition for professionalisation in the adult learning sector. Academy of Continuing Education (wba), Austria* (European Commission, DG Education and Culture, in cooperation with CEDEFOP). London: GHK Consulting. http://libserver.cedefop.europa.eu/vetelib/2011/77481.pdf. Accessed 15 Jan 2014.

Raffe, D. (2011). The role of learning outcomes in national qualifications frameworks. Bohlinger and Münchausen, op.cit., pp. 87–104.

Republic of Korea. Ministry of Education, Science & Technology. (2013). *Second national lifelong learning promotion plan (2013–2017)*. Seoul: Ministry of Education, Science & Technology.

Republic of Korea. Ministry of Education, Science & Technology. (2009). *Development and state of the art of adult education and learning: National report of republic of Korea* (UNESCO's 6th international conference on adult education, CONFINTEA VI). Hamburg: UIL.

Republic of Korea. National Institute for Lifelong Education. (2011). *Lifelong learning account system*. Seoul: NILE.

Republic of Korea. National Institute for Lifelong Learning Education (NILE). (2013). *Manual for academic credit bank system*. Seoul: NILE.

Republik Österreich. (2011). *Strategie zum lebensbegleitenden Lernen in Österreich LLL: 2020*. Wien: Republik Österreich. (In German).

Richards, P. (1983). Ecological change and the politics of African land use. *African Studies Review. Vol. 26, No. 2, Social Science and Humanistic Research on Africa: An Assessment* (pp. 1–72). African Studies Review.

Rodrigues, S. P. (2009). *Guia de operacionalização de cursos de educação e formação de adultos*. Lisbon: National Qualifications Agency (ANQ). (In Portuguese).

Rogers, A. (2014). *The base of the iceberg: Informal learning and its impact on formal and non-formal learning* (Study guides in adult education). Opladen/Berlin/Toronto: Barbara Budrich Publishers.

Samuels, J. (with input from SAQA's research directorate). (2013). South Africa: Contextual and institutional arrangements for lifelong learning. Singh and Duvekot, op.cit., pp. 70–77.

Savadogo, B., & Walther, R. (2013). Burkina Faso: A new paradigm for skills development. Singh and Duvekot, op.cit., pp. 41–44.

Sawchuk, P. H. (2009). Informal learning and work: From genealogy and definitions to contemporary methods and findings. In R. Maclean & D. Wilson (Eds.), *International handbook of education for the changing world of work: Bridging academic and vocational education* (pp. 319–331). Dordrecht: Springer.

Schneeberger, A., Petanovitsch, A., & Schlögl, P. (2008). *Development and the state of the art of adult learning and education: National report of Austria.* (UNESCO's 6th International Conference on Adult Education, CONFINTEA VI). Hamburg: UIL. http://www.unesco.org/fileadmin/MULTIMEDIA/INSTITUTES/UIL/confintea/pdf/National_Reports/Europe%20-%20North%20America/Austria.pdf. Accessed 17 Jan 2014.

Schön, D. (1983). *The reflective practitioner.* New York: Basic Books.

Schön, D. (1987). *Educating the reflective practitioner: Toward a new design for teaching and learning in the professions.* San Francisco: Jossey-Bass.

School for New Learning (SNL). (1994). *Qualities and principles for assessing learning at SNL.* Chicago: DePaul University School for New Learning.

Schuetze, H. G., & Casey, C. (2006). Models and means of lifelong learning: Progress and barriers on the road to a learning society. *Compare, 3*(3), 279–287.

Schuller, T., & Field, T. (1998). Social capital, human capital and the learning society. *International Journal of Lifelong Education, 17*(4), 226–235.

Schuller, T., & Watson, D. (2009). *Learning through life: Inquiry into the future for lifelong learning.* Leicester: NIACE.

Scottish Credit and Qualifications Framework. (2005). *Scottish Credit and Qualifications Framework (SCQF) guidelines for the Recognition of Prior Informal Learning (RPL).* Scotland: SCQF. http://portal3.ipb.pt/images/sa/SCQF_GUIDELINES_RPL.pdf. Accessed 16 Jan 2014.

Scottish Government. (2007a). *Skills for Scotland: A lifelong skills strategy.* Holyrood: Scottish Parliament Information Centre.

Scottish Government. (2007b). *The government economic strategy.* Holyrood: Scottish Parliament Information Centre.

Seddon, T., & Billet, S. (2004). *Social partnerships in vocational education: Building community capacity.* Adelaide: NCVER.

Seidel, S. (2011). Anerkennung informell erworbener Kompetenzen in Deutschland: Vom Flickenteppich zum umfassenden System? Bohlinger and Münchausen, op.cit., pp. 349–368.

Sen, A. (1993). Capability and well-being. In M. Nussbaum & A. Sen (Eds.), *The quality of life* (pp. 30–53). Oxford: Oxford University Press.

Sen, A. (2000). *Development as freedom.* Oxford: Oxford University Press.

Šiliņa, B. (2008). *Development and state of the art of adult learning: National report of the Republic of Latvia* (UNESCO's 6th international conference on adult education, CONFINTEA VI). Hamburg: UIL.

Singh, M. (2008). *Creating flexible and inclusive learning pathways in post-primary education and training in Africa: NQFs and recognition of non-formal and informal learning – The key to lifelong learning.* (ADEA Biennale on Post-primary Education, Maputo, Mozambique, 5–9 May). Paris: IIEP

Singh, M. (2009). Recognition, validation and accreditation of non-formal and informal learning and experience: Results from an international study. In R. Maclean & D. Wilson (Eds.), *International handbook of education for the changing world of work: Bridging academic and vocational education* (Vol. 6, Part VIII, pp. 2597–2614). Dordrecht: Springer.

Singh, M. (2011). Skills recognition in the informal sector. *NORRAG NEWS,* No. 46, September 2011, pp. 79–81.

Singh, M. (2012, February). Educational practice in India and its foundation in Indian heritage: a synthesis of the East and West? *Comparative Education, 49*(1), 88–106.

Singh, M., & Barot, E. (2012). UNESCO guidelines for the recognition, validation and accreditation of the outcomes of non-formal and informal learning: Critical success factors in applying them. *Webinar. September 7, 2012*. Canadian Association for Prior Learning Assessment, in cooperation with the Canadian Commission for UNESCO.

Singh, M., & Duvekot, R. (Eds.). (2013). *Linking recognition practices and national qualifications frameworks: International benchmarking of national experiences and strategies on the recognition, validation and accreditation of non-formal and informal learning*. Hamburg: UIL.

Smith, L., & Clayton, B. (2011). Student insights and perspectives on the validation of learning outcomes. Bohlinger and Münchausen, op.cit., pp. 443–460.

Soliven, P. S., & Reyes, M. A. N. (2008). *Development and state of the art of adult learning and education. National report of Philippines* (UNESCO's 6th international conference on adult education, CONFINTEA VI). Hamburg: UIL.

South African Qualifications Authority. (2012a). *Working document on the recognition of prior learning* (National RPL conference, Bridging and expanding existing islands of excellent practice, 23–25 February). *SAQA Bulletin, 12*(3): 1–9.

South African Qualifications Authority. (2012b). *South African qualifications authority. Government notice. no. 802. Policy and criteria for the recognition of prior learning*. Pretoria: SAQA. http://www.info.gov.za/view/DownloadFileAction?id=175610. Accessed 17 Jan 2014.

Spencer, B., Briton, D., & Gereluk, W. (2003). The case for prior learning assessment and recognition for labour education in Canada. *Just Labour: A Canadian Journal of Work and Society, 2*, 45–53.

Spencer, J. (2008). *Have we go an adult education model for PLAR?* In Proceedings of the Canadian Association for the Study of Adult Education (CASAE) annual conference. Available at http://www.casae-aceea.ca/sites/casae/archives/cnf2008/OnlineProceedings-2008/CAS2008-Spencer.pdf. Accessed 17 Sept 2014.

Stárek, J. (2013). The Czech Republic: The qualifications system and the national lifelong long learning strategy. Singh and Duvekot, op.cit., pp. 143–148.

Stecher, B. M. (2005). *Developing process indicators to improve educational governance: Lessons for education from health care*. Santa Monica: Rand Education.

Steenekamp, S., & Singh, M. (2012). *Recognition and validation of non-formal and informal learning, and NQFs: Critical levers for lifelong learning and sustainable skills development. Comparative analysis of six African countries* (ADEA Triennial. Ouagadougou, Burkina Faso. 13–17 February). Tunis: Agency for the Development of Education in Africa.

Straka, G. A. (2005). Informal learning: Genealogy, concepts, antagonisms and questions. In K. Künzel (Ed.), *International yearbook of adult education* (Vol. 31–32, pp. 93–126). Köln: Böhlau.

Straka, G. A. (2006). Zertifizierung informell erworbener Kompetenzen? neu für die bundesdeutsche Berufsbildung? In M. Eckert & A. Zöller (Eds.), *Der europäische Berufsbildungsraum? Beiträge der Berufsbildungsforschung* (pp. 205–216). Bielefeld: W. Bertelsmann Verlag. (in German).

Sullivan, S., & Thompson, G. (2005). The development of a self-assessment instrument to evaluate selected competencies of continuing education practitioners. *Canadian Journal of University Continuing Education, 31*(2), 59–94.

Sultana, R. G. (2009). Competence and competence frameworks in career guidance: Complex and contested concepts. *International Journal for Educational and Vocational Guidance, 9*, 15–30.

Switzerland, Office fédéral de la formation professionnelle et de la technologie OFFT. (2008). Reconnaissance et validation des acquis. État des lieux: rapport de la Suisse à l'attention de l'OCDE. Berne: Office fédéral de la formation professionnelle et de la technologie –OFFT.

Taylor, M., & Evans, K. (2009). Formal and informal training for workers with low literacy: Building an international dialogue between Canada and the United Kingdom. *Journal of Adult and Continuing Education, 15*(1), 37–54.

Thailand. Ministry of Education, Office of the Non-Formal and Informal Education. (2008). *Development and state of the art of adult learning and education: National report of Thailand* (UNESCO's 6th international conference on adult education, CONFINTEA VI). Bangkok: ONIE.

Thailand. Ministry of Education, Office of the Non-Formal and Informal Education. (2011). *Country Response on consultation on UNESCO Guidelines for the recognition, validation and accreditation (RVA) of the outcomes of non-formal and informal learning.* Bangkok: ONIE, Thai Ministry of Education.

Thompson, J. (2002). *Bread and roses: Arts culture and lifelong learning.* Leicester: NIACE.

Travers., N. L. (2011). United States of America: Prior learning assessment (PLA) research in colleges and universities. Harris, Breier and Wihak, op.cit., pp. 248–283.

Travers, N. L., & Evans, M. T. (2011). Evaluating prior learning assessment programme: A suggested framework. *International Review of Research in Open and Distance Learning, 12*(1), 151–159.

Trinidad and Tobago. National Training Agency Trinidad and Tobago. (n.d.) *Trinidad and Tobago National report on Technical and Vocational Education and Training (TVET):* A contribution to the regional discussion on reforming TVET institutions and accreditation systems for improved skills and enhanced employability in Caribbean labour markets. Trinidad/Tobago: National Training Agency. http://www.ilocarib.org.tt/cef/national%20employment%20reports/TandT%20NAt%20TVETFinal%20report2.pdf. Accessed 14 Jan 2014.

UNESCO. (2005). *United Nations decade of education for sustainable development, 2005–2014: International implementation scheme.* Paris: UNESCO.

UNESCO Bangkok Office. (2006). *Equivalency Programmes (EPs) for promoting lifelong learning.* Bangkok: UNESCO Asia and Pacific Regional Bureau for Education.

UNESCO Bangkok Office and UNICEF. (2011). *Equivalency programmes and alternative certified learning* (13–17 September, 2013). Bangkok: Asia and Pacific Regional Bureau for Education.

UNESCO Institute for Lifelong Learning. (2005). *Recognition, validation and certification: Synthesis report.* Hamburg: UIL.

UNESCO Institute for Lifelong Learning. (2011). Draft synthesis report. Responses by member states to the consultancy questions in preparation of the UNESCO guidelines for the recognition, validation, and accreditation of the outcomes of non-formal and informal learning, Hamburg, UIL.

UNESCO Institute for Lifelong Learning. (2012). *UNESCO guidelines for the recognition, validation and accreditation of the outcomes of Non-formal and informal learning.* Hamburg: UIL.

UNICEF. (2010). *Country information, Botswana.* www.unicef.org/infobycountry/botswana_statistics.html. Accessed 3 Aug 2010.

United Kingdom of Great Britain. Quality Assurance Agency for Higher Education. (2004). *Guidelines on the accreditation of prior learning.* London: QAA.

Us-Sabur, Z. (2008). Non-formal education in Bangladesh. In C. Duke & H. Hinzen (Eds.), Knowing more, doing better: Challenges for CONFINTEA VI from monitoring EFA in non-formal youth and adult education. *International Perspectives in Adult Education (IPE)* (Vol. 58, pp. 41–51). Bonn: DVV International.

Usher, R. (2008). Consuming learning. *Convergence, XLI*(1), 29–45.

Van der Velden, M. (2006). *A case for cognitive justice.* See http://Creativecommons.org/licenses/by-nc-nd/2.5/

Van Kleef, J. (2011). Canada: A typology of prior learning assessment and recognition (PLAR) research in context. Harris, Breier and Wihak, op.cit., pp. 44–84.

Van Kleef, J. (2012). PLAR: Finding quality in the dynamics of social practice. *PLAIO: Prior Learning Assessment Inside Out, 1*(2). http://www.plaio.org/index.php/home/article/view/30. Accessed 14 Jan 2014.

Van Noy, M., Jacobs, J., Korey, S., Bailey, T., & Hughes, K. L. (2008). *Non-credit enrolment in workforce education: State policies and community colleges practice.* Washington, DC: American Association of Community Colleges.

Visvanathan, S. (2001). Knowledge and information in the network society. *Seminar, 503,* 64–71.

Walsh-Goya, M., & Morrissey, M. (2014). RPL and Labour Mobility, Department of Labour and Advanced Education (LAE), Government of Nova Scotia. *UIL Global Observatory of the Recognition, Validation and Accreditation of Non-formal and Informal Learning.* Hamburg: UIL.

Walther, R., & Filipiak, E. (2007). *Vocational training in the informal sector, or how to stimulate the economies of developing countries: Conclusions of a field survey in seven African countries* (Notes and documents no. 33). Paris: Agence Française de Développement.

Watson, S. (1996). The national qualifications framework. A cognitive development perspective. *DELTA, 48*(1), 77–92.

Weinert, F. E. (2001). Concept of competence: A conceptual clarification. In D. S. Rychen & L. H. Salganik (Eds.),*Defining and selecting key competencies*. Göttingen: Hogrefe and Huber.

Welsh Assembly Government. (2010). *Credit and qualifications framework for Wales*. Cardiff: Welsh Government.

Wenger, E. (1998). Communities of practice: Learning as a social system. *The Systems Thinker, 9*(5), 1–12.

Werquin, P. (2007). Moving mountains: Will qualifications systems produce lifelong learning? *European Journal of Education, 4*(4), 459–484.

Werquin, P. (2008). Recognition of non-formal and informal learning in OECD countries: A very good idea in jeopardy? *Lifelong Learning in Europe, 3*, 142–149.

Werquin, P. (2010). *Recognising non-formal and informal learning: Outcomes, policies and practices*. Paris: OECD.

Werquin, P. (2012). Enabling recognition of non-formal and informal learning outcomes in France: The VAE legislation. *SAQA Bulletin, 12*(3), 55–88.

Werquin, P, & Wihak, C. (2011). Organisation for Economic Co-operation and Development (OECD): Research reveals 'islands of good practice'. Harris, Breier and Wihak, op.cit., pp. 161–171.

Westman, K. (2005). *Development of national qualifications framework and recognition of prior learning: Establishing new pathways for inclusion or exclusion in Kenya? Master programme in adult education and global change*. Linköping: Linköping University.

Whittaker, R. (2005). *Report on consultation on SCQF RPL guidelines*. Scotland: SCQF.

Whittaker, R. (2008). *Scottish credit and qualifications framework (SCQF) social services: Recognition of prior learning (RPL) pilot* (Evaluating report). Dundee: Scottish Social Services Council.

Whittaker, R. (2011). Scotland: Recognition of prior learning (RPL) research within a national credit and qualifications framework. Harris, Breier and Wihak, op.cit., pp. 172–199.

Whittaker, R. (2012). Challenging practices: Streamlining recognition of prior informal learning in Scottish higher education. *PLAIO: Prior Learning Assessment Inside Out*, 1(2). http://www.plaio.org/index.php/home/article/view/31. Accessed 23 Jan 2014.

Whittaker, R., Mills, V., & Knox, K. (2006). *Flexible delivery quality enhancement theme: Supporting the development of the flexible curriculum* (Final report). Glasgow: QAA Scotland.

Wihak, C., & Wong, A. (2011). Research into Prior Learning Assessment and Recognition (PLAR) in university adult education programmes in Canada. Harris, Breier and Wihak, op.cit., pp. 311–324.

Wilbur, G., Marienau, C., & Fiddler, M. (2012). Authenticity for assurance and accountability: Reconnecting standards and qualities for PLA competence and course-based frameworks. *PLAIO. Prior Learning Assessment Inside Out, 1*(2). http://www.plaio.org/index.php/home/article/view/28. Accessed 23 Jan 2014.

Winch, C. (1996). Quality in education. *Journal of Philosophy of Education, 30*(1), 1–155.

Wittgenstein, L. (1953). *Philosophical investigations* (cited from the 1967, 3rd ed.). Oxford: Blackwell.

Wong, A. (2004). *E-portfolios: Implications for University teaching and learning. University of Saskatchewan sabbatical research report*. Saskatoon: University of Saskatchewan.

Wong, A. (2011). Prior learning assessment and recognition (PLAR) and the teaching – research nexus in universities. Harris, Breier and Wihak, op.cit., pp. 284–310.

Young, M. (2010). Alternative educational futures for a knowledge society: (Keynote, ECER 2009). Vienna. *European Educational Research Journal (EERJ), 9*(1), 1–12.

Young, M., & Allais, S. (2011). *Options for designing an NVQF for India* (Submitted to the ministry of labour and employment). New Delhi: ILO/World Bank.

Youth Forum Jeunesse (YFJ). (2008). *Policy paper on non-formal education: A framework for indicating and assuring quality.* Adopted by the Council of Members/Extraordinary General Assembly 2–3 May 2008. Castelldefels, Catalonia, Spain.

Zepke, N. (1997). Student-centred learning, knowledge and the New Zealand qualifications framework. *The New Zealand Journal of Adult Learning, 25*(2), 82–96.

Author Index

© UNESCO Institute for Lifelong Learning 2015
M. Singh, *Global Perspectives on Recognising Non-formal and Informal Learning*,
Technical and Vocational Education and Training: Issues, Concerns and Prospects 21,
DOI 10.1007/978-3-319-15278-3

Subject Index

© UNESCO Institute for Lifelong Learning 2015   215
M. Singh, *Global Perspectives on Recognising Non-formal and Informal Learning*,
Technical and Vocational Education and Training: Issues, Concerns and Prospects 21,
DOI 10.1007/978-3-319-15278-3